W. S. Buye
Father's Day, June 19, 1955
Love from
Ruth and Laura

GENTLEMEN, START YOUR ENGINES

Gentlemen,

WILBUR SHAW

Start Your Engines

Illustrated

COWARD-McCANN, Inc. · NEW YORK

FOREWORD

THIS was the "big show" and I was a part of it.

To me it was a world's series, a heavyweight championship fight, a National Open, a Rose Bowl game and a Kentucky Derby all rolled into one tremendous spectacle—with a touch of the pomp and ceremony of a coronation.

Eight years earlier, when I was only sixteen, the original Howdy Wilcox had given Indianapolis its first hometown winner of the annual 500-mile automobile race. On that occasion I had vowed that some day I would drive in the International Classic, too, and win it.

Now, a few minutes before ten o'clock on the morning of May 30, 1927, I was about to start an automobile on the world's greatest race course where all of the motor sport immortals of the last eighteen years had performed. I was about to get my first chance to join that exclusive list of "500" victors, which is the ultimate goal of racing men all over the world.

To the ears of a race driver, I'm sure, there are no sweeter words in the English language than the traditional command at the Indianapolis Motor Speedway:

"Gentlemen, start your engines."

But until you actually hear your own engine roar into life on the starting line, you worry about each of the hundreds of mechanical parts which might fail you.

My stomach was full of butterflies. My heart was in my throat. Almost every organ of my body was acting in some strange manner and each nerve seemed to be screaming "Let's go!" But in spite of the terrific tension, which had been mounting to this relentless peak with each passing moment over a period of many days, I was extremely happy.

I had qualified my little Jynx Special in nineteenth position among the thirty-three eligible starters. With the field poised for the takeoff, there were six rows of three cars each ahead of me. I was in the No. 1 spot of the seventh row, flanked by two cars on my right. Four more rows of three cars each were behind me.

The Jynx was the fastest thing on four wheels I had ever driven. I was ready, mentally and physically, to give it the best ride possible. I was extremely proud to have won a place in such illustrious company, but I wasn't kidding myself and my attitude was one of determination rather than of confidence, because the Jynx didn't compare with the cars assigned to such veterans as Tom Milton, Harry Hartz, Leon Duray, Eddie Hearne and other favorites.

It was what the racing fraternity calls a re-built job. The engine had been designed four years earlier with a piston displacement of 122 cubic inches. To met the technical requirements for this 1927 race, open only to cars with a displacement of not more than 91.5 inches, it had been necessary to change the crankshaft in order to shorten the stroke.

I definitely lacked the speed and power which most of my more experienced rivals had at their command. If I hadn't learned anything else from dirt track racing, however, it had convinced me that the only way to make any money was to be among those still running at the finish. I was all set to drive as fast as the engine would permit without flying apart. But I was going to make sure of finishing the full five hundred miles so that I could count on another—and better—chance of winning next year.

Above everything else, I was going to do my level best to make my bride of a few months—as well as my father and mother and friends—proud of me.

6

CHAPTER 1

MY father was the most successful man I have ever known.

While very young, he had managed to squander a moderate inheritance. And he had done it the quick way—on women, race horses and bird dogs. His brother had helped a little, but Dad always was willing to admit that most of the expensive ideas had been his own. After that, he never amounted to much financially. Some income, of course, was necessary to make life enjoyable, but as long as he had enough for today, he saw no reason to worry about tomorrow.

Dad hated towns. His one ambition was to live in the woods and he achieved that desire most of his life.

He never got very far on the Shelbyville, Indiana, police force, because he had little respect for laws made by men.

He probably was the least productive salesman the Prudential Life Insurance Company ever had on its payroll. There were too many other things to do besides work.

He found the institution of marriage too confining and there was a divorce while I was still quite young.

By ordinary standards he was rather shiftless.

But from the day my parents separated until I was in the sixth grade of school, I continued to spend almost as much time with my dad as with my mother; and I know James Oliver Shaw was more successful than any of the business tycoons now living from ulcer to ulcer.

He was a whole man and a happy one. He had sampled

every flavor life had to offer and decided on the ones he liked most. Then he lived his life to the hilt, according to his own preferences, with complete freedom from worry.

The little gentleman was quite a dandy, who hated sloppy dressing. His auburn hair was wavy, with a big stubborn cowlick over his right eye, and he made up for his lack of size by a magnetism you could actually feel.

When Dad was around, everyone knew it. Yet he never was loud in speech and seldom had much to say except when he was with people he liked. Ordinary conventions never worried him. He chewed tobacco almost constantly—Piper-Heidsieck, the Champagne of Tobaccos, they called it—and I used to think he didn't even take that cud out of his mouth to eat.

One thing, for which I'll always feel indebted to my dad, was his desire to teach me everything he knew. That's about all any father can do, other than set a good example; and too many parents depend almost entirely on the schools, or the Boy Scouts, or church organizations to do the job for them.

All of these fine agencies eventually contributed to my physical and mental development. But long before I was old enough to take advantage of what they had to offer, Dad developed my sense of self-reliance and imparted to me a generous portion of his own intense love for the big outdoors.

Whenever he went into the woods, even on those occasions when he should have been working, he usually took me with him. His amazing knowledge of nature made every trip an unforgettable memory. Unless you have experienced it yourself, you probably will never realize how much a boy can learn while watching a busy squirrel or listening to the sad message of a whippoorwill.

Dad had a code of his own, which certainly did not conform to the strict conservation rules governing such activities today. He didn't pay much attention to man-made laws, because he believed nature's own laws were more important; but good sportsmanship and the love of competition dominated every move he made.

Until I was six or seven years old, I learned by observation.

8

And, believe me, I was observing a master. Then he bought me my first rifle and taught me to use and respect it. At the same time he helped me establish my first trap line and informed me I was "in business" for myself.

It wasn't many days later before I learned one lesson I've never forgotten to this day. Along with the usual number of muskrats, I found one trap holding a nice fat possum. He really was a beauty and I started to skin him as my father had taught me. But I was so eager to get back home and show off the pelt that I slit it right in the middle while scraping it.

The going price for prime possum at that time was thirty-five cents and this was the finest possum I'd ever trapped or shot on my own. I could use the money for more ammunition. So I tossed the damaged pelt in with the good ones and received full price for it at the general store because I didn't mention the tear.

I thought I had made a pretty good deal for myself, but when I told Dad about it he took me apart. He made me feel small enough to crawl into a mouse hole. Then he explained that I had received full value for the pelt only because the man at the store believed he could accept me, Wilbur Shaw, at full value on the basis of our previous dealings in which I never had cheated him. I went back to the store and returned the thirty-five cents, wishing I'd never caught that darn possum. But I learned the hard way that no amount of money can pay for the loss of self-respect.

In his attitude toward the fish and game laws, Dad's code often was confusing. He'd laugh—and sometimes curse—at the accepted ways of doing things. But what he did was done openly. All the game wardens in the surrounding territory knew he shot fish and hunted out of season. At the same time, they knew that anything he shot or caught was going to be eaten and they didn't interfere. I profited by their understanding too.

On more than one occasion, while returning home with a big bass in one hand and my rifle in the other, I'd be scared silly when I encountered a game warden. Invariably he would laugh and kid me about my "fishing rod" and it didn't take me long to realize that he secretly agreed with my dad's concept of conservation.

Nothing irritated Dad more than the sight of a big string of little fish, barely up to legal limit. A hungry man would need twelve or fifteen of them for a single meal. Such a fisherman always caused Dad to comment on the number of even smaller fish which probably had been thrown back to die with their mouths or guts torn by the hook.

I learned it was just as much fun—and much easier on the supply of fish—to wait patiently for some fat bass or an occasional pike to swim near enough to the surface for a bullet to take effect. Then you got the one you wanted without killing the little ones.

Hunting squirrel and duck was an even greater thrill and one squirrel-hunting trip which stands out in my memory was made a few days before the season opened officially. Because everyone and his grandmother would be out in the woods with guns on the opening day, Dad reasoned correctly that if we wanted a mess or two of squirrels, the only smart thing to do was to get there first. So we had gone by train to a favorite spot on the other side of Columbus.

The first squirrel I shot looked as though it had cauliflower ears and I took it to my dad for an explanation.

"It's full of ticks," he warned.

True enough, that squirrel probably didn't even hear the shot which hit him because there wasn't room in either ear for one more tick. With vague visions of a painful death due to the effects of Rocky Mountain spotted fever, which someone had told me was transmitted by ticks, I dropped that squirrel like a hot potato and started scratching.

As soon as we had the pockets of our hunting coats filled with squirrels, we hurried back to the little cabin in which we had spent the night with one of Dad's friends. Then both of us peeled off our clothes and went over each other like a pair of monkeys looking for fleas. I don't remember finding a single tick, but I couldn't get my mind off the subject until the whippoorwills started their weird songs at dusk. Positively fascinated by the sound, I sneaked within three feet of one perched on a rail fence and watched him perform at close range until something frightened him away. Then, at the end of a long hard day and successful hunt, I slept the complete sleep of blissful exhaustion until it was time to catch the train for home.

We had cleaned the squirrels the night before and placed them in a five-gallon lard can half full of salt water. Dad found a comfortable seat for me with the big lard tin between my legs and the hunting gear beside me. Then he went visiting. It seemed as if he knew everyone on the train and I didn't see him again until we reached Greensburg. Even when the train made a long stop at Columbus, I didn't leave my seat. Dad had told me to watch those squirrels.

The coach was almost deserted, because everyone else had stepped to the platform to stretch his legs. I occupied myself for several minutes looking at the station and the parts of town I could see beyond it. When I finally glanced away from the window, I noticed a big policeman coming down the aisle toward me. Visions of a prison cell filled my mind. The squirrels under me must have squirmed too. They weren't supposed to be there, because the season wouldn't open for another day or two.

A strange policeman presented a different problem than a friendly and understanding game warden, but he passed on by and I began to breathe again. Then his footsteps stopped, and without looking I could almost see him turn and come back toward me. I heard his voice over my shoulder.

"Hello there, young man."

I felt absolutely speechless, but I swallowed hard and managed to say "Hello."

"What've you got in that lard can?"

"Just lard."

"Traveling far?"

"Greensburg."

"All alone?"

At that particular instant I certainly felt all alone and I said

11

"Yes, sir," because if I was caught I didn't want to involve my father.

"Good for you. I like to see youngsters able to take care of themselves. Have a good time and take care of that lard."

Dad rejoined me as we reached Greensburg, but before I could tell him about the policeman we bumped into Frank Eubank on the station platform.

"You should have been with us, Frank," he exclaimed, ruffling my hair. "The woods were full of squirrels and I'll bet Wilbur won't forget this trip for a long time. I put him in charge of the squirrels on the way home and when we stopped at Columbus I ran into a friend of mine who's a cop. I told him we'd had quite a bit of luck, even though the season wasn't open yet, and then sent him into the coach to question Wilbur. You should have seen the little guy handle the situation."

I felt silly and a little bit resentful as I listened to the details of the gag. Apparently Dad had kept his eye on me all of the time and enjoyed my discomfiture. But before he had finished the tale, I suddenly realized it was the type of practical joke he might have pulled on any of his grown-up friends. The fact that he had told Mr. Eubank about it was proof he was pleased with my reaction. Frank was the town barber, who would spread the story before nightfall, and I'd be somewhat of a hero—at least to his son, Wayne.

Wayne Eubank and I were friendly rivals during most of our boyhood days and there was something wrong with any youngster who experienced a single dull moment if he lived in one of Indiana's county seat towns during the early 1900s. Shelbyville and Greensburg, where I spent most of my early childhood, were typical of that day and age.

Aside from the usual Sunday afternoon baseball games, there were no spectator sports as we know them today. But we had no trouble devising our own methods of recreation. Almost every red-blooded American boy is born with an intense competitive spirit and our "gang" engaged in races of some sort almost every day—on foot or with roller skates, bicycles and goat carts.

At other times we'd fight the battle of "Bunker Hill" or go

12

swimming under the cooling coils at the ice plant. The smell of ammonia wasn't pleasant and it made our eyes sting. But the water in the tank, at least, was wet and cool.

Our Bunker Hill was a huge pile of corn cobs at the grain elevator. Wayne and I usually were the ones who would choose up sides and we had some terrific battles with the "Americans" often suffering as many casualties as the "British."

I still have a locked muscle in my left cheek as the result of one fight in mid-winter. There wasn't enough snow for a snowball battle, so we had gone to the cob pile at the elevator. The fact that the cobs were frozen as hard as rocks didn't matter. That situation simply placed a greater premium on agility and alertness.

One of Wayne's "shots" hit me flush on the cheek that day and I almost passed out. But I got even with him before many weeks had passed. I gave him the mumps. My case was rather mild, but he really had 'em.

Like most fathers, my dad always tried to give me the important things I wanted. Usually I had to wait a while for them, due to financial circumstances, but the delay brought only added happiness with their actual possession. One of the gifts I remember best was a goat Dad purchased for me while I was in the third grade of school. With very little imagination, I named him Billy.

It's said that a goat and his odor are inseparable. But I'll swear to my last breath that Billy didn't smell after I got his hair brushed out and almost sleek-looking. He was downright handsome, at least to me. Riding behind him in a four-wheel cart, I felt like the King of Shelbyville.

Billy wasn't afraid of man or beast and he definitely had a one-track mind. When he started in a given direction, he never varied an inch from a straight line unless I turned him to the right or left. Then he would adopt the new course and stay on it until I gave him another command with a tug on the reins. Almost every other boy in Shelbyville also had a goat and the acquisition of Billy set the stage for my first formal race on any track. It took place at the Shelby County Fair of 1910.

13

Those were the days when every Hoosier man, woman and child had a particular interest in his county fair. Even if they didn't have from one to a dozen or more entries themselves— livestock, vegetables, grain, baked goods, preserves, handiwork and hundreds of other things for which cash prizes were at stake—they would be on hand to see how their neighbors fared in the distribution of awards.

Against a noisy and colorful background of horse races, girl shows, ferris wheels, merry-go-rounds and gambling games, the county fair was *the* event of the year. And for the first time in my life I had the necessary equipment to participate in the annual goat race. It was a blistering-hot July day, the kind that bakes you instead of stewing you, but the weather didn't bother me a bit. I was too intent on winning. At some time or other during recent weeks, Billy and I had run away from everyone who had challenged us to a test of speed. Now we had the opportunity to make our supremacy official and I had my own ideas of the "perfect" finish which would bring the crowd to its collective feet as we came from behind to win.

The start was good and I was sure all of the applause from the stands was intended for Billy and me as we moved up quickly to second place in the field. I was certain the leader would "come back to me," whenever I chose to give Billy free rein, and equally certain that no one in the rear could overtake us. My father would be at the finish line to shake my hand and we would go downtown that night to do a little indiscreet boasting at the ice cream parlor.

As we neared the finish line I gave Billy a tug on the rein and he veered to the right in order to gain sufficient racing room to pass the leader. Everything was proceeding according to plan but I couldn't resist the temptation to glance at the grandstand and wave nonchalantly to my friends. The crowd was cheering and applauding. It was a sight I'll never forget and I was completely entranced by the commotion I was caus- ing—until I suddenly realized we were getting extremely close to the outside rail.

When I had pulled Billy to the right in order to pass the

leader, I'd forgotten to get him squared away for the dash to the finish line. He had kept right on running at a tangent. We had covered twelve or fifteen feet more than our rivals but we still were in second place by a half length and it was too late to do anything about it.

I was almost sick with disappointment and ready to cry as Dad found me. When I started to explain what had happened, he interrupted me and put his arm around my shoulder.

"I know, son," he said. "I saw it all. Might be the luckiest thing ever happened to you. Next time, I'll bet, you'll keep your mind on your job. But let's forget about it right now and have an ice cream cone."

The lessons I learned from experience always seemed to remain with me longest. Another incident I've never forgotten took place in Greensburg after Dad had given me my first bicycle. My legs weren't long enough for me to reach the pedals when I straddled it. But I could ride as well and as fast as any of the other boys by thrusting one leg through the frame.

A high brick wall, topped by a narrow strip of stone and cement, encircled the school yard. It certainly wasn't intended as a bicycle track, but one day some of my pals dared me to try it. They boosted me to the top and handed the bike up to me. It didn't look very safe, but I couldn't back down after going that far.

Summoning a little extra courage, I finally managed to get rolling in a straight line. The faster I went, the easier it seemed to be to keep the bike in the exact center of the strip. It really was fun and I was moving along at a fairly good clip when I glanced ahead and saw the corner of the wall coming at me much too fast.

Bikes aren't designed to make sharp right-angle turns on a "track" only ten or twelve inches wide and I didn't have time to stop. I sailed right on out into space and did a perfect nose dive as the front wheel of the bike hit the ground. I heard the rim split and then the frame of the bike wrapped itself around me. Although I wasn't hurt much, I dreaded taking that dam-

15

aged bike home to Dad. In his opinion, failure to take good care of your equipment was inexcusable.

It was easy to tell he didn't like what he saw as I trudged up the front walk with the wreckage on my shoulder; but as usual he withheld judgment until after I had had a chance to tell my story. The tightness around his mouth seemed to soften as I explained that I simply didn't have any place to go when I reached the corner of that wall.

"Did you learn your lesson?" he asked.

"Well, I'm sure I don't ever want to get into a spot like that again," I replied. "It's no fun when you get into a situation where you find you're absolutely helpless."

"Okay. Take it down to the shop tomorrow and have it fixed. I'll give you enough money to pay for the job."

Dad was quite a guy.

CHAPTER 2

THE major emotional blow of my childhood was the shock of my parents' divorce. It's easy, now, to see that such a decision was inevitable because of their lack of common interests. But it wasn't easy to adjust myself to the situation even though Mother permitted me to continue spending considerable time with Dad.

For many days, before the abrupt break was made, there was a depressing atmosphere about our household. Unlike Dad, who could forget his troubles by communing with nature, Mother had been unable to shake off the grief caused by the death of my younger twin brothers during an attack of pneumonia before they had reached their first birthday. An older brother also had succumbed to the same disease at an early age, reducing our family to myself and my sister, Joenita.

Possibly due to Mother's despondency, Dad began to spend more and more time away from home. We had moved to Greensburg, where Dad had taken over the Prudential Insurance agency after resigning from the Shelbyville police force, but he continued to make the thirty-mile trip back to Shelbyville on frequent occasions to visit his many friends.

When he returned, often late at night after I had retired, I would hear the murmur of their voices and this was unusual because I had noticed they no longer had much to say to each other on the evenings he did spend at home. That troubled me, but it wasn't until after one particular incident, in which I was the principal figure, that I suddenly realized they had lost their love and respect for each other.

Several of us youngsters were playing in our back yard on the day before Halloween, which always was a special occasion for me because I had been born on October 31, 1902. We were sailing the lids of empty paint cans back and forth among us. In those days, the cans were made out of heavy material which required a series of chisel cuts in order to remove the top. Although the jagged-edged discs were dangerous "toys," because they would cut like a knife if they hit you, it was fun to sail them high in the air. They would dart and swoop like swallows.

Dodging them was no great difficulty, as long as you remained alert and kept your eyes on any of them coming in your direction. I lost sight of one in the sun, however, and it hit me smack in the face, almost cutting off my nose. The tip of it actually was hanging only by the skin when I cupped my hand around it to hold it in place. Screaming at the top of my voice, with the blood pouring out, I ran for the house.

It seemed only a few minutes until all of our neighbors were on hand with a lot of advice, but Mother insisted the wound was too serious for anyone except a doctor to touch. When he arrived, he declared it would be necessary for him to take a few stitches and he suggested that I sit in a kitchen chair on the edge of the back porch where he would have ample light to see what he was doing.

17

By the time he was ready to start the project, quite an audience was assembled. The place was so crowded, in fact, that several people had to cling to our clothesline in order to keep from being jostled off the porch entirely. One end of the clothesline was anchored to a big nail in the wall above my head and a large wash tub also hung from the nail. The extra strain was too much. The nail pulled loose without warning and the edge of the heavy tub hit me right on top of the head, splitting my scalp open as it barely missed the doctor.

Someone applied a cool wet towel to the new injury in order to control the bleeding while the doctor finished putting the stitches into my nose. Additional stitches were necessary in my scalp and my head must have resembled the cover of a baseball when the job was completed.

The bandages, of course, came next. Yard after yard of gauze was wrapped around my head until I looked like a Hindu whose turban had slipped down over the front of his face. Except for two tiny holes in front of my eyes, so that I could see, I was covered from the crown of my head to the bottom of my upper lip.

Dad had returned home during all of the excitement and he was the first person I saw through the little openings in my turban. He had both arms around Mother in an effort to comfort her and I realized suddenly that it was the first time I had seen them embrace in many weeks.

"Hot diggety, that did it," I said to myself, kind of pleased about the whole episode because of this happy ending. "Everything is going to be all right again."

But it didn't work that way. The breach already was too wide. During the next few weeks they drifted even farther apart and Mother finally decided it was foolish to let the situation continue any longer. Early one morning, after Dad had spent another full night away from home, she packed our bags and boarded an interurban for Shelbyville with my sister and me.

For a time, we lived with our maternal grandfather and grandmother, but it wasn't long until Mother was in the milli-

18

nery business, first at Manilla and then at Fairland. Each time she took her children with her. In Manilla I contributed to the family purse by working up a Saturday Evening Post route. In Fairland, I carried the Indianapolis News, with a big knot tied in the shoulder strap to keep the heavy bag from dragging the ground.

Mother was a practical and industrious person who valued security. She was a cultured and God-fearing woman, who believed her children should be raised in the church. She demanded obedience, too, and was a strict disciplinarian. She may have lacked Dad's ability to teach us—especially me—how to do things with our hands, but, with more than ordinary talent for music and art, she devoted considerable time to giving us an appreciation of the finer things of life. In anything she did, Mother took pride in doing it well. She always insisted that we do likewise.

Invariably she had the right answer to any problem we brought to her and the extra time to explain when we asked "why?" In that way, we soon learned to reason things out for ourselves. Except when Dad was involved, she also seemed to have the knack of knowing the right thing to say in any situation and sensing the right time to say it in order to achieve the desired result.

During each summer, when she permitted me to spend a few weeks with Dad, I would get out of the habit of going to Sunday School. Hunting or fishing was much more fun. But whenever I was at home, Sunday School attendance was an ironclad requirement for participating in any type of Sunday recreation or doing my job as mascot of the Fairland Grays.

On one occasion, when I recovered from a Sunday morning "illness" in time to report for duty at the baseball diamond, she told me that anyone too ill to attend Sunday School was too ill to do anything else on Sunday. She made it clear that I was expected to stay in the house for the balance of the day. But when something—probably the extreme quiet—caused her to check on my whereabouts a little later, she was greeted by an empty room and an open window. Few incidents in my life

19

have been more embarrassing than when she stormed out to the players' bench during a late-inning rally and dragged my protesting body home.

My days in the small towns were numbered, however. After I had finished the fifth grade of school, Mother remarried and moved to Indianapolis to establish a new home for us with Charles Morgan as my stepfather. For a brief time I felt completely lost. Then I found new friends at Benjamin Harrison School, located near the downtown district at Delaware and Walnut Streets.

They introduced me to the facilities of the Central Y.M.C.A., where I could swim the year around. During the winter I won a regular place on the team as a diver and I also was a member of the tumbling squad. Some of the fellows I met at the Y also were members of Boy Scout Troop No. 37 at the First Baptist Church. Most of them were older than I, but they needed a little guy like me for their own tumbling routine. They would toss me around like an Indian club and, because I could take it and loved it, they quickly induced me to join.

I owe a great deal to the Boy Scouts of America for sharpening my determination to excel at anything I undertook. The merit badge system created in me a desire for more knowledge and ability. Before I could earn a rating as a first class Scout, however, my step-father took the entire family to Florence, Alabama, where he had obtained employment on the Muscles Shoals project. I was in the eighth grade of school at the time and Mother insisted that I continue my studies at Florence.

One morning was all I could stomach. I could hardly understand the pupils and teacher because of their thick southern drawls. They made no secret of the fact they had little use for a "damyankee." I couldn't get interested in my lessons because they were at least a year behind the Indianapolis schools. I'd studied the same stuff the previous fall. I left the classroom at the noon hour and never returned.

Mother and I had a long session, lasting most of the afternoon, before I was able to win her consent. But she finally agreed that it wouldn't do me any good to spend all my time

20

at school reviewing things I already had learned. I sold her on the idea that I actually would learn more by getting a job during the few months we were to spend in the South and Mr. Morgan was sure there was something I could do at Muscles Shoals.

The following morning I was on one of the big trucks which always hauled a full load of men out to the employment office at the construction site and a man by the name of McNamara hired me as a timekeeper at thirty-five dollars a week. He was in charge of all plumbing installations in the barracks and his office was the dirtiest I had ever seen. Each morning and evening, the workmen stomped in with their muddy boots and the place was a mess most of the time.

As soon as I had a few extra minutes I found a broom and started to sweep. I had dust flying in all directions when Mr. McNamara shouted, "Put that damn broom down before I hit you over the head with it."

A few minutes later, however, he came over to the table where I was working on the time cards.

"I don't mind you cleaning the place up," he said. "It needs a good cleaning. But if you're going to swing a broom, swing it right. Get the broom again and I'll show you what I mean." Using careful, short strokes, he gave me a quick lesson in sweeping, demonstrating how easily the dust could be swept up without getting it all over everything in the room.

I thanked him and from then on I swept the place out every morning. By devoting an extra thirty minutes a day to the office, I soon had it in respectable condition and about two weeks later he asked me if I wanted a better job.

"How would you like to be a spotter?" he asked.

"What's a spotter?" I replied.

"All you have to do is walk from one building to another and make sure that none of the men is loafing on the job," he explained. "Government inspectors won't stand for anything like that. If we have such men on the payroll I want to get rid of 'em before I'm told to fire 'em. And the job pays fifty dollars a week."

21

That's all I needed to know. I assumed my new duties the next morning. Before the end of the day everyone knew I was the boss's "bird dog" and whenever I got near a building you could hear the hammers begin to sing a faster song on the caulking irons.

I told Mr. McNamara what was happening and after about a week of it I said, "If I had a horse to ride between one building and another the men would get even more work done every day."

"I think you're just trying to make your own job easier," he laughed; "but maybe it's a good idea."

A couple of days later, sure enough, he got me a horse. No longer was it necessary for me to walk around in that red mud or choking dust. There never was a happy medium. If the slimy clay wasn't ankle deep, the dust was so heavy you could hardly breathe. But it was a great life and a big-time operation for a boy of fourteen—a thrilling truck ride to and from work each day, a horse to ride, fifty dollars a week and a couple of cute girls in the neighborhood to help me spend it.

The only trouble with this pleasant situation was that it didn't last very long. An epidemic of influenza almost wiped out the community. It was dreadful. People were dying so fast that it was impossible to obtain coffins—or even cheap wooden boxes—for the dead. At the peak of the epidemic, bodies were stacked up like cordwood until it was possible for officials to set up a temporary sawmill in order to provide lumber for simple pine boxes in which to bury the victims. Mother was ready to go back to Indiana on the next train.

At the same time, union organizers moved into the Muscles Shoals area and my stepfather would have no part of their tactics while our nation was at war. His job was to help get the barracks and buildings ready as quickly as possible for the nitrate plant, which was to be the Muscles Shoals contribution to the war effort. It made him furious to have union organizers interrupt the normal working day with speeches designed to create discontent among the men in regard to their working conditions and their already generous pay scale. Rather than apply for a union card, he packed up the family, bag and baggage, and returned to Indianapolis.

Only a few weeks remained before my class was to graduate. But the first day we were home, Mother accompanied me to school and talked with my teachers. With their assurance that I probably would be able to make the grade by working real hard, I buckled down to the job. I was the proudest guy in the world when I received my diploma. The honor of making the class speech was like an extra layer of icing on a piece of cake.

CHAPTER 3

I WAS too busy catching up with my lessons during that month of May, 1916, to devote much attention to the 500-mile race. The magic name of Stutz, however, had been extremely prominent in all of the pre-race speculation. Even though a combination of a foreign car and driver won the big classic that year—for the last time, incidentally—Stutz made a better showing than any other American car. For that reason, I headed straight for the Stutz factory when it became time for me to look for a summer job.

For ten weeks I installed batteries in the new Stutz cars. But my principal accomplishment that summer was to learn to chew tobacco. I didn't feel like a full fledged member of the Stutz organization until I could chew as well as the rest of the men in the plant.

In the fall, I enrolled at Arsenal Technical High School, but from the first day I felt like a lost soul on the big seventy-six-acre campus. I had failed to register properly at the completion of grade school and my name wasn't on the freshman list. I bounced around at loose ends for more than a week. By the time the situation was straightened out, I was behind in my work and felt like a stranger in every class on my schedule.

I was completely disgusted with school. On top of that, I missed having my own spending money, a factor which had made life quite enjoyable in Alabama as well as during the summer in Indianapolis. Mother wasn't a bit happy with my attitude. Each evening, however, I told her a new tale of woe and at last she agreed I could quit and go to work again if I continued to study at home. I enrolled immediately with ICS for a mechanical drawing course and went to work for my step-father as an apprentice plumber.

Most of my associates were older than I and many of them were among the first to enlist when the United States entered World War I. John Carney probably was my closest friend at that time. When he finally went off to service, too, with the Marines, I was so lonely I couldn't even sleep that night until after I had formulated a definite plan of action. The next morning I invested in my first pair of long trousers.

"I'll wear 'em," I told the clerk, after he'd finally managed to fit me. "Wrap up the old ones and I'll take 'em home." But the minute I had the new pants on, I knew I'd never be happy in short pants again, so I tossed the package in the first corner trash can I passed. Then I found a fruit stand, ate all the bananas I could hold, took on a quart or two of water and walked into the Marine recruiting office with all the confidence I could muster.

Before I could say a word to the husky sergeant at the desk he said, "What can I do for you, young man?" If I had been a little smarter, that salutation would have been enough to let me know it was going to be "no dice"; but I stuck out my chest and said: "I want to enlist in the Marine Corps." I meant it, too.

He looked me over from head to toe—all five feet of me, weighing no more than 100 pounds, bananas, water and all—and smiled.

24

"I'm sorry, young man, but we can't possibly use little fellows like you."

"Maybe I'm little," I replied, "but I can lick a lot of guys you've got in the Marine Corps."

This time he laughed and made me as mad as I've ever been in my entire life by saying, "Look, sonny, the place for you while we're fighting this war is home with your mother."

I was so fired up and intense that I either had to fight or cry. He was big and I was a disappointed kid of fifteen, so I let the tears come. I wanted to run away and hide in a corner some place until I could get control of my emotions. But the big sergeant came around from behind the desk and led me over to a window so that no one else in the room could see my face. Then, with his arm around my shoulder, he told me how important it was for fellows like me to stay at home and grow up in a hurry so that we'd be ready when our turn came.

When he finally got me started downstairs, I still was mopping tears with the sleeve of my shirt and thinking what a lousy world it was when a fellow who really wanted to fight wasn't given a chance to show what he could do. If a gun was the "equalizer" most people thought it was, I was better equipped for combat than a lot of men already in uniform.

I had a terrible time walking home in those long pants. It seemed to me that both knees had started to stiffen up and the cuffs, flapping around my ankles, almost tripped me as I climbed the front steps.

Mother took one look, threw up her hands and exclaimed, "Good gracious, what have you done now?" I started to explain about my trip to the recruiting office. Half way through the account, however, I started to cry again. In another moment Mother was doing the same thing. She, undoubtedly, for one reason and I for another.

At the next Scout meeting, Mr. Purvis, our scoutmaster, showed up in army uniform with orders to report at an officers training camp. I told him of my attempt to enlist. Probably to ease my disappointment and keep my mind occupied, he suggested that I act as unofficial assistant scout master in his absence, helping Mr. Jacquart and Mr. Reid. I stuck it out for two weeks. When Mr. Reid showed up in army uniform, too, that was the last straw.

During the winter my sister had come to live with us again— her husband had died of tuberculosis of the throat—and one evening she said she thought she would enjoy visiting Dad for a few days. He was working in Detroit at the time. The mere mention of him awakened the same desire in me and we took off for the Motor City the following Sunday.

Dad was working at the American Car and Foundry Company, making more money than he had ever made in his life. To Sis and me, Detroit was a terrific place and Dad could think of something different for us to do every day while he was on the job.

One morning Sis and I were strolling along Woodward Avenue, looking in the show windows. Suddenly she said, "Wait right here a minute," and disappeared into the Saxon show room. After she'd been inside for what seemed like a long time, I entered too, in time to see her emerge from an office which had the name Harvey G. Wilson painted on the glass door.

"I've got a job!" she exclaimed, with a big grin on her face. "I'm going to start work here tomorrow morning."

"What about me?" I asked.

"You'd better go back home in a few days and stay with Mother," she said.

I didn't give her any argument, but I had other plans. I liked Detroit, too.

That night I looked up the address of two battery companies, whose names were familiar—Exide and Willard. The next morning, as soon as Sis and Dad had started for work, I jumped on a streetcar and went down to 1150 Cass Avenue, which at that time was the address of the largest electric storage battery station in the nation.

I walked in the door, located the manager, told him I was looking for a job and that I knew everything about batteries.

26

He hired me as a service man, at $40 a week, and told me to report for work in the morning.

"Do you care if I look around a bit and see exactly how you like to have your men do things?" I asked, as soon as the details were settled. He told me to make myself at home and I walked up to the most capable looking man in the repair department and confessed.

"They just gave me a job here in the service department," I explained. "I told them I knew a lot about batteries and I'm supposed to start work tomorrow morning. But I've never done anything to a battery in my life except install one in a car. What do I have to know to do my job?"

"I like a cocky little guy like you," he grinned. "Stick around and I'll show you." Within an hour I knew how to read a hydrometer and a discharge volt meter, how to recognize positive and negative battery posts, how to fill a battery to the proper level and everything I'd need to know, at least to get started.

Before the end of a month, my worries were over. Customers were asking for me by name, because of my willingness to do little extra things in the way of service for them. In 1917 and 1918, there were no storage batteries such as we have today. With wooden case, the life of a battery was comparatively short. They required attention every two weeks and they got it, because even a Ford battery cost between $30 and $35. One for a Cadillac or a Pierce Arrow ran as high as $55 or $60. Any intelligent car owner had his battery checked as often as his oil and water.

It wasn't long until I was made service manager at $100 a week, and that was a lot of money for a young man in those days.

Sis had to relinquish her job because of failing health, however, and her death was a terrible blow to Mother. After returning to Indianapolis for the funeral, I realized I was needed at home for a while. Because of the tremendous emotional strain which Mother was experiencing, there was nothing else I could do with a clear conscience.

27

That decision meant I had to look for another job and my first stop was Churchman & Taylor, the local Exide distributor. There was no other line of business in which my brief experience would be of any value.

"You can start in our electric vehicles department tomorrow," said Mr. Churchman, "but your salary will depend on how good a salesman you are. We can't pay you more than fifty dollars a week. But, on top of that, we'll give you a ten per cent commission on all of the batteries you sell."

At that time, there wasn't anything I despised more than an electric vehicle. As far as I was concerned, no red-blooded man should ever be seen in one. But the commission idea interested me because it seemed like an opportunity to make a lot of money. A battery for the average electric vehicle at that time sold for $300 to $550.

"It's a deal," I said. But it didn't take me many weeks to realize I had made a mistake. My heart wasn't in the job. For a while I kept my interest alive by purchasing a Milburn Light Electric and seeing how fast I could make it run. By installing the highest experimental gear I could obtain and using special thin-plate batteries to obtain the greatest possible acceleration, I managed to call upon potential customers in a vehicle which would attain a speed of fifty miles an hour. That was the absolute ceiling, because the limitations of any electric vehicle made further experimentation useless.

I lacked the patience necessary to deal with the elderly ladies who dominated my list of prospects. Most of them knew nothing about batteries and weren't interested in learning about them. They made their purchases from the salesman who listened most attentively while they talked about influential friends, rich relatives and memories of their younger days.

Mother was operating a rooming house at the time—the old Sterling R. Holt home at Meridian and 16th Streets. One of her boarders was Mac McConnell, an Illinois University graduate and an advertising salesman for the Chilton Class Journal. Occasionally he borrowed my Milburn to make business calls

28

and I accompanied him on one of these trips to the Speedway Engineering Company on North Illinois Street.

There I met Bill Hunt and realized immediately that I wouldn't be happy until I was in the same kind of business as Bill. I was sold on him personally too. Bill built race cars and drove them. In order to keep from starving, he also manufactured 8-valve and 16-valve cylinder heads for Model T Fords.

Ten minutes after I'd met Bill, I propositioned him for a job.

"You're nuts," said Bill. "There isn't any money in this business. I can't pay you enough to live on even if you're the best mechanic in the world."

"That doesn't make a bit of difference," I replied. "I'll work for nothing if I have to. I want to find out all about race cars—how to build 'em and how to drive 'em. I don't know of any better place to start than right here."

"I don't need another man right now," was Bill's comeback, "but if you want to wash parts and do all the other dirty work around the shop I'll pay you twelve-fifty a week."

I said "Okay" and went tearing back to Churchman & Taylor.

When I told Mr. Churchman I was quitting in order to go to work for Bill Hunt he exclaimed, "Wilbur, you're crazy. I know Bill Hunt, and I know you're making more money right now than he does. How much did he offer you?"

"Not nearly as much as you're paying me," I replied. "But I want to be a race driver and that's as good a place to start as any."

"If you've already made up your mind, I won't try to change it," he said. "But when you get your belly full of junker race cars, come back here. We'll have a job for you."

CHAPTER 4

IN ORDER to celebrate my transition from electric to gasoline vehicles, I borrowed Mac McConnell's Dort that night for a date. It wasn't much of an automobile, but it had a gasoline engine in it and that was all that was necessary. I spent half of the night driving around town and telling my companion what a great race driver I was going to be. Finally I took her home. But when I climbed back into the Dort in order to go home myself, I couldn't start it to save my soul.

After the selling I had given her—as well as myself—on what a whale of a mechanic and race driver I was going to be, the situation was embarrassing to say the least. I certainly wasn't going to let her know I needed help to get an ordinary gasoline engine started. So I took a streetcar home, filled my pockets full of tools, and rode another streetcar back to her house.

It was daylight before I finally located the trouble in the ignition system and made the necessary repairs. I was due at Bill's shop at eight o'clock, so I didn't bother about going home to clean up. But right at the busy intersection of Meridian and Ohio Streets, in the midst of all the morning rush hour traffic, the engine died again.

A quick examination revealed something else was wrong this time, but I had no idea what the trouble might be.

It was like swallowing a bitter pill to call Bill for help and I could tell by his voice on the phone that he wasn't enthusiastic about coming down town to tow me home. I didn't get any sympathy when he arrived, either.

"Just who do you think is working for who on this job?" was

30

his greeting. "The quickest way for you to get fired is to make a habit of stunts like this!"

I was glad he didn't have a chance to rake me over the coals at greater length as he towed me back to his shop. When we rolled to a stop, however, he said, "Now get busy and find out what the trouble is. That's your first job and you've got plenty of tools to work with. I'll call your mother and Mac so they'll know where you are."

Without even taking time out for breakfast, I went to work. The distributor points looked okay, but I couldn't detect any spark. I grabbed a new battery off the rack and tried it again with results that were not much better.

I told Bill what I had discovered and asked "What do I do now?"

"Get a new condenser," he replied.

Thirty minutes later the Dort was running as smoothly as a sewing machine. Bill suggested that I take the car back to Mac and get some breakfast at home. Only then did I realize I was hungry.

Mac was mighty happy to see his Dort running and all in one piece. Mother took one look at me and said, "Get upstairs and take a bath before you dare sit down at the breakfast table. I'll feed you after you get rid of all that dirt. Then you're going to bed to get some rest."

Admittedly, it was a bad start on my new job, but as I became more useful around the shop with each succeeding day, I finally summoned enough courage to ask Bill if he'd help me build a race car of my own.

"I've got all I can do to keep my own car running and take care of my business," he answered, "but if you want to start building a car on your own time, you can use any equipment here in the shop after hours. Just remember that you're working for me during the daytime."

The very same evening I started making the rounds of all the junk yards in search of suitable parts, full of confidence that I finally was on my way toward becoming the best race driver in the business. But it became evident, almost immediately, that the junk yard was no place to look for race car parts. Apparently no race driver ever discarded anything which might possibly be repaired at some future date. It was going to be necessary for me to change my tactics.

Finally I decided that the best approach to the problem was to get acquainted with as many race drivers as possible. While continuing to work for Bill during the day, I could lend a hand to some of the other fellows at night in exchange for used parts which were not quite ready for the junk yard. With this idea in mind, the first thing I had to do was learn how to be useful.

Bill's shop was well equipped. After spending a few days chasing parts for him in a stripped-down Model T Ford, I talked him into giving me an opportunity to do some of the inside work. It was well that he did, because I was becoming quite unpopular with the traffic officers of the Indianapolis Police Department. I had been operating on the theory that any time I was sent after something it was important for me to get back as quickly as possible. Every trip, consequently, was a race against time.

The day before Bill decided to give me a chance inside, I had almost run over a red-faced Irish cop at Illinois and Market Streets. While making a left turn around his stop-and-go semaphore with a little touch of what I regarded as a bit of Shaw flourish, the rear end of the model T failed to "break loose" for the anticipated skid. Consequently, the left rear wheel rolled over the corner of his small wooden platform and almost nipped his toes.

He really read me the riot act in his dripping Irish brogue and ended the incident by saying, "Git on out o' 'ere now and if ye iver come near this corner agin while I'm on dooty I'll put ye in the brig."

My first important inside job for Bill was case-hardening parts in a hand-operated forge and a cyanide pot. Later I learned that I was given the job because no one else wanted to take the chance of breathing those cyanide fumes. Before long I was running the acetylene welding outfit and practicing on some of the other equipment whenever I had a few spare moments.

I was beginning to think I was doing all right when I almost lost my job. Bill had hit a curb with his Keaton, which I believe was the only one in Indiana at that time. The accident had bent the metal ring used to hold the tire on the demountable rim. As a rule, no one but Bill ever touched the Keaton, but on this occasion he asked me to take off the rim and heat it in the forge so that he could attempt to straighten it. I got the fire going, bedded the ring down in it and then started to wind the forge with everything I had. I suppose I should have known better, but that's the way I tackled the job when I was heating cyanide and I didn't know that a different technique was needed for the rim.

After a few minutes of high speed cranking, I looked down and saw little sparks jumping out, so I called Bill.

"I think it's ready Bill," I said. "It's sparkling."

Never have I seen another man in all my life get so mad as he did, instantly. Without looking, of course, he knew I had burned his rim-ring beyond salvage. It was a crippling blow to the Keaton, because replacement parts for it were almost unobtainable. Considering the temper he had, it's a wonder he didn't kill me on the spot. As it was, I absorbed the worst tongue lashing I've ever received and he reminded me of my mental shortcomings every time he saw me for the next several days, even though I did my best to stay out of his way.

Gradually our relations returned to normal and I helped Bill get his 16-valve dirt track car ready for the coming season. I would have given my right arm for the privilege of driving it in the opening event at Hamilton, Ohio. This was out of the question, of course, because I hadn't even seen an automobile race up to that time. Bill gave me a real break, however, when he decided to send the car in advance by truck instead of driving it over to Hamilton on the morning of the race as most of the fellows did.

The National Road from Indianapolis east was all gravel at

the time and Bill didn't want to take the chance of damaging the car in any way.

"It's in tip top shape right now," he declared, "and we're going to keep it that way until the race starts. The other fellows can drive over on Sunday if they want to but this car is going in style.

"Here's fifteen dollars," he said, handing me three five-dollar bills and a road map. "Get the car loaded on the truck the very first thing Saturday morning and take off. I'll see you Sunday."

As I headed for Hamilton, wearing Bill's helmet, I was the proudest guy in the whole United States. Near Centerville, however, I heard a rod bearing go out in the truck engine. That took the wind out of me in a hurry. I pulled over to the side of the road, in front of a little shoe repair shop, and sat there for several minutes wondering what I should do.

While I was trying to solve the problem, I watched the cobbler going about his business through the window in the front of the shop and I suddenly had an idea. Why wouldn't a leather bearing do the job, at least until we were able to get back to Indianapolis after the race?

It took me an hour to get the pan off, because it was so hot. I tried to keep the oil in the pan so I could use it again, but a lot of it spilled on my face and chest when the pan came down. I was really a mess when I took the rod cap into the cobbler and asked him to cut a piece of leather to fit the space formerly occupied by the babbit metal in the big end of the connecting rod bearing.

He acted as if he thought I was crazy and I wasn't real sure he wasn't right, but I had to try something. It was difficult to make him understand what I wanted. Finally I sketched a rough pattern and he cut a piece of oak-tanned sole leather that fit almost perfectly. When I wrapped it around the journal on the crank shaft and pulled up the cap it looked as if it might work. So I took the leather out again, soaked it in oil for several minutes and then put it back into place.

The cobbler was getting more interested in the operation all of the time. He was able to provide a lard can and a piece of cloth for use in straining the babbit out of the oil. He watched me put the pan back into place and then helped pour the oil back into the engine. But when the task was completed, he said he still didn't think it would work, and he wouldn't accept a thing for his services. That probably was the cheapest connecting rod bearing replacement ever installed and I limped into Hamilton without further difficulty.

It was almost midnight when I arrived, so I drove straight to the race track and curled up in the cab of the truck to get as much sleep as possible. Bill found me there the next morning, still snoring, and he was hopping mad because the race car was covered with dust. After hearing my story, however, he changed his tone and it was music to my ears to hear him tell some of his friends of what I had done.

I was a busy guy until Bill qualified. After that, I had some time to see what was going on and my eyes almost popped out of my head. I'd never seen so many race cars at one time in all of my life. They certainly were not very hot by today's standards, but they looked wonderful to me. Some of the top mid-west dirt track drivers of that day were on hand. Among those ready to run were Skinny Clemons, Ford Moyer, Charlie Brown, Chance Kinsey, the Ormsby boys, Ralph and Homer, as well as eight or ten others of almost equal ability.

I must have acted like a kid going berserk, trying to help everyone do anything which needed doing. For at least thirty minutes I pushed my heart out on every car which needed pushing. A few minutes before the race was scheduled to start, I returned to Bill's pit and climbed on top of a stack of spare tires to get a better view of the proceedings. As the field got under way, the dust became so heavy it was impossible to see anything except what happened immediately in front of me.

On about the fifth lap, Bill failed to come around with the rest of the pack and I noticed a lot of the spectators running toward the north turn. I couldn't see what had happened up there, but there wasn't any doubt in my mind that Bill was in trouble. I took off as fast as I could run along the inside rail until I could see a gap in the outer barrier with a crowd of people in the background. In some way, without being hit, I managed to sprint across the track. Then, like a football player with the instincts of a mad bull, I dove through the outer rim of the crowd and fought my way to Bill's side.

He was stretched out on the grass and I emerged from the inner rim of the crowd with such momentum that I fell right on top of him. Then, regaining my balance, I knelt alongside of him and took his face in my hands. He was as pale as a ghost and his shirt was soaked with blood.

"Bill! Bill! Are you badly hurt?" I shouted above the engine noise of the other cars.

Without even opening his eyes he said, "What?"

"Can't I do something for you?" I asked.

"Don't worry about me," he replied. "I'll be all right by tomorrow or the next day. Tell Chuck to take care of the truck and the car and then have him check with me at the hospital."

About that time they came up with a stretcher, put him on it and slid him into the ambulance. I tried to climb aboard, too, but he wouldn't let me.

"You do what I told you to do," he ordered. "And get back home tonight the best way you can." Then, probably thinking that he might be able to steer me away from racing after what I had just seen, he added: "This isn't a very safe business. Anyone who doesn't want to die young ought to stay out of it."

I watched the ambulance until it was out of sight, more convinced than ever that I liked the excitement of automobile racing. I also delivered Bill's message and asked Worth Slowman if he had any idea how I could get home. He suggested that I might get a ride with Brownie in the Lexington, which was the only race car at the track with headlights. The Lexington was a converted passenger car with two bucket seats attached to the frame. But Brownie would be in the driver's seat and his mechanic, Fuzzy Davidson, would be in the other.

"I've got a load," said Brownie, "but if you want to hang on all of the way to Indianapolis I'll get you home."

"I'll manage," I answered. When we finally headed for Indianapolis, I was spread out like a dancer doing the splits. I had one foot on each side of the frame with a finger tip hooked over the back of each bucket seat. Five minutes of that was all anyone could stand, so I tried putting my right foot on the rear axle housing. It was jumping up and down so fast it scared me at first, but it was a much more comfortable position than I had taken originally.

By the time I became tired in this position I had gained considerable confidence and I finally placed my right foot squarely on the rear axle. It was awfully rough on my legs and it sounds silly now, but we travelled almost seventy miles an hour most of the way home and I enjoyed every minute of the ride.

This was the life for me despite the dust and danger and disappointments and hard work which went with it!

CHAPTER 5

ALMOST overnight, my already intense desire to become a race driver developed into what might be termed a mania. I didn't even want to take time out to sleep or eat.

After working all day for Bill Hunt, I'd spend most of the night helping some other driver get his car ready for a race on the coming Sunday at one of Indiana's county fair half-mile ovals. I wasn't particular who I worked for, either, as long as he was willing to exchange spare parts—or even rejected parts —for my services.

One of my most frequent haunts was Ford Moyer's little brick barn at the corner of the alley on Fourteenth street, between Meridian and Pennsylvania. Moyer preferred to sleep during the day and work at night, when it was cooler, and I had to pass right by the shop on my way home from Bill's place. Often I would forget all sense of time and work with Moyer until Mother came after me.

In those days, dirt track drivers all used motorcycle tires on their race cars, which in most cases were powered by Ford engines with Frontenac cylinder heads and were called Fronty Fords. Ninety pounds of air and a generous application of shellac kept the tires on the clincher rims, but it was necessary to mount them a couple of days in advance of a race to give the shellac time to dry. I mounted almost all of Ford's tires. We became close friends and he helped tremendously in assembling the parts I needed to start work on my own car.

As soon as I thought I had enough to begin the job, I didn't hesitate to take advantage of Hunt's offer to use his tools on my own time. The frame, alone, required hour after hour of patient work because the only one I had been able to find was rusted and cracked. In order to make it strong enough, after cleaning off the rust, I must have done almost as much welding as the steel workers who erected the Empire State Building.

Before I could make much additional progress, however, Bill went out of business. He wasn't making any money out of Imperial Motors, building and installing special equipment for stock engines, largely because he was too busy fooling around with his own race cars to take care of what business came into the shop. But he owned the building and needed money. With a chance to rent the lower floor, he took it immediately and moved all of his equipment upstairs. Then he handed me a duplicate key and walked out, after telling me to keep right on working until the car was finished.

That's the kind of a friend Bill was. To this day, I think he would have turned down any prospective tenant who would have interfered with my private little project. He understood how much it meant to me to have a place where I could try to fulfill what at that time was my only ambition.

Before casting my lot with Bill, I had managed to save several hundred dollars. It was enough to get me through the winter. By early spring, the car was practically finished. Late at night, I fired it up for the first time. In that otherwise empty second-floor room the noise was deafening. Engine vibration loosened many weeks of accumulated dirt from the walls and ceiling. An overly-rich fuel mixture resulted in clouds of smoke which covered the woodwork and windows of the building with an oily film.

A hasty inspection of the damage to the lower floor furnishings convinced me it was time to vacate the place immediately. That posed a new problem, which I hadn't even considered, although it had existed for many weeks. I had been so intent on building that race car, I hadn't paid any attention to what was going on around me. Like the man who built a boat in his basement, I was stuck with it.

In remodeling the lower floor, the new tenants had divided it into a number of small offices. The area in front of the freight elevator still was open, but there was no possible way to get the car out of the building—after bringing it down to the first floor—without tearing out all of the office partitions. Swearing at myself didn't seem to help matters, so I went back upstairs to see what could be done.

From every angle I studied the problem, it was very evident the only solution was to remove the window casement and knock out enough bricks to make an opening large enough to accommodate the car. That operation would create another problem—getting the car down to the ground without damaging it. As I looked out the alley window, however, I noticed several 2 x 12 planks which the decorators had used as scaffolding. It would be a gamble, but it was worth a try. I couldn't do the job alone, however, so I headed for home to catch up on my sleep.

The following afternoon I recruited the help of a couple of friends and we tackled the job as soon as the building was vacated in the evening. The window casement came out easily. Then we started the tedious work of chopping the mortar from between the bricks and removing them, one at a time. We took 'em all out, down to floor level, and widened the opening on both sides until it was large enough for the car to pass through.

We even stacked the bricks in a neat pile, with good intentions of returning later to put them back into place.

The alley wasn't wide enough for us to run the car straight through the opening. We had to install the heavy planks on an angle and this complicated the problem because the left front wheel would be two or three feet down the left ramp—and several inches lower than floor level—before the right front wheel would begin to roll down the right ramp. It was very evident that such procedure would tilt the car into a precarious position, but we had no choice in the matter. Finally everything was ready for the attempt with both planks braced securely. We rolled the car up to the opening and tied a heavy rope to the rear axle. Then we ran the rope through a convenient pulley at the top of the elevator shaft and took our respective positions. I climbed into the cockpit, one of my pals eased the car out on the planks cautiously and the other member of our trio hung on to the rope in order to regulate the speed of my descent.

It's a wonder I didn't break my neck and I suppose I should have been scared silly—especially when the planks began to sway and sag as they felt the weight of all four wheels. My only thought, however, was to get the car on the ground without damaging it. Near the halfway mark, I suddenly felt as if something was ready to snap under the strain and I yelled at the top of my voice: "Let her go!"

It was all over in a matter of seconds. Because the bottom of the left ramp was braced against the wall of the building on the opposite side of the alley, it was necessary for me to cut my wheels to the right while the nose of the car was still fifteen or eighteen inches above the ground. It resulted in quite a jolt, but the car was intact and that was all that mattered. We jerked the planks down and stacked them against the wall. Then, pushing the car ahead of us, we ran out of the alley as if we had robbed a safe. I doubt if we turned out the lights. I know we didn't protect the interior of the building from the elements, by covering the hole we had made in the wall. And I never went back to see if the necessary repairs ever were made. I was too busy getting the car ready for the race program on the coming Sunday at the Hoosier Motor Speedway, which was a half-mile course on the outskirts of Indianapolis.

Roscoe E. Dunning was the starter at the track and he prided himself on looking after the safety of all the drivers. He didn't care about hurting anyone's feelings if he thought a special ruling was necessary in the interests of the majority. He always acted as if he felt personally responsible for everything that happened on the race course and he ran the show without much backtalk.

I'd only completed two practice laps when he flagged me off the track before I'd even had a chance to see how fast the car would run. I certainly wasn't ready to come into the pits, but I eased off the throttle and coasted up to him on the next time around.

"Get that iron off the track," he shouted, before I had even had a chance to ask why he had flagged me. He meant it, too, and I doubt if I've ever been as mad at any other man in my entire life as I was at that instant. I cut the switch, jumped out and charged up to him like a mad bull.

In his opinion, I was nothing but an eighteen-year-old kid without enough brains to realize that my "bag of bolts" was a hazard to every other driver on the track. Before I ran out of breath, however, I let him know how long I had been dreaming about this particular day, when I would be driving a race car of my own in actual competition. I don't remember exactly what I said, or how I said it. But when I had finished screaming at him, I'm sure he knew how much work and worry and sweat and tears had gone into the building of that little car which I had proudly named the Imperial Special.

I said some things I'm ashamed of, too, because he couldn't have hurt me more if he had sentenced me to death. It was the end of the world, as far as I was concerned. I didn't want to go on living if I couldn't be a race driver.

Not a muscle in his grim countenance moved until I had finished my tirade. Then he smiled, sympathetically, and put his hand on my shoulder.

41

"Look, son," he said, "you're not going to run on this track today. You want to be a race driver and that's not hard to understand. But the only thing for you to do now is calm down. Drop in to see me some afternoon next week and we'll talk things over."

It was evident that further argument would be useless, but I made up my mind right then I would go to some other track and show him how wrong he was in not letting me run.

The opportunity came two weeks later at a half-mile fairgrounds track in Lafayette. Although Hunt didn't plan to run that day, he was on hand in the pits when I arrived and he was anxious to see what kind of a car I had put together. I regarded his presence as a good omen. His interest in me had made the car possible and I told him I was mighty happy to have him there to watch me win my first race.

After I had turned a few practice laps, he took the car out himself and seemed to like the way it handled. Then I took it again and tried to get into the turns the same way he did. Although I hated to admit it, I still had a lot to learn. Bill watched me closely and appeared to be considerably worried when he finally had a chance to talk to me as the starter cleared the track in preparation for qualification.

"Why don't you wait until you've had a chance to get a little more practice?" he asked. "Racing is a risky business and these dirt tracks can be treacherous until you get used to them."

I laughed at him.

"I'm not kidding," he said. "You haven't got a chance today."

"I've got to start sometime," I replied, "and it might as well be now."

"If that's the way you feel about it," he said, "let me qualify the car for you so that you won't have to start from way back in the field."

Under AAA rules that would not have been possible, but this wasn't an AAA race. His suggestion sounded like a good one and the race officials offered no objections. Bill did a good job, too, turning in the second fastest time to give me the outside position in the front row as the field lined up in pairs for the flying start.

"How fast should I go on the turns?" I asked Bill, as I waited for the starting signal. I hadn't even thought about it until then.

"That's something you'll have to learn for yourself," he answered. "It's almost impossible to turn one of these little cars over. But if you are going too fast on a turn you'll begin to slide off the track. Then it's time to ease up a little. Don't worry about it," he added. "You'll feel it in the seat of your pants after you've made a few laps."

That's all the time we had to talk about it. Whatever else he might have told me wouldn't have helped much anyway because I had very little judgment of speed in those early days. That's something every driver has to learn the hard way and it doesn't come quickly.

When the flag dropped, Ralph Ormsby was in the pole position on my left and "Chance" Kinsley was immediately behind me. They were two of the "hot shots" during that 1921 campaign, but I beat them into the first turn—probably because they didn't want to get too close to an inexperienced rookie they never had seen in action before.

It was a wonderful feeling to be out in front and, for a few seconds, the world was my oyster. I wasn't smart enough to realize that the chief reason I had got through the first turn safely was because I hadn't been running fast enough to get into trouble. By the time I was half way through the backstretch, however, I was running wide open. I headed into the turn without easing off of the throttle and a bit of everything happened all at once.

First, the car started "skipping" sideways. Then it slid into a rut and I was riding only on my two right wheels with no knowledge of what to do under such conditions. After about fifty feet of this involuntary stunt driving, the car leveled off again and the left wheels hit the ground with a jolt. It seemed as if the whole frame was being twisted out of shape as another rut grabbed at the right wheels and this time the car did a complete roll, taking a big section of fence with it.

I have no recollection of ever lifting my foot from the accelerator as these developments occurred with lightning rapid-
ity. But I did have sufficient presence of mind to scoot "down
in the basement" as we call it. I was small enough, too, so that
the cowling protected my entire body as the car rolled.

I climbed out of the wreckage with no more personal damage
than a variety of painful bruises, but one glance at the car was
enough to convince me that the Imperial Special was beyond
repair. In thirty seconds I had wiped out six months of the
toughest kind of work imaginable.

Hunt was among the first to reach me.

"Are you the guy who said it was impossible to turn one of
these things over?" I challenged.

"I'm the guy," he answered. "But, honest, Wilbur, if you
learn to stay out of those ruts, it probably won't happen again
in ten years."

That was small comfort. There wasn't a more dejected individual in Indiana as I loaded the wreckage on a rented truck
and started the trip home. On the way, I recalled Dunning's
invitation to "talk things over" and I was waiting on his door-
step the following morning.

CHAPTER 6

IT DIDN'T take me long to tell Dunning what had
happened at Lafayette. I also apologized for what I had said to
him two weeks earlier and reminded him of his suggestion that
we talk things over.

"What do I do now, Mr. Dunning?" I asked. "I haven't got
a car and I haven't got any money to buy a car. But I still want
to be a race driver."

44

"If you're sure you've learned your lesson," he answered, "I've got something you might be interested in. I like your spirit and there's a Fronty Ford over in my garage which doesn't need much work on it to be as fast as any dirt track car in this neck of the woods. Go over and take a look at it. I need a driver. If you like it, and if you're willing to follow instructions, I think maybe we can make a deal."

"I don't have to look at it!" I exclaimed. "I know I'll like it."

"All right. Go on over and get to work on it then," he said.

Neither of us had mentioned percentage. I had no idea whether I'd be driving for money or peanuts. But I didn't care. He brushed aside my thanks and pretended to be too busy to bother with me any more that day. I walked over to the garage and feasted my eyes on a sleek shining, firewagon-red race car.

After a couple of days of work, with some help from Dunning in the evenings, I had that engine purring like a kitten. Because of the color of the car, and the fact that his initials were R. E. D., we named it the RED Special. His official connection with the Hoosier Motor Speedway as starter made it possible for me to get in some practice and three weeks later he "turned me loose" for a series of sprint races at the same Lafayette track which had been the scene of my first race.

The new, unpainted boards in the fence on the east turn served as a reminder of my inexperience. But this time I had some idea of how to go about the job I was trying to do—how to steer with my throttle—how to drift on the turns in order to keep from losing any more momentum than absolutely necessary—and how to keep out of trouble. It was a grand and glorious feeling to collect the winner's share of the purse for one of the shorter events on the program, even though it amounted to only $18. There was even greater satisfaction in the knowledge that I was being "accepted" by the racing fraternity.

Unquestionably there is more of that "one for all and all for one" spirit in automobile racing than in any other sport. Every day during those early years I learned something new from another driver or mechanic or car owner. None of them, including Hunt and Dunning, ever was under any obligation to help me. But they did; and the same situation has prevailed down through the years, even in the "big time."

Any race driver will tell you that it's no fun beating someone who is handicapped by inferior equipment. If one driver has a spare part he isn't going to need on a particular day, it's common practice for him to lend it to some rival who needs it and then go out and try to beat him anyway.

By the spring of 1924, after I had won the National Light Car Championship with the RED Special, promoters were beginning to offer me "appearance money." That's the term used for the system which assures a driver—who is a favorite with the fans—of a stipulated fee for participating in a race even if he doesn't win any prize money. During the next three years I believe I raced on every mile and half-mile track in Indiana, Illinois and Ohio—except the few which were open only to AAA drivers.

That was the life!

We not only raced on those tracks. We raced to them in the morning and then raced all of the way home at night. It's quite true that such proceedings were against the law. But it's equally true that we were mighty hard to catch and we regarded this "cops and robbers game" as a regular part of our racing experience. Traffic on the unpaved roads was comparatively light. The hazards of speeding in those days were not nearly as great as they are now. There was no state police force to patrol the highways. Sheriffs had jurisdiction only in their own counties. Most of them lacked the necessary equipment to catch us from behind, unless we ran into trouble. All we had to do was reach the county line to be safe from arrest until another sheriff took up his unsuccessful pursuit.

Actually it was the noise of our engines, on which we used no mufflers, which aroused more animosity among townsfolk and farmers than our speeding. Honestly, I didn't blame them, and I certainly wouldn't condone such practices under the conditions existing today. But it was less expensive to pay an

46

occasional fine than it was to buy trailers in order to transport our cars from track to track.

I got the whole gang into trouble one day on the way home from the Roby Speedway near Chicago. We had raced there on a Saturday and then "worked" until almost dawn spending our prize money in some of the night spots. It was mid-morning when I roared into Lebanon at the head of the pack. People were visiting with one another in front of the churches and it was a shame to shatter the quiet Sunday atmosphere. A local shower had washed the streets clean and it was really a lovely scene which made me feel somewhat sacrilegious because of all the clatter I was making.

I eased off the throttle a little as I approached the corner of the courthouse square, where the street made a right-angle turn. But the rain had left the asphalt slicker than I realized. I wasn't expecting any trouble and when the tires suddenly lost their grip on the pavement, I did a full loop quicker than it takes to tell about it. The RED Special crashed into the hitching posts in front of the row of stores bordering the square. The motor stalled and everything was quiet. The car remained on all four wheels. But with the engine dead, I was in trouble. Race cars with battery ignition and automatic starting devices are extremely rare. In order to get rolling again, I would have to persuade some one to push me. Before I succeeded in that, the "law" probably would have me in its clutches.

This time, however, I was lucky. With people converging on the scene of the accident from all directions, the first to reach me were eight or ten children, their scrubbed faces shining with awe at the sight of an honest-to-goodness race car and the oil-stained countenance of its driver.

"Come on, gang," I shouted. "Give me a push, quick."

They jumped to the job as my ears caught the roar from the approaching cars of my fellow drivers. One mighty shove from five or six of the boys—and a couple of girls—was sufficient to bring my engine back to life. Some of them probably were spanked soundly when they got home because of the oil and grease and dust on their previously spotless "Sunday-go-to-

47

meeting" clothes. But I was on my way an instant before the town constable arrived to place me under arrest.

I found out later the other fellows were not so fortunate. They had to reduce speed to avoid the chance of hitting someone in the crowd, which had gathered at the spot. The constable waved them to a halt, demanding to know who was driving the car which had knocked down the hitching posts and then "escaped" with the help of the Sunday School pupils. He got an immediate answer from Ford Moyer.

"If you'll give me a push, officer," Ford suggested, innocently, "I'll catch him and find out."

"Smart guy, huh?" grunted the constable. "You're not going to catch anybody for a while. You and all of your pals are going down to the JP court with me. And if I have anything to say about it, he'll make the fines stiff enough to take care of the guy who got away."

They didn't have enough money among them to pay the fines and had to cool their heels in Lebanon until some of their friends could drive out from Indianapolis with sufficient cash to get them out.

Even some of the cops were race fans at heart, however. On one occasion I was cruising back alone from a race and it was necessary for me to drive through the very center of Fort Wayne. There was no chance of "slamming through town" with the same surprise tactics which usually worked in the smaller villages. It was safer to "sneak" through, cutting the engine speed to its bare minimum of approximately forty miles an hour and "slipping the clutch" to reduce actual speed another ten or twelve miles without stalling.

I was guilty of driving without a muffler, but I was making an honest effort to comply with the speed laws when a huge policeman stepped off the curb in front of me and held up his hand. I had to kill the engine to keep from hitting him and I was mad.

"You big ape," I shouted. "Now I'll have to sit here until I can get some one to push me. And it's all your fault."

"Okay, Okay," he answered, impatiently. "I just wanted to

48

know who won today. If I hadn't had to be on duty, I'd have been over there to watch you. Tell me what happened and I'll get someone to push you."

Darned if he didn't too. We talked about racing for several minutes, while a small crowd began to gather. Then he recruited a couple of young fellows to help him give me a push and I was on my way again—hoping that I'd pick up a fast mail train to race from Anderson to Indianapolis.

We often raced trains, while also racing each other, especially on the way back from Frank Funk's track at Winchester. We always returned by way of the National Road (US 40), which paralleled the Pennsylvania railroad tracks between Richmond and Indianapolis. We would park on the crest of a hill, so that we could get started again without a push, by releasing the brake and coasting downgrade until we attained sufficient momentum. We'd give the train a flying start and then see who could overtake it first.

That was rough. The road was gravel and with ninety pounds of air in our tires to keep them on the rim, twenty or thirty miles at top speed would almost jar the insides out of you. By that time, however, we'd be out in front of the train. We'd stop on the crest of another hill to get a little rest, while waiting for the train to overtake us, and then take off on another "lap" of the homeward journey.

I'm not proud of these incidents when we violated the law and ignored the fundamental principles of highway safety. In those days, however, it was necessary for us to drive our cars over the regular roads in order to reach a track on which to race. We turned each trip into a race to keep from getting bored on the way and we participated in an even greater number of foolish and impetuous stunts on the race track.

On more than one occasion, I even rode the tail of a race car out at the old Hoosier Motor Speedway. My first attempt of this kind was the result of a dare. But I got such a kick out of the experience, that I did it often. It was almost like riding a bucking horse. I'd "mount" from behind, reach forward with both hands to get a good grip on the back of the cockpit and

49

clamp my knees around the tail of the car. Then the driver would start circling the track at steadily increasing speed in an effort to make me say "uncle."

Usually they "went along" with the stunt and didn't make it too tough on me. I never was thrown off and I don't remember ever being forced to ask one of them to stop although Dutch Bauman came close to "curing" me. On that particular ride he was determined to make me ask for mercy. After reaching top speed, with no indication from me that I'd had enough, he began hunting out every hole in the track surface. On one turn, he finally jolted my knees loose from their grip and knocked the wind out of me. He must have heard me grunt. Or else he suddenly realized no human could stand much more of such punishment.

"Had enough?" he shouted.

Even though I had, I wasn't ready to admit it.

"I'm not ready to quit unless you are," I gasped.

But after another lap, he began to reduce speed and I was able to get a grin on my face again, so no one would know how scared I had been.

"I want to make a couple of more practice laps," he yelled back at me. "But I'll slow down in front of the pits on the next trip around and you can drop off. I'll tell you when to let go."

To this day, I don't know whether he did it intentionally, or not. His judgment of pace, while slowing down after running at top speed, might have been as far from accurate as that of most average drivers on the highway when they enter a small village. You've probably had the experience yourself when you've hit the outskirts of a little community while running seventy or seventy-five miles an hour and suddenly seen a sign: "speed limit, 20 MPH." You ease up on the throttle. Your speed drops off gradually. You're sure you're not running more than four or five miles an hour over the specified limit until you glance at your speedometer and then you're surprised to see that it shows forty-five or fifty.

Maybe that is what happened in this case. When Dutch shouted "now" he was travelling at least forty. I didn't realize it, myself, until my feet hit the ground. The instant they touched, I was thrown in what would have been a bone-breaking head-long sprawl on the track if the instincts developed in tumbling had not come to my rescue. Automatically, I did a half somer-sault and doubled up into a ball, with my arms and legs tucked as close to the trunk of my body as was physically possible.

I landed on the back of my shoulders and rolled down the track until my momentum was exhausted. Aside from a few minor bumps and bruises, I wasn't hurt. But I was mad and it didn't help matters when Dutch pulled into the pits after one more lap with a big grin on his face.

Even if it had been his intention to ask if I was all right, I didn't give him a chance. The instant he was out of his car, I started swinging with both fists. Taking him by surprise, al-though he was at least forty pounds heavier with a definite physical advantage in every department, I got in a half-dozen good licks before he could retaliate in any way. By that time, the other fellows had started to separate us and the "battle" was over. Without actually apologizing, he let me know he had not tried, deliberately, to "mess me up." We continued to be the closest friends—and at the same time the most intense rivals on the race track—of anyone in the racing business.

During my entire racing career, I always derived greater pleasure in beating Dutch Bauman than any other driver. He must have felt the same way because, if no one else wanted to race us, we'd race each other.

One of our most unusual "duels" took place one rain-drenched afternoon on a muddy track at Chicago. The grandstand was well filled and about thirty of us were ready to start the time trials when the heavens opened. The downpour lasted almost a half-hour, washing out all hope of staging any part of the scheduled program.

The disappointed customers began to leave as soon as the rain diminished. Hundreds of them had driven many miles to see us put on a show. But their disappointment was mild in comparison with the feeling of frustration which we drivers were experiencing. There's nothing worse than getting yourself

51

"fired up" to win a race and then have no way in which to work off all of that pent-up emotion.

Dutch and I had been scheduled for a match race against each other. Although the elements had conspired against us, I knew I wouldn't be able to "cool off" until I'd had a chance to beat him, so I challenged him to go on with our regular plans in the mud. He was willing and, together, we went in search of the officials.

Even though we intended to race for nothing—not even a side bet of our own—they didn't want any part of the idea. It took a lot of talking to change their minds. Finally, of all things, I sold them on the idea that such a race would be perfectly safe and would serve to bring the crowd back to see us again a week later.

"We can't get enough traction in that mud to go over thirty or forty miles an hour," I argued. "We probably will be half a lap apart most of the time. With no other cars on the track, no one's going to get hurt. But the fans really will get a kick out of watching us slide around."

With some reluctance, they gave the announcer instructions to tell the crowd we had agreed to put on the match race in spite of the slippery track. Fans who already had reached the parking area, came back to the grandstand to watch us and we climbed into our respective cars. Never before or since, have I seen so much flying mud. Despite everything we did, neither of us was able to hold the lead for more than a lap. Usually we changed positions on each turn. Almost invariably, whichever one of us succeeded in attaining sufficient speed to get out in front on the straightaway, failed to negotiate the next turn. It seemed as if I was traveling backwards half of the time and Dutch wasn't faring any better. I passed Dutch while I was going sideways on one occasion.

He was leading again at the start of the last lap, but he went into another spin on the final turn and the tail of his car was pointed toward the finish line when I slithered by him to get the checkered flag from a mud-spattered official. It didn't mean a thing, except that I was luckier than Dutch on that par-

52

ticular afternoon. But the tension was gone, the crowd had enjoyed our little show and we weren't concerned about the extra work ahead of us in order to get the mud off of our equipment.

Racing was fun under any conditions. I had my share of bad luck—along with the good—but it didn't matter because I realized each mile of competition brought me a little closer to the "big time."

I lost a 1924 Labor Day race at the Hoosier Motor Speedway because of a broken clutch shaft, after leading for forty-four laps. A month later, at Detroit, I had a 100-mile race "in my hip pocket" when an axle shaft broke with only ten laps to go. Things took a turn for the better at the start of the 1925 season and my early victories included a 100-mile event at Toledo on June 15. Three weeks later I had a chance to prove my ability in a 200-lap race before hometown fans at the Hoosier track. I really wanted to win this one, but I took one chance too many and lost control of the car on the first turn during the 125th lap. It tore down a lot of fence and did a one-and-three-quarters "barrel roll," sliding to a stop on its side.

I ducked under the cowling at the first sign of trouble and wasn't scratched. In fact, I don't even recall being excited at the time. I fit into the cockpit of the RED Special so tight that I couldn't get into or out of the car without removing the steering wheel. I always carried a special wrench with me in order to perform this operation quickly and the Indianapolis papers used feature stories on the accident because I was able to remove the wheel and extricate myself from the wreckage before help reached me.

By the middle of 1926, I'd had a chance to drive for several prominent car owners, including Skinny Clemons. After winning the Red Grange Sweepstakes at the Hawthorne track in Chicago, I felt certain I was ready for AAA competition. Several of my friends, who also were my most formidable rivals, had the same idea.

We were reluctant to take such action because we didn't want to "walk out" on the promoters who had made it possible for us to get into racing. But Jack Leach and Frank Funk, who promoted races at the Roby Speedway near Chicago and on the high banked track at Winchester, Indiana, respectively, were sympathetic with our desire for a chance at the larger purses—including the Indianapolis "500."

Frank was particularly helpful. In looks, as well as actions, he always reminded me of what I had learned about Abe Lincoln. He knew that what we wanted to do was the only logical step for us to take if we ever intended to amount to much in racing. He talked things over with Jack and both of them decided to join the AAA along with us, so that we could continue to race for them most of the time and still be eligible for all of the top events in the country.

With their cooperation and approval, we worked out the details so that we would be embraced by the AAA in a body, drivers and promoters alike, at the beginning of the 1927 campaign.

One more important race remained on our 1926 schedule, following the meeting with AAA officials. I celebrated the occasion by driving one of Art Chevrolet's Fronty Fords to a new track record of 1:21:56.1 for one hundred miles at Hawthorne.

CHAPTER 7

LIVING dangerously, no matter how you do it, has a certain amount of romance and fascination which appeals to the girls. I don't ever recall being hungry for feminine companionship after becoming a race driver. Even though they occasionally infringed on the amount of time necessary to get my car ready for a race, it was nice to have them around when the pressure was off. You can't beat 'em, for a pleasant change of pace and an outlet for the pent-up energy untapped by the thrills experienced on the track.

No one girl, however, had occupied my attention for any length of time until a few weeks before the end of that 1926 season. Then I met Beatrice Patrick while I was back in Indianapolis to repair an engine I had torn up in a race at Akron, Ohio. It was the night of the first Dempsey-Tunney title fight. Ted Elliott, my close friend and ex-mechanic, had invited a bunch of us out to his home to listen to the radio account of the battle. But I don't remember anything about the battle—except that Tunney won—because another friend of Ted's walked in at about that time with a girl who took my mind completely off the fight and racing and everything else.

If you can imagine a blond Irish Madonna, she was it. Five feet and five inches tall, weighing 115 pounds and built like a Greek goddess. If I had been struck by lightning, the effect wouldn't have been more devastating than my first glimpse of her. Every time she looked at me and smiled, I felt like a helpless puppy caught near a wet spot on a new carpet.

I don't know whether it was the home brew or only the way in which she looked at me, but my stomach tied itself in knots and I had the first taste of indigestion in my entire life. I didn't know whether I'd swallowed a skyrocket or a cannonball, but never have I had a more dreadful feeling. This embarrassing experience, however, turned out to be a blessing in disguise. When she realized I really was ill, she became the most solicitous and sympathetic person in the room. Maybe the pain in my tummy didn't actually stop when she put her cool hands on my forehead, but at least I didn't feel it any more. The hands did something that made me forget about everything except her intimate presence.

I had enough presence of mind, however, to continue getting "sicker and sicker." At the same time, I managed to get the idea across to her—without everyone else knowing it—that the one thing I needed above everything else in my future life was to have her around all the time. I probably did it in a stumbling and awkward manner, but I meant it. And the won-

derful part about it was that she believed me. She didn't say
so, but I knew it by the almost imperceptible little squeeze she
gave me with those soft cool hands on my forehead.

Clara Elliott, Ted's wife, finally broke the spell. Apparently
I was overdoing my sick act, because Clara left the room for a
minute and then came back to us and said, "Here's a dose of
bicarbonate of soda that should put you back on your feet
again."

I said "Thanks," without much sincerity, but I did sit up and
begin to take part in the general conversation again. After the
friendly bets on the fight had been settled and the party was
beginning to break up, I suddenly realized that I didn't even
know the girl's name. They called her Bea, but I didn't know
her last name or where she lived or anything about her except
that she was wonderful. I cornered the fellow who had brought
her to the party and said, "That girl of yours certainly is a
honey. Does she have any sisters?"

"She has one cuter than she is," he replied.

I was certain that couldn't be true, but I said, "If you're
going to have another date with Bea tomorrow night, why
don't you pick me up about eight o'clock and take me along so
I can meet her? If she isn't busy, all four of us can go out
together and the party will be on me."

As soon as they had headed for home, however, I knew I
couldn't wait until tomorrow to see Bea again. I didn't want
anything to happen to that girl; and most of all, I didn't even
want to let her get out of my sight. So I said "Good night" too,
somewhat brusquely perhaps, in my haste to get out of the
door in time to see which direction they were headed. Their
car was just turning the corner. My Jordan Playboy roadster
was headed the wrong way, but I vaulted over the door,
started it quickly and made a U turn in the middle of the block
to be sure I wouldn't lose them.

They weren't in any particular hurry and I loafed along behind them at a discreet distance. When they pulled up in front
of her house, he stopped and turned off his lights. I did the
same thing almost a block behind them and then started into a

slow burn because they didn't get out of the car immediately. My blood pressure was mounting every second, thinking about someone else petting "my" girl. I'd almost made up my mind to walk up and take charge of the situation, which probably would have ruined everything, when they finally climbed out and strolled up on the porch. Her stock went up instantly, when she gave him a little peck of a kiss and went inside almost immediately.

As soon as he drove off, I started my engine again and pulled up exactly where he had parked. I ran up her front steps as if the law was after me and knocked on the door. But it wasn't Bea who answered. Instead, it was her father who opened the door and I could have sunk straight through a crack in the floor. I was totally unprepared for such a development and he didn't help matters any by standing there, silently, with an inquiring expression on his face. He didn't even ask me what I wanted, or anything.

That was one of the few times in my life I felt absolutely speechless. It seemed as if it took me all of five minutes to regain my voice and get across the idea that I wanted to see Bea for a moment.

"Do you know what time it is?" he asked.

"Yes," I answered; "but I know she hasn't had time to get to bed and I've got to tell her something yet tonight."

"Well, if it's too important to wait until morning," he replied, "come right on in and tell all of us about it."

That probably was the moment to retreat, but I've always believed that the best defense is a good offense. And, strangely enough, some inner voice seemed to tell me that he was the kind of father she ought to have.

We went on in and when I met Bea's mother I knew I hadn't made a mistake. She had the nicest eyes of any I've ever looked into. One glance was enough to tell me I was "home, free." While Mr. Patrick called upstairs for Bea, I pulled a chair up alongside her mother and started to tell her the full story of what had happened that evening. I didn't even slow down when Bea's father came back into the room. He'd be easy, if I could sell myself to Mrs. Patrick, because anyone could tell in a hurry who was boss in that household.

Bea was only a minute or two getting back downstairs, but by that time I had covered most of the territory I wanted to cover. And it was well that I had, because as soon as she entered the room I found it impossible to keep my mind on what I was saying. That helpless puppy feeling engulfed me and I looked to Mrs. Patrick for help. There it was, in the form of a wonderful smile of understanding and sympathy. I could have climbed right up on her lap and kissed her.

Through what remained of the short conversation, Bea sat there with the quiet self-assurance of a beautiful conqueror. And believe me, she was. In desperation I finally got around to blurting out, "Do you think it will be all right if Bea and I have dates?"

Without giving Mr. Patrick a chance to answer, Bea's mother turned on that wonderful smile again and said, "I'm sure it would."

With that, I leaned forward and kissed her. And I don't mean Bea. I kissed her mother. Then I shook hands very formally with Bea and her dad, said "Good night" to everyone and headed toward home—driving that roadster of mine like a mad man. I had the feeling that I was the luckiest guy in the whole world and I had to tell someone all about it.

Mother was in bed and sound asleep when I entered the house. The first she knew of my being there was when I jumped right in the center of her bed and started to talk as fast as I could.

Coming up out of a sound sleep, she grabbed me by the shoulders and said, "Wait a minute, Wilbur, wait a minute. What's this all about?"

I started all over again and as the story unfolded she began to realize that I really was in love for the first time.

She kept saying, "Slow down, slow down."

Each time, I'd answer, "Mother, I can't slow down," and then keep right on talking as fast as the words would come.

It was almost daylight before we quit talking—or maybe I

58

should say until I quit talking because Mother did very little but listen until I ran out of things to say about Bea. When I finally went to bed, after considerable persuasion, I was almost afraid to go to sleep because I didn't want to wake up and discover it was all a dream.

After a whirlwind courtship, which reached hurricane proportions at times, we were married six weeks later in the little church on Monument Circle and we spent most of the winter enjoying a Florida honeymoon.

CHAPTER 8

THE outlook never was brighter and I was the happiest guy in the world as we returned north in the early spring.

At last I was eligible for the "500" and I wasted no time trying to line up a ride. Skinny Clemons convinced Fred (Fritz) Holliday of the Holliday Steel Company that I was a better-than-average prospect. Fritz was ready to put up the necessary cash if we could find a suitable car—and if I could prove to him that I was half the driver Skinny said I was. A few days after the big track was open for practice, we were "in business."

The car we chose was the one in which Jimmy Murphy had driven to his death at Syracuse in 1924. Frank Elliott had purchased it from the Murphy estate and, with the help of a comparatively unknown California mechanic named Louie Meyer, had cut the piston displacement from its original 122 cubic inches to the required 91½ by reducing the stroke. After getting it ready for Indianapolis, however, Frank had grabbed at the opportunity to drive a new car in the big classic and was offering the old rebuilt Miller for sale. It certainly wasn't the "hottest" car entered in the race, by far. But it had four wheels and an engine and that's all I thought I needed.

When we had looked it over thoroughly, Fritz suggested that I hop in and see how it handled. They pushed me off and it was just like driving into paradise. I picked up speed going through the first two turns and the backstretch looked as if it was a mile wide and ten miles long.

"This is going to be a breeze," I told myself. "Anyone who can't drive on this kind of a course doesn't even belong in an automobile."

Two laps were ample to warm up the engine. On the next trip I "cut" one. It was a little better than 104 miles an hour and Elliott ran out on the track, waving a sheepskin coat, to flag me in. To me it didn't seem particularly fast. I knew I could have gone faster. But it was fast enough to suit him, because he owned the car and didn't want it skinned up. I hated to interrupt the symphony of that Miller engine, but I followed instructions. The music of it probably wouldn't get any applause at Carnegie Hall. But to me it sounded like a violin and a pipe organ and bagpipe performing together as an accompaniment for the song of the tires on the bricks.

One look at my beaming countenance, as I took off my goggles, convinced Fritz I was thoroughly satisfied with the car's performance. The deal was closed immediately with Meyer's agreement to serve as mechanic. I was so jubilant I didn't even offer any objections when Fritz said he planned to name the car the Jynx Special. Some of the boys were quick to point out that this put a double "hex" on my chances—a name like that for a car which already had been branded "Murphy's death car." But I would have carried a dozen "hexes" around the track on my back for a chance to drive in the "500" and Fritz had good reason for selecting the name.

He had been offered the Indianapolis distributorship for a new product designed to end the tire worries of the entire motoring public and the race car gave him an opportunity to advertise it. Like other youngsters, I had used canned condensed milk to good advantage in my bicycle tires many years earlier

60

and I imagine that is where this idea had originated. Whatever the sticky substance was, it was to be injected into the tire tube through the valve stem for duty as a puncture-sealing material.

After a couple of days of practice and experimentation with various plugs and fuels, we had the car running like a watch. We had managed to work out every problem without a great deal of trouble and we finally found time to put Jynx into the tubes. Everything seemed to be perfectly normal as I gradually picked up speed through the first turn. But when I stepped on it at the start of the back stretch, the car quivered and bucked and jumped like an outlaw horse. It semed as if no two wheels ever were in contact with the track surface at any one time. The car was almost unmanageable. Owing to the tremendous centrifugal force developed at high speed, the sticky substance all had collected at one particular spot in each tube and thrown all four wheels out of balance.

I made my first contribution to safe driving by throwing away the puncture-sealing "goo" immediately, but we were stuck with the name and we raced with it. Although my car lacked the power to come within ten miles an hour of the top speed of the newer creations, I qualified comfortably. Then Louie and I tore it down, inspected every moving part and reassembled it with painstaking care. It ran like a charm. All we had to do was wait until race day to see what fortune had in store for us.

Several of the boys against whom I had been campaigning on the smaller tracks—Cliff Woodbury, Louis Schneider, Jack Petticord, Fred Leckleider, Dutch Bauman, Al Cotey and Benny Shoaff—also had managed to earn starting positions and I was thankful for their company on this first "big league" attempt.

The favorites were such veterans as Tom Milton, Frank Lockhart, Pete DePaolo, Harry Hartz, Eddie Hearne and Leon Duray. Milton was my personal idol—a gentleman at all times, a supermechanic and a terrific competitor who drove with his head as well as his hands and feet.

He had announced his retirement two years earlier, but had been persuaded to climb back into the cockpit for this particular race as a replacement for Cliff Durant, who was too ill to drive. It was a real thrill, just to be on the same track with him and the other former "500" winners—even in practice.

As race day approached, the tension grew with each succeeding hour. On the morning of May 30, I actually was trembling with excitement before I came within sight of the Speedway. I did my best to appear nonchalant as we pushed the car out on the track in front of our pit and placed all of the necessary tools and equipment into their proper spots. But my hands and limbs actually were tingling. My heart was beating a steady tattoo on the inside of my ribs. I felt as if my stomach was full of butterflies as large as blackbirds. Even my kidneys got into the act. But three trips to the men's toilet—when it seemed impossible for me to wait until I could get there—all proved to be false alarms. Friends spoke to me. And sometimes I answered. But I have no recollection of any word which actually was said.

It's extremely difficult to describe my complete mental and physical approach to that first "500," but men who have gone into battle probably will understand. The realization that others were experiencing the same sensations, or even worse, didn't help.

"The world's biggest band" (anyone who wanted to carry an instrument could march and then seen the race free of charge in those days) finished its parade on the main straightaway and the command finally was given for us to assume our starting positions. The long wait was about over.

The job of pushing the car to its designated spot in the No. 1 position of the seventh row came as somewhat of a relief from the mental strain which had almost reached the breaking point. Walking to the starting line for the traditional panoramic picture of all participants and officials provided another brief but welcome interlude.

The tension mounted again, however, as we returned to our cars. My temples were throbbing. My lips seemed dry and parched, even though I moistened them with my tongue every five or ten seconds. With my heart in my throat it was all I could do to swallow. The muscles in my chest seemed to have such a stranglehold on my lungs that I had to make a conscious effort to breathe.

"What will I do if my engine fails to take hold?" I asked myself. But when the signal finally was given, my worries were over. Louie spun the crank. I hit the switch on the third or fourth revolution and the engine roared into life instantly.

With the other thirty-two cars contributing their full share of noise to the bedlam, my eardrums felt as if they would burst. I couldn't hear a single word spoken to me by any member of my crew as each of them wished me good luck with a handshake or a slap on the back.

All of the tension built up during weeks of work and worry exploded into unbridled excitement. It was impossible for anyone to conceal his emotions any longer. Tears and prayers were intermingled with laughter as the excitement of that final moment affected each of us in different fashion. Then I was rolling forward on the pace lap.

Although racing men, as a rule, are not religious in a demonstrative way, it's a rarity to find any successful person who doesn't admit the need for Divine help if he expects to do a good job at anything. Men who live dangerously, I believe, always are a little closer to their Maker than the average individual. From the time you climb into a race car until you bring it to a safe stop, you never are out of a precarious position. It's difficult to really love racing without being more or less of a fatalist, and—as we began to gain momentum—I'm quite sure that a great many shared my private little prayer of "Thy will be done."

As I passed the grandstand, from which I knew Bea and my mother were watching every move I made, I waved in the general location of their seats even though I couldn't pick them out in the crowd. With the wave, went a message of reassurance over the ever-reliable heart "telegraph system." Their answer came instantly. And as we moved slowly into the first turn I settled down to the important business at hand.

With the entire field in perfect formation by the time we

63

reached the northeast corner of the course, the pace became faster. We made the turn into the main straightaway at about sixty miles an hour and picked up a little more speed. I punched the throttle in order to maintain my position. Then we hit the north cross-over on the main stretch, used earlier in the day by race fans desiring to park in the infield, and all hell broke loose. I was enveloped immediately in a regular sand storm because of the dirt left on the track by their shoes and tires. Momentarily, that beautiful all-brick racing strip was no better than a dirt track. I couldn't see a thing because of the dust kicked up by the cars ahead of me. I couldn't lift my foot from the throttle without running the risk of being hit from behind. But my years of dirt track experience came to my rescue and I didn't flinch.

Still enveloped by a cloud of dust, we were doing better than a hundred miles an hour a few seconds later when instinct warned that it was time to ease off a bit in preparation for the southwest turn. I lifted my foot and nothing happened. If anything, I seemed to be going faster. I didn't realize it at the time, but I had become a part of a 100-mile-an-hour "tornado."

Have you ever stood close to the edge of a highway when a truck rolled by at fifty or sixty miles an hour and felt the vacuum created by it almost suck you along with it? If you have, you probably can visualize the tremendous force generated by thirty-three closely-bunched race cars traveling twice as fast. It's an awesome experience to be a part of such a rapidly-moving mass of air.

Such speed on a turn, in heavy traffic, was a new experience. I never was more scared in my life as I felt the tremendous pull on the tires. But, somehow, I managed to avoid disaster. The entire field began to string out in single file on the short south straightaway and the danger diminished almost as suddenly as it had materialized. I was on my own again, at the wheel of a familiar car with a clear view of the track ahead of me.

The scenery on either side of me, however, was a complete blur. I couldn't even pick out my own pit on the first time or two around the course. But gradually my faculties adjusted

64

W. S. at the time of his grade school graduation in 1916.

An excellent photograph of W. S. at the wheel of the Boyle Maserati Special in which he scored two of his three "500" victories. 1940.

The Red Special with W. S. at the wheel and R. E. Dunning at the right. 1923.

Another view of the Red Special. 1923.

W. S. in the Jynx Special which he drove in his first 500-mile race. 1927.

The C-1 Clemons Car which W. S. drove in 1926, prior to his first 500-mile race the following spring.

Barney Oldfield modeling W. S.'s crash helmet, the first ever worn in competition by an American race driver. Presented to W. S. by Major H. O. D. Segrave of England. Spring of 1932.

The starting line-up for a race at California's Ascot Race:

In this picture, according to their starting positions, are Ernie Triplett, Mel Keanely, Sam Palmer, Chet Gardner, Stubby Stubblefield, W. S., Babe Stapp, Les Spangler, Mel McKee, Herman Schurch, Louis Tomei, Carl Ryder. 1932.

Wilson Photo

Former heavyweight champion Jim Jeffries awarding a trophy to W. S. after his victory in a helmet dash at the Ascot Track in California. 1932.

Frank Lockhart's Stutz Black Hawk Special at Daytona Beach before his fatal accident.

The remains of the Lockhart car after the accident. April 25, 1928.

W. S. in the Blu-Green Special which he drove to a new world's record on Muroc Dry Lake, California, in the spring of 1932. From left to right are "Doc" Betz, chief timer; Harold Harper, assistant timer; Waldo Steih, Firestone Tire & Rubber Company; Art Pillsbury, AAA Zone Supervisor; and George Stephenson of the AAA Technical Committee

W. S. in the Blu-Green Special with his lion cub mascot, Hannibal. 1932.

W. S. in the Mallory Special which he drove in California, 1932.

W. S. and Otto Wolfer in the Ford which W. S. drove in the Mines Field Stock Car Race in California. 1934.

Wilson Photo

W. S. in the Vance Car which was called "Red Pete" and which he drove in his first California race in the fall of 1930.

A general view of the Mines Field course.

The most serious accident in W. S.'s early racing career, which occurred during a race at Ascot. His body can be seen between the underneath side of the rolling car and the top of the guard rail. 1933.

W. S. helping to extricate his car from the Atlantic Ocean after deliberately driving it into the water when the motor caught on fire. Daytona Beach, 1928.

The Whippet is finally brought back on the beach after the disastrous fire.

W. S. in the Whippet Special before the record attempt at Daytona Beach, Florida, which ended in the racer catching on fire. 1928.

W. S. in the Gilmore Red Lion Special before a California race. 1933.

O'Dell & Shields

O'Dell & Shields   *O'Dell & Shields*   *O'Dell & Shie*

Frank Lockhart   Harry Hartz   Ralph Mulford

O'Dell & Shields   *O'Dell & Shields*

Eddie Hearne   Gaston Chevrolet

Howdy Wilcox   Jimmy Murphy   Tommy Milton

O'Dell & Shields   *O'Dell & Shields*   *O'Dell & Shie*

W. S. with a raccoon mascot at the Speedway in 1937.

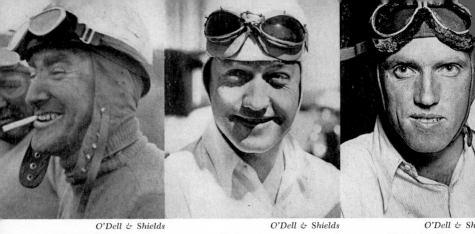

Al Gordon

Babe Stapp

Francis Quinn

Stubby Stubblefield

Chet Gardner

Ernie Triplett

Arval Brunmier

Les Spangler

Dr. Fred Loring

themselves to the high rate of speed. I located my pit on about the fifth lap and recognized all the familiar faces of my crew on the next trip around. By the tenth lap I was reading their signals without any difficulty and I managed to find time for a glance at the special drivers' scoreboard which identified the cars in the first five positions. Frank Lockhart, winner the previous year, was the leader.

I wasn't doing so well and Clemons wasted no time calling my attention to the matter. His signals told me I had dropped back to twenty-third position, but I was beginning to regain my confidence with each succeeding minute. If I ever was going to get up near the head of this pack, it was time to start. I passed a couple of stragglers and then had to ease off again for a few minutes because of three spectacular accidents in rapid-fire order. None of them happened within my own range of vision. As I came down the main stretch on my twenty-fourth lap, however, I saw Norm Batten's empty car blazing alongside the inner rail, where he had jumped to safety after bringing it to a halt. On the next trip around the course I saw Jules Ellingboe being lifted from the wreckage of his car on the north turn. And a few minutes later I got a glimpse of an emergency crew carrying Henry Kohlert from the track after he had been thrown from his car when it hit the wall on the south turn.

With the course clear again, I moved up steadily to seventh place. But the physical beating I was absorbing was terrific. In those days, before most of the track was resurfaced with Kentucky rock asphalt, the bricks were really rough. Except for the Duesenbergs, with their wider and longer springs, there wasn't a car in the race which didn't make a good try at the job of beating its driver into a pulp. The shorter, narrower springs didn't begin to do the work expected of them and the friction type shock absorbers were a far cry from the hydraulic units of later years.

Such veterans as Frank Elliott, Milton, Hearne and Dave Evans already had asked for relief when I had to make my first scheduled pit stop for fuel, oil and a right rear tire. I felt as if I had served as a punching bag for Jack Dempsey, but I was still "on my feet" and confident of going the distance. I had no thought of getting out of the car. As Skinny and Louie serviced it, however, Fritz handed me a cup of water and said, "Why don't you let Louie take a few laps while you're getting a little rest?"

"I'm all right," I replied.

"Maybe you are, now," he said. "But all of the smart boys, who know what it takes to win this race, already have asked for relief so that they'll feel like 'punching it' at the finish. Come on and get a little rest," he urged. "Let Louie take it for fifteen or twenty minutes and then you'll feel fresh when it counts the most."

The pit work had been fast. The car was almost ready to roll again. There wasn't much time to argue and I certainly didn't want to offend the man who had made it possible for me to get into this race in the first place.

Reluctantly I said "okay" and climbed out. Meyer jumped in and took off like a scared rabbit, but I didn't relax a minute. I would watch him out of sight into the south turn and then lean far out over the pit wall to focus my eyes on the north corner until he came into view again.

Three or four laps of this inactivity on the sideline was about all I could take. I wanted to get back into the race so bad I could taste it and this desire was magnified tremendously when Bauman and Lockhart both were forced out of the running by mechanical trouble while leading the field. Dutch had moved into the number one spot when Lockhart made his first pit stop at about the same time as mine. Almost instantly, however, a broken pinion gear had ended Bauman's hopes of winning. As the result of this misfortune, Lockhart had regained command briefly, only to have a connecting rod break.

Although we had lost two positions on our own pit stop, these developments moved us up to seventh place again and I felt as if I couldn't wait a minute longer to get my hands on the wheel once more.

"Get out the board and tell Louie to come in on the next

66

time around," I shouted. "With a little luck, I've got a chance of winning this race."

"Certainly you have," Fritz agreed. "But keep your pants on. We can't afford to waste any time. If we call him in now, you'll have to make another stop later for enough fuel to finish the race. If we let him go ten or twelve more laps, a full tank should carry you the rest of the way."

That made sense, despite my impatience.

"Start getting the board ready, anyway!" I exclaimed.

Each lap seemed interminably long. Louie acknowledged the command, however, as soon as Fritz gave me permission to hold up the board. He eased into the pit on the next trip with a big smile on his face. He had moved up to sixth place and I knew he had enjoyed every minute of his ride. Now it was my turn again.

A quick inspection of the tires indicated that all of them were in good shape. We filled the fuel tank to the brim, added oil and water, and I was off.

The pit stop had set me back one position, to seventh, and Pete DePaolo was leading the pack as a relief driver for Bob McDonogh. It was the third car Pete had been in that day. Earlier he had "spelled" Tony Gulotta for several laps. And even if he stayed in this one during the remainder of the race, I knew he would have to make at least one more stop for fuel. I was fairly certain, too, that everyone else in front of me was in the same boat as Pete.

I was too far back to win unless the real front runners failed to finish; but the mechanical "death rate" already was high and climbing steadily. I was resolved to make sure no one caught me from behind and I was praying that luck would give me at least an even break on every attempt I made to improve my position.

DePaolo was the first to run into trouble. His pit stop on the 149th lap appeared to be routine procedure for fuel and tires. But he lacked his former speed when he got back into action. Souders, the only driver who had not asked for relief up to that time, moved into the No. 1 spot. Then Benny Shoaff, Earl Devore, Tony Gulotta and Dave Evans—the only others still ahead of me—made their last scheduled pit stops in quick order. When they were running again, Souders was about three laps ahead of Shoaff's car, with Babe Stapp driving it in a relief role. Stapp enjoyed a similar margin over the third-place Devore. Gulotta was next in line, two laps farther back, and I was right on his tail. I had moved ahead of Evans while he was still in the pit and also had passed DePaolo, whose speed had been cut sharply because of supercharger trouble.

Barring unexpected developments, neither Gulotta nor I had a chance at the top prize, but we certainly put on a whale of battle for fourth place. Despite the extra horsepower at his command, I'd almost catch him on the turns, only to have him widen the gap on the long straightaways.

When Stapp was forced out of the running late in the race, because of a broken rear axle, Souders suddenly found himself with a lead of eight full laps over his nearest challenger, Devore, who in turn was two laps ahead of Gulotta and me.

As the two of us continued our duel for third place, too far back to challenge them, they finished at reduced speed to minimize the danger of mechanical trouble. I made a supreme bid to pass Tony on the 197th lap, cutting his advantage to such a short distance that I could almost reach out and touch the tail of his car on the turns. But he pulled away again and finished ahead of me with one final display of his superior power. He simply had too many horses under his hood.

For a guy who seldom was satisfied with anything short of first place, I was a happy individual when I accepted my fourth-place prize money of $3,500 at the traditional Victory Dinner. I was sure anyone who could finish fourth in a car whose top speed was ten or twelve miles an hour under that of most other entries, could win with a good automobile. Next year I intended to prove it.

CHAPTER 9

BEFORE running in the "500" for the first time, I had made arrangements to drive for Floyd Smith of Detroit on the dirt tracks during the summer after the race. He owned a Frontenac which Shorty Cantlon had been campaigning without too much luck. I had been driving for Slim Heinly of Chicago and when I heard that Shorty was dissatisfied with the Frontenac I suggested that we trade cars. He jumped at the chance.

Floyd and I had been teamed up only a few weeks, however, when he suddenly decided to buy another car offered for sale by the Miller brothers of Hollywood. It was even faster than the Frontenac, but the maintenance cost during the past year had been far in excess of the prize money won with it by Cliff Bergere. Floyd thought he knew how to keep it running.

He closed the deal by phone and received a wire authorizing him to take possession of the car in Hammond, where Cliff had been working on it. Cliff usually kept his cars in meticulous condition. This one was reported to be ready to run, so we planned to pick it up on the way to Roby and race it the next day.

Floyd's sense of humor often took peculiar quirks. Our opening conversation with Cliff indicated he had not been informed of the deal and when Floyd glanced into the cockpit he noticed a picture of Cliff's wife, Ramona, pasted on the instrument panel. With no explanation of any kind, Floyd reached under the steering wheel and peeled off the photo.

"Women haven't any business around a race car," he exclaimed. Then, with Cliff mad enough to tear him apart, Floyd

69

handed him the picture along with the telegram confirming the sale of the car. It was a peculiar way of declaring ownership, but Floyd often did things differently from anyone else.

We towed the Frontenac to Roby and I qualified it on the pole. It ran like a scared rabbit, jumping at the slightest pressure on the throttle. But it also raised the immediate question as to how long it would run. Cliff had a gear in the rear end which enabled him to reach peak speed about half way down the straightaway—quicker than anyone else. But from then, until it was time to ease off for the turn, it seemed as if the engine would tear itself loose from the frame.

"This thing will really run," I told Floyd, "but unless I miss my guess, it won't stay in one piece very long. It's likely to cost you a small fortune before the season is over."

"Quit worrying about it," he ordered. "Just go ahead and pour it on."

When the starting flag dropped, I proceeded to run away from the field. There wasn't another car on the track with comparable acceleration and I added to my lead steadily, even without running wide open at any time after the first lap.

Despite this consideration for the engine, however, it seemed to be screaming its head off. Near the end of the straightaway, at about the 40-lap mark, without any other warning, the scream suddenly changed into a bedlam of expensive noises. I hit the switch and kicked out the clutch, but it was too late. The damage unquestionably was considerable.

At Roby there was a driveway on top of the hump at the start of the first turn. I steered the car right off the track and sat there until the race ended, wondering how long it would take to make repairs and knowing that the cost of the necessary parts probably would run into four figures.

I was a mighty dejected individual, when Floyd finally was able to cross the track and join me. It irked me no end to see a big grin on his face—after my earlier warning.

"You've got nothing to grin about," I exclaimed. "Those noises you heard didn't come from the universal joint. It's going to cost some dough to get this thing back into shape."

70

"Quit worrying about it," he answered. "It doesn't bother me a bit."

"Don't kid yourself, brother," I replied. "You're hurt, plenty, right in the pocketbook. If you don't believe me, take a look under the hood."

"I'm not hurt and neither are you," he explained, still grinning.

"When you took the lead and started to run away from the field," he continued, "Horace Dodge walked up to me and asked how much I wanted for the car. I added $2,000 to the price I had paid the Miller brothers and Dodge wrote the check right there. Here it is."

That was a surprise which left me with mingled emotions. I was glad Floyd wasn't saddled with the expense of repairs, but I regretted the fact I apparently wasn't going to get another chance in the Miller. I never had driven a dirt track car which handled so easily. I said as much to Floyd and then he came through with his second surprise.

"I forgot to tell you," he laughed. "You're part of the deal. In fact, everything is just the same as it was except that Dodge is paying the bills and we're working for him on a percentage. He wants us to travel first class, too."

We shipped the car back to Detroit and found we had broken a crankshaft, ruined a cylinder block and ruptured the case in a couple of places. While we were putting it together again we changed the gear ratio in an effort to minimize the risk of repeating the damage. This time we made the mistake of being too conservative and I had to drive like hell in order to get fourth place in a 100-mile race at Kalamazoo, Michigan, in our next start.

Again we changed the gear ratio for a race at Langhorne, Pa., on July 4. Because Langhorne always had been one of the fastest dirt tracks in the country, we decided to take out the standard gears for dirt tracks and use a gear similar to that employed on the bricks at Indianapolis.

If Langhorne had been in its usual condition, I still think we would have had a distinct edge on the other entrants. But the

71

promoters had made some changes. In an effort to eliminate the dust, they had given the track a generous coating of oil on the day before the race and worked the top dirt loose so that the oil could penetrate better. The course was as "heavy" as I had ever seen it and it was too late for us to do anything about it, even though it was evident we didn't have a chance to win. Quick-change rear ends were unknown in racing circles at that time. With the track in that condition, I didn't have enough power to pull a sick woman out of bed.

I was on an "appearance deal," however, making me feel obligated to compete as advertised, so I ran the entire race in second gear with one eye on my tachometer to make sure I wouldn't tear the engine apart. It really worked out better than I anticipated. Most of the other cars also were geared improperly for the conditions that existed that day and I managed to get fourth place at the finish.

The official records still credit me with a third in that race, but Freddie Winnai actually finished in that spot—right in front of me—and both of us knew it. He was ahead of me in the starting lineup, neither of us had been required to make a pit stop and I never had passed him. When they paid us off, however, the third prize was handed to me and the fourth prize was given to Freddie. He objected immediately and I supported his argument, but the promoter insisted he was going to pay off according to the final standing given him by the official scorers.

Together, Freddie and I then went to the scorers and told them of their error. They wouldn't listen to us and claimed that they couldn't possibly be wrong. Disgusted by their refusal to admit their mistake, I called Freddie aside and suggested that we take care of the situation ourselves.

"The points don't make any difference," I said, "Because neither of us has a chance at the National title. Since first place in the race isn't involved, the only thing that really matters is the prize money. I'll endorse my check to you. You endorse your check to me. Then everybody will be satisfied, including the scorers."

72

That's what we did, too.

The following day, Floyd and I shipped the car by rail to Chicago for our next race at Roby. We'd taken Dodge at his word when he said he wanted us to go "first class." But when we reached Chicago we could find no trace of the race car.

The freight office told us there was no record of it ever having arrived so I went direct to the yard master in an effort to get a full-scale search under way. I'd always wondered how the railroads managed to keep track of all the freight cars, anyway, and I was getting a little bit of a kick out of finding that they didn't.

It was an interesting experience to watch the yard master turn loose his "bird dogs" on the job of tracing the car. Messages began to fly back and forth by morse code along the entire route and it wasn't long until he was able to tell us the car had been located at Gary, Indiana. He seemed to be quite satisfied with the results he'd obtained so quickly, but our problem still wasn't solved.

"That doesn't do us much good," I said. "I'm supposed to drive it in a race tomorrow and I've got to have enough time to change gears before I even try to qualify. How can we get it here in a hurry?"

"Just keep your pants on, young man," he replied. "I'm going to give you an engine and let you get it right now."

"I can't operate a steam engine," I said.

"I don't expect you to," he answered. "But I'm going to give you an engineer and a fireman to take care of that part of the job."

It was the best offer I'd had for a long time, as far as unusual excitement was concerned, so I sailed merrily out of the door in the direction of the nearest switch engine. He accompanied me and, after giving the crew its instructions, told me to climb into the cab.

"They don't need any help from me to run this big brute," I exclaimed, jumping on the cow catcher. "I'd rather ride out here in front." I had seen trainmen do that occasionally and I thought it would be a new thrill. Believe me, it was. During

73

the next few minutes I had ample reason to wish I hadn't been so darned cocky.

As soon as we were rolling along at a pretty good clip, the wind began to tear at my clothes and bother my eyes. I missed the usual protection of cowling and goggles. The strangest feeling, however, came on the turns. Because my position was several feet in advance of the front wheels of the locomotive, I'd continue straight ahead for an instant on each turn. Then as the wheels followed the rails, it seemed as if I were traveling directly sideways until the track straightened out again.

To a person trained as I had been for several years—to respond instantly to side movements of only a few hundredths of an inch and always to keep headed in the exact direction I wanted to go—this experience was plain poison. I'd had my fill of it even before we reached Gary and was glad to climb into the cab for the return trip.

We worked most of the night to make the necessary changes on the car and finished the job about ten o'clock in the morning, after getting a few hours of sleep.

This time we had hit upon the correct gear ratio and I was doing all right until late in the race when I began to "feel" the faint tap-tap-tap which is the signal of impending trouble in a small engine turning at a very high rate of speed. I eased off the throttle and managed to salvage third place. As soon as the race was finished, however, I told Floyd I thought we were in for another repair job. It wasn't much trouble to remove the side plates, so we took a quick look and the No. 8 rod was loose.

At this rate we were going to continue doing an awful lot of work for very little money. We discussed the prospects on the way back to Detroit and then had a long talk with Dodge. The car was his, to do with as he wished, but we were going to devote our time to something we knew would stay together and we got Smith's Frontenac ready again for the next race at Roby. It was fast enough to win that event, but on Labor Day the entire world seemed to collapse around me.

Bea and I were expecting a son late in the fall. Early in the

74

season she had accompanied me on almost all of our trips, but when traveling began to make her uncomfortable, she'd made up her mind the safest thing to do was to remain at home with Mrs. Smith.

Floyd and I were scheduled to race at Milwaukee on Labor Day and everything had been fine when we started the journey. When we registered at the hotel about seven o'clock in the evening, however, there was a message for me to call Detroit. It required almost an hour to get the call through, because of some unexplained delay, and I paced the floor of our room every minute of the time. At last I heard Mrs. Smith's voice on the phone.

"Don't be alarmed," she said. "I'm sure everything is going to be all right. But Bea started to hemorrhage this afternoon and I wanted you to know that her doctor has taken her to the hospital so that she'd be sure of getting all of the care she may need."

She gave me the name of the hospital and I placed another call to check direct with the doctor. The hospital switchboard operator couldn't locate him immediately. But when I identified myself and asked for news of Bea, she said, "Just a minute, Mr. Shaw."

Then the voice of a strange nurse came on over the wire.

"We've been trying to get you for several minutes, Mr. Shaw," she exclaimed. "We have bad news for you, so brace yourself. The baby was born prematurely and—despite everything we could do—it was impossible for us to save Mrs. Shaw."

I couldn't say a word. I couldn't even hang up the receiver. Floyd finally took it out of my numb hand, obtained a few additional details from the nurse and then placed his arm around my shoulders in silent sympathy.

Within an hour we were on our way back to Detroit by train. For me, it was the end of the world. All of the way home I kept asking myself what I could possibly have done to deserve such a raw deal from the One who governs all of our lives here on this earth.

Somehow I managed to get through the ordeal of bringing

the bodies of my wife and baby back to Indianapolis for the funeral services at her parents' home. With their burial everything was finished as far as I was concerned. There was no place to go, nothing I wanted to do, and no one I wanted to see. I simply didn't give a damn about anything.

CHAPTER 10

FOR several days I stayed close to home, spending much of my time with Mother. Floyd called twice from Detroit, urging me to rejoin him and resume racing in an effort to forget my grief. But I wasn't interested.

Finally he called again. After severing our connections with Dodge, we had discussed the possibility of buying a little Miller chassis from Charlie Abell, who had dumped his engine apart earlier in the season. I had suggested it would make a "hot" car with the Frontenac engine in it.

"I've just closed a deal with Abell for the Miller chassis you wanted," Floyd said. "Now I need a lot of help in order to get the Frontenac engine installed in time for the 100-mile race at Cleveland.

"The chassis is right there in Indianapolis," he added. "Why don't you bring it up here and give me a hand?"

I still wasn't interested. But with the proposition put to me in that manner, I couldn't let Floyd down.

The installation was quite a job. The one piece of mechanical equipment we had at our command was a drill press. The engine definitely was too big to fit into the narrow frame without the necessity of a great many changes. But we finally worked out every problem with the help of a hack saw, a file, a ham-

76

mer and a welding torch. When we finished, the car may not have looked like much, but it really would run.

The only trouble was that my old eagerness for competition was gone. All of my life I had concentrated on whatever seemed to be fun, with a terrific desire to excel at everything I attempted. Bea's loss had changed all of that. Nothing was fun anymore. Because of that feeling, I didn't think it would be fair to Floyd to resume our former relationship. Some one else, with an honest yearning to win, could do a better job for him.

At his insistence, however, I raced the car in promoter B. Ward Beam's 100-miler at Cleveland and finished second. Another driver in the same car, I thought, might have won. I told Floyd so and went back to Indianapolis.

A sprint race program was scheduled in Detroit a couple of weeks later and Floyd wanted to make a good showing in his own home town. He urged me to try it again and I consented, grudgingly, because he simply wouldn't take "No" for an answer.

I got a second, third and fifth, respectively, in the three sprint events on the card. He seemed satisfied, but I knew I should have done better.

Once more I went back to Indianapolis and into virtual seclusion, spending the winter months with Mother until another telephone call from Floyd finally brought me out of my doldrums.

"How would you like to try for the four-cylinder world's record over the measured mile at Daytona Beach?" he asked.

The thought of a chance to break the world's record, then held by Bob Burman in a Blizen Benz, presented a new challenge and swept everything else out of my mind.

"I believe the Overland Company will pay us enough money to take care of our expenses if we agree to call the car a Whippet Special so that they can use the publicity to call attention to their new lowpriced product," Floyd explained.

"After we break the record," he added, "we can collect a lot of appearance money too, for exhibitions."

It sounded wonderful to me and I agreed to head for Detroit

77

the following morning. When I arrived, Floyd already was on his way to Toledo to see how much financial backing he could obtain from Roy Peed, Overland sales manager. Mrs. Smith, late for a luncheon date, asked me to give her a ride downtown and I was glad to oblige because there was nothing for me to do until we heard from Floyd.

"If we are going to change the name of the car to Whippet," she said, "someone has to break the news to Mr. Boyer." Boyer had sponsored us during the previous season, paying us a considerable sum to carry the name of his products on the car, and we wanted to continue the arrangement during the coming year after making the record attempt for Overland. "He's out of town," she continued, "but I'm having lunch with his secretary and it might be a good idea for you to join us. I'm sure you can do a better job of explaining the situation than I can."

For lunch, we went to a place called "The Den of Forty Thieves," which was a little tearoom featuring a lady fortune teller who "read" the tea leaves. Having absolutely no faith in fortune tellers, I didn't pay much attention to the usual chatter as she started to tell my two companions about their past and future lives. One sentence, however, suddenly caught my attention.

"Your husband is away on a trip," I heard the fortune teller say to Mrs. Smith. "He'll return home tonight with a negative answer and he'll be very depressed. But if you can induce him to go right back to the same place tomorrow, the answer will be satisfactory."

Soon it was my turn. Complying with her instructions, I placed my cup upside down on the saucer and turned it three times. Apparently that was the accepted formula for getting the tea leaves arranged so that she could tell what was going to happen. She mentioned a recent death in my family and a number of other incidents which might have been said of almost anyone without missing the truth too far. I decided to test her further by asking about my occupation.

"The leaves tell a very strange story," she said. "I can't quite understand them. I see you going 'round and 'round like a merry-go-round, but you always come right back to your starting point."

All three of us laughed, of course, and I'm sure she didn't appreciate our amusement. I asked her one more trite question: "Am I going to be able to continue to do that successfully?"

She said, "Yes, I think you are."

I could hardly wait until she had left our table to ask Mrs. Smith if she had made an advance appointment or given the woman any clue concerning our interests and she assured me she had not.

That evening we were not surprised when Floyd arrived home in low spirits. Both of us went to work on him immediately in an effort to talk him into going back to Toledo the following morning. Finally, thoroughly irritated by our "campaign," he exclaimed, "It's the silliest thing I ever heard of, but I'll do it, by golly!"

The next morning at 11:30 the phone rang. Floyd was calling from Toledo. "It's a deal," he said. "They want us to call it the Whippet Special and we'll go to Daytona Beach in February to get the four-cylinder record." The lady with the tea leaves had called the turn.

We installed the Frontenac engine in a Miller chassis, which was much lighter, and did a complete overhaul job on the car in the Overland factory.

Our part in the proposed series of record attempts at Daytona Beach was comparatively small. Chief attention centered on Captain Malcolm Campbell of England, Ray Keech and Frank Lockhart. All three were seeking the world's land speed record in the unlimited class over a measured mile course. Interest was particularly high because of the tremendous contrast between their respective cars.

Campbell placed his hopes on a huge, streamlined Campbell-Napier Special called the Bluebird. Lockhart was ready to try for the same record in a comparatively small Stutz Blackhawk with a 183 cubic-inch engine. Keech was to drive a veritable monster of a car called the Triplex Special. It consisted almost entirely of a long wide frame with one engine mounted in front of the driver's seat and two above the rear axle, side by side. It was the ugliest thing I'd ever seen on four wheels, but it certainly had the appearance of tremendous power.

They were shooting at a record of 203.79 miles an hour, which Major H. O. D. Segrave had established in his Sunbeam Special the previous year. Segrave was in England at the time, making preparations to try for the world's record on water with his Miss England.

Most of the group interested in the record attempts was staying at the Claridge Hotel in Daytona Beach. The weather was absolutely miserable and it was due to get worse before we would have a chance to run at peak speed. The beach is at its best only after a heavy storm out of the northeast. To keep from getting bored, we did a lot of swimming and played practical jokes on each other as rapidly as we could devise them. In the evenings we often played cards or demonstrated our pet parlor tricks.

One night, after most of us had exhausted our repertoires, Mrs. Art Means, wife of the AAA Contest Board's Assistant Secretary, offered to tell our fortunes by reading our palms.

"I'm strictly an amateur," she said, "but since you haven't anything better to do, maybe you'll enjoy it."

Some one recalled how she had "hit the nail on the head" the previous year in regard to Segrave's successful record attempt.

"Yes," she explained, "I could tell from his palm that he would succeed. But I hate to hear that he intends to try for a new record on water, because he's headed for serious trouble. According to his palm, water is not his element. He can't possibly succeed on such an attempt and it might end in disaster."

After a little more conversation, Frank and I volunteered to have our palms read and she took Frank's hand first.

She studied it for a few seconds and said, "You might just as well pack up and go home right now. You will not succeed in breaking the land speed record at this time. And it will not be wise," she added, "for you to make any subsequent attempts."

80

I knew Mrs. Means quite well, because of her interest in dirt track races, and was expecting somewhat of a ribbing when she took my hand. Instead, she examined it for what seemed to be an unusually long time without saying a word and then looked me straight in the eye.

"Can you take it?" she finally asked in dead seriousness.

"Go right ahead and dish it out, Baby," I replied.

"You can't possibly live more than two or three years!" she exclaimed.

"Can't you be more specific than that?" I asked, jokingly.

"I wouldn't even attempt to forecast the exact date of your death," she answered. "But, according to your palm, you've almost run out your string. It could happen anytime between now and June 15th of 1930, at the very latest."

"The last thing I'm going to do is worry about it," I said.

Then we all had a good laugh about the entire episode. We were grown men, who thought we knew what we were doing and how to do it. Each of us felt quite capable of taking good care of himself. And in the first place, she had admitted she was only an amateur.

A few days later, on February 19, Campbell set a new world's record of 206.856 miles an hour as an average speed with and against the wind over the measured mile course. The following day, Keech fell approximately twenty miles short of that mark. Lockhart's first serious record run was a fraction of a mile above 200 miles an hour. But on another attempt he lost control as the result of a sudden gust of wind and wound up with his car in the ocean.

My car caught on fire and I ran it into the water deliberately to avoid being painfully burned. The ocean was the handiest fire extinguisher I've ever used. But it certainly ruined a good engine.

Keech realized additional work was necessary on his car to make it a serious record contender. Lockhart and I returned to Indianapolis and Campbell headed for England, with the speed crown apparently still out of America's reach. Tom Milton, driving a Duesenberg, had been the last American driver to wear it—in 1920.

Lockhart called me about two weeks later.

"How would you like to go back to Daytona in April and make another try for the record?" he asked. "If the Willys Company will share expenses with Stutz—for policing the beach and getting the necessary officials and timing equipment— maybe we can get the records after all."

The plans were completed within a few hours and I headed for Detroit to help Floyd get the Whippet ready. As the result of running it into the ocean, my engine was beyond repair. But on our earlier Florida visit I had seen a marine engine of the 151 Hydroplane Class built by Harry Miller and I thought it would be ideal for our purpose.

Harry assured me it would not be difficult to make the necessary changes for automotive use and we purchased it for $3,800.

When we reached Daytona, the beach was in no condition for record attempts, but we were able to make some test runs— very expensive test runs. We blew one piston right after another. After working all night to put in a new set, we'd grab a couple of hours sleep and then blow some more as soon as we tried to run again. About the fourth or fifth day we cracked a cylinder block and phoned Harry Miller for a new one to be sent via air express.

Keech also had returned to Daytona with the Triplex and was the first to make his record attempt, April 22, before I was ready to run. It seemed very evident that he had broken Campbell's mark and brought the speed crown back to America by a margin of two or three miles an hour. The crowd was jubilant. But officials announced the timing device had not been functioning properly and that the result could not be considered a world's mark.

Seldom have I seen a man quite so mad. Keech really "blew his top." Then, speaking with teeth clenched, he told them to "make damn sure the apparatus is working this time, because I'm going right back out on the course and do it again."

He did, too, with a two-way average of 207.552.

Two days later, Lockhart announced that he planned to run early on the following morning. I stayed with Odis Porter in the timing stand as Frank averaged better than 203 miles an hour against the wind. Even under normal conditions, with only a slight breeze, it was possible to add as much as fourteen or fifteen miles an hour while running with the wind and Frank needed to pick up only ten miles an hour on the return trip for a new record of 208.

We waited as his crew re-iced the engine, which was cooled in this manner instead of by a conventional radiator. We watched his car gather momentum as he finally started back and approached the measured-mile section of the course.

Half way through the measured mile, a rear tire blew out. The car veered suddenly to the left into soft sand. The body of the car tore loose from the frame and somersaulted, end over end, for almost five hundred yards. On the third somersault it seemed to leap high in the air. Then it crashed hard on its nose and pitched Frank at least seventy-five yards ahead of where the car, itself, finally stopped.

I was one of the first to reach him, but he was beyond help.

His death was a terrific blow to me. We had been very close friends and he ranked second only to Milton as a driver in my opinion. But I couldn't abandon my own plans for an assault on the four-cylinder record because too many other people had invested too much of their own time and too much of their own money in the project for me to let them down.

I finally got the engine back together again and five days after Lockhart's crash I was ready to shoot for Burman's record of 141.732. I missed it by seven miles an hour, averaging 134.-831 for the two-way run. I still had hopes of success under ideal conditions, but on my next attempt I blew another piston as I reached top speed. Thoroughly disgusted, I packed up the same day and headed for home with the spectre of bad luck still casting its shadow over me.

It looked as if things would change for the better when Phil Shafer offered me the opportunity of driving a new Miller Special he had entered in the 500-mile race that year for a big automotive accessory company which was preparing to place a new automatic fuel pump on the market. The company was interested only in proving the efficiency of this new product by using it on the car in the Indianapolis race, but trial runs convinced us that the device had not yet been developed to the point where it would perform properly at such high speeds.

Instead of giving us permission to run the car with the usual hand pump, which was standard equipment on all race cars at that time, the company offered it for sale. I didn't have enough cash to handle the deal, but Louie Meyer persuaded Alden Sampson to buy it for him and I was without a car with May 30 only a few days away. Meyer installed a conventional fuel pump immediately and proceeded to win the race.

At the last minute, I also managed to get a ride after Pete DePaolo had wrecked his front-drive Flying Cloud Special while qualifying. Cotton Henning rebuilt it in Louis Chevrolet's shop in time for me to qualify—with special permission from AAA officials—on the morning of the race. Cliff Durant had been kind enough to let me use his front-drive car for several practice laps while the repairs were being made and my prospects appeared to be taking a turn for the better. But the trend didn't last long.

After forty-two laps in pursuit of Leon Duray, who set a record-breaking pace for the first 160 miles before experiencing mechanical trouble, I was through for the day in my own car. The special timing gears in the Flying Cloud, manufactured at a cost of $3,400, had failed.

George Souders took the lead when Duray encountered trouble and I got back into the race for a while as a relief driver for Ray Keech. Ray was having trouble because of a leak in his fuel line. He had to pump like the devil to maintain sufficient fuel pressure and he was almost exhausted when he came into the pits. I was able to move the car up from ninth to seventh position while he rested.

Meanwhile, Jimmy Gleason and Babe Stapp took turns at the head of the pack until Tony Gulotta moved to the front with approximately 130 miles to go. Lou Meyer and Lou

84

Schneider, driving relief for Lou Moore, also were ahead of me when I turned the car back to Keech.

It certainly looked like Gulotta's race, especially after Gleason was forced out of the running by mechanical trouble during a final bid for the lead with only twenty laps to go. Gulotta's car stalled on the 181st lap, however, because of a clogged fuel line and Meyer took command to win by forty-five seconds over the Moore-Schneider combination. Souders finished third, Keech fourth, Norm Batten fifth and Stapp sixth. Gulotta, completely crushed by his bad luck, finally got his car running again in time to take tenth place, crossing the finish line more than a half-hour after the winner had been given the checkered flag.

Ten days later I failed to finish again, while driving the patched-up "Whippet" in a 100-mile race at Detroit.

I was completely disgusted. Beginning with Bea's death, I'd had nothing but bad luck for almost ten straight months. It was impossible to compete successfully on the AAA championship circuit without good equipment. The Flying Cloud, being a front-drive car, wasn't suitable for dirt tracks. All of the good cars had regular drivers.

Some of the other drivers, who had joined the AAA with me in 1927, also found it impossible to obtain cars fast enough for the championship circuit. Our decision to go "big time" actually had backfired, because a few of the better drivers with good equipment occasionally invaded the half-mile tracks, which had enrolled under the AAA banner with us, and cut into our prize money.

None of us was earning enough to stay in the business. The promoters conducting races on the smaller tracks, however, couldn't operate without us because not enough top flight "names" would show up to assure them of full fields for their programs.

Together the promoters and most of the drivers involved in the 1926–27 decision withdrew from the AAA in a body. My racing luck began to change immediately and late in the summer I got the best "break" of my entire life when Fritz

Schneider asked me to take a ride in a "hopped up" Packard which he thought was about the fastest pleasure car in town.

CHAPTER 11

WHILE Fritz was demonstrating the Packard's speed for my particular benefit, he also mentioned the fact that one of Eddie Updyke's Auburn-Cord salesmen had challenged him to a race.

"I'll leave that guy so far behind it will take him all week to catch up," Fritz exclaimed.

"You have a surprise coming," I said. "This car is pretty hot, but I'll bet money one of the new 115 Auburns will run away from it and hide on any straight-out test of speed."

Before the argument had continued many more minutes, we were on our way to Updyke's show room in search of Herb Groff, who had issued the challenge. He happened to be on duty and Fritz proceeded immediately to arrange a date for the race, which was to be staged on the open highway north of town.

While the usual bragging and bantering was in progress, one of the girls in the office left her desk and walked across the showroom floor to the water fountain. I hadn't taken a second look at any girl for a long time. But here was a cute little brunette with real class and I continued to watch every step she took on the way back to her desk. Then I interrupted the argument between Fritz and the Auburn salesman by putting my arms around their shoulders and whispering: "Don't look now, fellows, but there's the gal I'm going to marry, sitting at the desk near the door to Eddie's office."

"You're nuts," said Fritz.

"I'm not kidding," I answered. "I'm going to marry that young lady as soon as she'll have me."

Another salesman, who had joined our little group, didn't say anything. If I'd had eyes for anyone except the girl in question I might have noticed a certain coolness in his expression and attitude toward me as he quickly brought the discussion back to plans for the match race. It took place the following afternoon, with the Auburn winning easily and, instead of riding home with Fritz, I went back to Updyke's.

I smiled at the girl, without getting a very satisfactory response, as I walked into Eddie's office.

"You should be the first to know that I'm going to marry your secretary, Eddie," I exclaimed, "But I don't even know her name yet. How about calling her in and introducing us?"

"I think you're a little late," he answered. "She's engaged to one of my salesmen, but I'll be glad to introduce you and wish you luck."

He pressed the buzzer and in she came, with shorthand book and pencil in hand, looking very trim and smart. She acknowledged the introduction with a gracious smile, which made me more sure than ever that my judgment was good, but the smile didn't last long.

"Eddie doesn't have anything for you to do right now," I explained abruptly. "He called you in here just as a favor to me, because I wanted to meet you and ask you for a date."

She looked at Eddie, with a rather surprised expression on her face, and then turned back to me.

"No, thanks," she said. "I'm engaged, but it has been a pleasure to meet you."

Then she turned and walked back to her desk. The "torch" I had lighted the previous day really began to blaze then. From that instant my activities in her direction took on all of the momentum of a full-scale political campaign.

For more than a month I didn't make any noticeable progress with her, personally, except to get a smile from her with increasing regularity. But by the middle of November I had everyone in the office, except her fiancé, on my team—Frances Welker, Viola Starrett, Herb Groff, Don Delbrook, Emerson Thompson and the others on the staff.

As a last resort, I went to Eddie.

"Maybe if you'll sell me one of your Auburn Speedsters," I suggested, "it will help things along."

"Maybe it will," he agreed. "And I'll do even more than that. I'll make sure that she'll have to do the paper work on the sale and I'll also give her salesman friend an assignment to keep him out of the office for an hour or two. Come in tomorrow afternoon and I'll have everything all set."

He was as good as his word, too. When I showed up the following day, the salesman wasn't in sight. As soon as I entered Eddie's office, he punched the buzzer and in came my heart throb.

"I'm already late for an appointment downtown," he told her. "But Mr. Shaw is buying that cream and black Speedster on the showroom floor—the one with the red upholstering—and he wants to close the deal right now. You handle the details while I'm gone." Then he left and she started filling out the necessary papers.

"I hope you like this automobile I'm buying," I said, "because you're going to have to do a lot of riding in it."

She went right on filling out the papers, without saying a word, and finally pushed them across the desk for me to sign.

"I need this Speedster like I need a hole in my head," I continued. "The only reason I'm buying it is simply to impress you, because I already have a perfectly wonderful Jordan Playboy roadster."

"Well, it's all pretty silly," she replied. "Do you have any idea how much interest you are going to pay each month on the unpaid balance?"

"No," I said. "But it's nice to know that I'm making a little headway with you. At least I have you interested in my interest, and that's something."

I didn't get a date that night, but I did get an encouraging smile when I told her I'd be back to try again during the early part of the coming week—after racing at one of the half-mile tracks.

Monday morning I sailed back into Updyke's office and said, "I'm back and I still want a date. When are you going to let me take you to dinner?"

She floored me completely when she said, "How about Thanksgiving Day at five o'clock?"

From then on everything was wonderful. One date convinced me I was the luckiest guy in the world. I was extremely happy in her company and she seemed to feel the same way. Neither of us had many close friends and we didn't run around with any particular crowd, but we spent every possible minute together.

I've never been able to figure out how she managed to stand the pace. I seldom said goodnight until long after midnight and she had to be up bright and early each morning in time to get to work by eight o'clock. I was reading "The Prince of India" at the time. Almost every night I would give her a detailed description of the part of the story I had read during the day—while she was working—and often I would read a chapter or two aloud to her in the evening. We both enjoyed dancing. We also spent many hours singing together, with her at the piano. More than anything else, however, we loved to go for long rides in the country and talk about our plans—or at least my plans—for the future.

As the nights became colder, I bought a big black bearskin coat and a derby hat. For a fellow who was only five feet 7½ inches tall and weighed 130 pounds wringing wet, I must have been quite a sight. But I would climb behind the wheel, unbutton the coat and put my right arm along the back of the front seat in such a manner that part of the coat was spread over the particular spot where she would sit next to me. She'd cuddle up close, pull "her half" of the coat around her and we'd take off with the top down in the coldest weather.

I should have told you earlier that her name was Cathleen Stearns and that most of her friends called her Cass; but this particular bit of information isn't of much importance. On the night of our first date I started to call her Boots because she reminded me of the shapely girl who played the title role in the comic strip, "Boots and Her Buddies"—and I didn't let her keep her last name many months. In fact, we came mighty close to being married on Christmas day.

We had driven out to Updyke's home on Christmas eve and were locked in a tight clinch under the mistletoe when Eddie suddenly "popped the question" to both of us.

"You two kids have known each other long enough," he said. "What are you waiting for? Get married tomorrow and the whole party is on me. I'll even pay for the honeymoon."

I tried to press the point home, but Boots waved aside all argument.

"He's had too much Christmas cheer," she exclaimed. "Tomorrow he won't even remember he said that."

It was almost three months later before she finally said yes.

Ever since I had met Boots I had been considering the possibility of getting back into good standing with the AAA. She deserved nothing but the best, and if I ever hoped to get to the top in automobile racing, that was the only path open to me. In the matter of prestige and money, in fact every department, the AAA was in a class by itself among racing organizations.

Any little "push" I may have needed to actually make formal application for reinstatement, already had been received a few days before Christmas in the form of a letter from J. M. White of Philadelphia, who owned the Triplex Special in which Keech had set the world's land speed record the previous spring. He had been impressed with my performance in the Whippet, despite my bad luck, and the letter was an invitation for me to drive the car. Segrave was planning to visit Daytona in an attempt to regain the record for England and White was determined to meet this challenge.

I explained to him that I was an "outlaw" in the eyes of the AAA, but that I was interested in getting back into good standing. He promised to do everything he could to help me and suggested that I communicate with Val Haresnape, Secretary of the AAA Contest Board, to see what my prospects were. I wrote to Val immediately, telling him of White's plans and assuring him that I was ready to "straighten up and fly right" in keeping with AAA regulations for all time to come.

Val replied to my letter promptly, but his answer was "no." I would have to make a formal application in the approved manner, he explained, and it would be impossible for the Contest Board to act on it in time to make me eligible for the record run. I presented every argument I could think of in my favor during the weeks of correspondence which followed, but the answer was still "no" a week before the Florida date.

Never one to give up without playing the string out to the end, I decided to go to Daytona Beach anyway; and I persuaded Boots to live at our home while I was gone, so Mother would not be alone.

In my hurry to get started from Indianapolis I had forgotten to wire for hotel reservations and every room in Daytona Beach was occupied when I arrived. While glancing over the register at one hotel, however, I found that Ted Gill of the Associated Press had succeeded in getting a room. We were close friends. I was in a hurry, so I instructed the clerk to send my bags up to Ted's room and then headed for Lee Bible's garage, where I was to meet White and climb into the Triplex for the first time.

After giving me a few minutes to examine the big brute of a car, White brought up the subject of my AAA suspension.

"It looks as if you are out of luck, Wilbur," he said. "Those AAA so-and-sos will be glad to have you back in AAA competition, but they are determined to teach you a lesson first. Val told me yesterday that he wouldn't even consider recommending your reinstatement before June 1, and that means you won't be eligible to drive here or in this year's 500-mile race."

"Let's not give up yet," I pleaded. "Maybe if we talk to him together, tomorrow morning, he'll change his mind. I've simply got to drive this monster to a new record before I go back to Indianapolis."

We made a date for early the next morning and I returned to the hotel to have dinner with Ted. I told him of our plans to see Val and gave him the complete story so that he would be on the alert for Val's decision in the morning.

When White and I walked into Val's office, he greeted us as courteously as if we were important business acquaintances, but he still was as adamant as ever about my predicament. Even when White offered to pay a $2,500 cash fine for my immediate reinstatement Val refused to change his decision.

"It's not the money we are after, Mr. White," he said. "We want to be sure this boy has learned his lesson. If we make it too easy for him to get back into good standing, he probably will go outlaw again before the end of the year.

"There is no reason why you should feel that Shaw is the only driver capable of setting a new record for you," Val continued. "We have some very capable men here, in good standing, with a lot of experience behind them. Bob McDonough and Deacon Litz are two of the best and I'm sure either one would do a good job for you."

It was evident that further argument would be useless, so we left, and the first thing we heard when we reached the sidewalk was a newsboy shouting "Shaw definitely out as driver of record car."

My roommate of the previous night, Gill, had written the story and I was mad as hell because he had permitted it to get into print while we still had some slight hope of getting matters ironed out satisfactorily. I cooled off, later, when Ted explained he had checked with Val in order to see when a statement would be available for publication after our scheduled conference—and had been told very forcibly that there was absolutely no chance of any change in the original decision, regardless of what we had to say.

White and I read the entire story together and he was as mad as I was.

"Well," he exclaimed, "that does it. But I'll tell you one thing. We're not going to let any AAA official tell us who to put in the car even if I have to ship it back to Philadelphia without even firing it up."

We were still giving the AAA hell when we reached Bible's

92

garage and he stopped work on the car to listen to our conversation. When we finally ran out of cuss words, he laid his tools aside and joined us.

"How about me driving it, Mr. White," he asked. "I'm in good standing with the AAA. At least I've never driven on an outlaw track. And I think I know as much about this car as anyone else."

"Do you really want a shot at it?" asked White.

"Who wouldn't?" replied Bible.

"All right, you're it," said White.

I was sick with disappointment. Instead of going to the beach when Lee was scheduled to make his run, I accepted an invitation to spend the day at the winter home of Frank Neid, who spent the summer months in Akron, Ohio. It's history now how Lee lost control of the car on the northward run—wrecking it completely and killing himself as well as a cameraman.

As soon as I got the bad news, I headed straight for the hotel to pack for the trip home. Every newspaperman in town, it seemed, wanted a statement from me. Apparently they were hopeful that I would be in a mood to deliver a blistering broadside at AAA officials. But I didn't have anything to say, because the same thing might have happened to me.

Within an hour, I was on my way back to Indianapolis. I wanted to get back to Boots at the earliest possible moment. Since our first date on Thanksgiving Day, until I had headed for Florida, I don't believe a single day had passed that we had not spent considerable time together—and how I missed her! But the trip home was a rough one.

Most of the roads at that time were dirt and it seemed that half of the "Sunny South" was under water. When I stopped at a filling station in Atlanta, Georgia, the attendant told me I might just as well go to a hotel and spend the night there, because the roads to the north were impassable. The sun had been down for about an hour at that time, but I wasn't a bit discouraged about my chances of getting through.

"I'll manage, some way or other," I told him, and resumed my trip as soon as he had filled the fuel tank. I spent the next ten hours driving all over the northwestern part of Georgia. I doubt if I failed to try a single route headed homeward. Each time I came to a bridge, I would "feel my way" along the water-covered approaches until it was very evident the entire car would be engulfed if I advanced a few more feet. Then I would back out of trouble and look for another possible route through the flooded area. By seven o'clock in the morning, I was back at the same Atlanta filling station for more fuel. By that time, the attendant had received reports of one route which was supposed to be open by noon and I managed to get through.

My speedometer showed better than seventy-five miles an hour almost constantly on the open road until the car suddenly parked itself on the crest of a pile of soft dirt at the side of the road with all four wheels in the air, but still right side up. A farmer had driven a team of mules out of a narrow lane, right in front of me, and I had no place else to go without hitting him. It had taken only a fraction of a second to get the car in that precarious position, but more than an hour was required to recruit as much help as I needed to roll it back on the highway.

Boots and Mother ran down from the porch to welcome me when I pulled up in front of the house and—believe me—my two girls looked mighty good to me after what I had been through. It was late at night when I finished telling them all about my trip. Mother already had retired before Boots suggested it was about time for me to take her to her aunt's home, where she had been living in Indianapolis before agreeing to stay with Mother during my absence.

"I can't see any reason for you to move back with your aunt," I said. "Why should we wait any longer? Why don't we get married right away?"

"I guess you're right," she said, "but we can't get married right this minute."

So I took her home and gave her another kiss, with instructions to be ready at nine o'clock in the morning for the ride to the courthouse to get our license. With that detail taken care

94

of, we made arrangements to be married at eight o'clock the same evening at a little church on the south side of Indianapolis, where we had attended services occasionally with Wayne and Hilda Eubank. Wayne and Frances Welker, a lifelong friend of Boots, agreed to stand up with us for the ceremony and we swore them to secrecy because we didn't want anyone else to know about our plans. We didn't even tell Mother.

Earlier that spring, however, Mother had made Boots a suit with the stipulation that she save it to wear on her wedding day. Boots was wearing it when she came to the dinner table that evening and Mother immediately accused her of breaking her promise. Apparently there was only one way to handle the situation. Before either of them had a chance to say anything else, I took the license and ring from my pocket and placed them on Mother's plate.

She cried a little and laughed a little, giving us the dickens because we had not taken her into our confidence. I believe she really was hurt by our failure to make arrangements for her to witness the wedding ceremony. But she was happy for both of us and she gave us her blessing as we hurried out the door to meet Fran and Wayne.

Somebody had failed to keep our secret, however. When we walked out of the church, several friends were on hand to shower us with rice. They were all for forming a horn-honking parade behind our car, too, but Wayne came to the rescue.

"I'll help you give them the slip," he whispered, "and then I'll meet you at my drugstore. We'll celebrate by having a chocolate soda together."

That's exactly what we did, too, before joining a few other friends for an impromptu party later. And I've always regarded it as the happiest and most important day of my life—March 23, 1929.

CHAPTER 12

BOOTS continued to work for a few weeks, because my bank account was almost exhausted and I wouldn't have an opportunity to win any prize money until May or June.

The cash I had finished the season with had been barely enough to see me through the winter. The monthly notes for $88.09 each on the Auburn Speedster still were coming due regularly, too. But I had obtained a new type of valve spring from the L. A. Young Company of Detroit, Michigan, and preliminary tests indicated they were the perfect answer to my engine problem on the 151-inch Miller.

The AAA also modified its ruling, slightly, on my suspension. Although I still was listed as "ineligible" for the 500-mile race, permission was granted for me to compete in all other AAA races on the 1929 program, including those scheduled prior to May 30. The "don't-give-a-damn" attitude which I had assumed after Bea's death was eliminated quickly as Boots and I pulled together in double harness. I had something—and someone— to live for again and I devoted all of my mind and energy to the job.

The 500-mile race that year fell on a Thursday. The first 100-mile championship event of the season was held the previous Sunday at Toledo, Ohio, and I won it easily. On the day most of the other "hot shots" were racing in the "500" at Indianapolis, with Ray Keech victorious, I went to Bridgeville, Pa., to win another 100-miler. Three days later, a victory in the Cleveland "100" gave me three in a row.

Two broken valve springs knocked me out of the lead in the Detroit championship race, which Cliff Woodbury won. But

I limped home in fifth place and obtained some new—and even better—valve springs from the Young Company. In the return races at both Bridgeville and Toledo, I resumed my winning ways. A new world's record for a 100-mile championship race on a flat dirt track at Syracuse, N.Y., in late August resulted in an invitation from Mike Boyle of Chicago to drive his car in the 200-mile Labor Day event at Altoona, Pa.

I had never driven on the Altoona boards before and my 151-inch Miller was not eligible because officials had placed a 91.5-inch limit on engines for that race, the same as at Indianapolis. The Boyle car was a beautiful-handling front drive creation, which Woodbury had been slated to drive. It had not been run since the Indianapolis Classic, because front-drive cars are not suitable for dirt tracks. Cliff had been campaigning one of Boyle's rear-drive cars during the summer, but had wrecked it in an earlier race at Altoona on June 29 and retired from racing.

The last-minute invitation from Boyle made me hustle to reach Altoona in time to qualify. The trials ended at sundown on the day before the race and it was late afternoon when I arrived. With only a lap or two of practice, I qualified well at 124 miles an hour to earn a starting position well up in the field—but AAA officials refused to give it to me. Some of them contended that I might be a hazard to other drivers in such an advanced position at the start of the race, because of my lack of experience on the boards, and they finally ruled that I would have to start in last place. My arguments were to no avail. I would start last, or not at all, they declared.

Mad as hell, and determined to show them they didn't know what they were doing, I really stood on the accelerator when the starting flag dropped the following day. I didn't pay any attention to the gauges on the instrument panel or anything else, except the traffic around me, until I had worked my way into the lead. As mad as I was, and with the fine equipment I had, it didn't take long.

When I finally was out in front, with time to look at the gauges, I was shocked to find the tachometer showing 9,000 revolutions a minute. I'd never heard of an engine turning that

97

fast without flying apart, so I eased off a little bit and got "in the groove." Every track has a "groove," which is nothing more than a narrow, unmarked strip of the race course where you can run at peak speed with the least amount of physical and mechanical effort. Even after easing off to 8,500 rpm's, I continued to pass other cars regularly, picking my spots to avoid unnecessary engine strain. Soon I had a lead of two laps on the entire field.

It was a wonderful feeling. For a long time I had been hearing how much driving ability you had to have in order to get around the Altoona track at good speed, but it seemed to me to be one of the easiest jobs I had ever undertaken. After a few more laps, however, I began to experience the sensation of losing my sense of touch. I realized suddenly that I couldn't feel the steering wheel which I was gripping with both hands. I even looked, to make sure I had hold of it. Then the numbness began to creep up my arms. It was a perfectly dreadful sensation.

There I was, in complete command of the most important race I'd ever had a really good chance to win, and my entire body was becoming numb. I couldn't bear the thought of stopping, but I finally was forced to admit to myself that no other course was open. If I tried to continue, it was only a question of time until I would lose my grip on the wheel in one of the turns and wreck a perfectly good automobile. I was even too weak—or at least too numb—to pat myself on top of the helmet in order to warn my crew that I needed a relief driver. I simply took my foot off the accelerator and coasted into the pit, too far gone to get out of the car.

They lifted me from the cockpit and I began to shake all over. Although I was dripping with perspiration, I felt as if I was freezing to death. Some one had the presence of mind to rush me to the hospital and the nurses put me to bed under a huge pile of blankets. I was their only patient. They gave me a lot of attention and it wasn't long until I was enjoying every bit of it. One of the doctors handed me a drinking glass filled with water and ammonia. Then some one handed me another glass of straight gin and, as I began to snap out of it, they told me what had happened. All the symptoms indicated to them I had been "gassed" in some manner. This had caused most of my blood to concentrate itself in the two large receptacles of my circulatory system, leaving only a small percentage of the blood to pass through arteries and veins. The blankets, ammonia water and gin were being used in an effort to restore my circulation to normal and it didn't take long to get the job done. The only trouble was that the gin had made me as "tight" as a billy goat.

"Get me some dry clothes," I told one of the nurses. "I've got to get back to let Boots know I'm all right and to see how the race is coming out."

"We haven't anything to give you except a sheet that you could wrap around yourself," they laughed. "It looks as if you're going to have to stay here until some of your friends bring you some clothes."

"Give me the sheet," I replied, "if that's the only way for me to get out of here." But one of the doctors offered to go to the pits and try to borrow some coveralls for me. In a few minutes he was back.

"Here's an extra pair belonging to Deacon Litz," he said. "Don't forget to return them."

He might as well have rented a big tent for me. Deacon was six feet three inches tall and weighed two hundred and twenty pounds. The material in one leg of his pants would have been sufficient to make me a suit. I got into the coveralls, however, with some help from the nurses. They rolled up the pants legs so I could walk without tripping and used a couple of big safety pins to take the necessary tucks in the waist. With long sleeves flapping the breeze, I must have looked like a grotesque scarecrow when I stepped out of the door. Because I was still feeling the effects of the gin, a nurse and an interne insisted on accompanying me. Apparently they had decided it was easier to humor me than to keep me confined.

Boots told me later I was the silliest looking thing she had ever seen. "I could tell you were tight as soon as you waved to

99

me, even though you were quite a distance away," she said, "and I wondered how you had gotten that way so quickly."

At the pits, I learned that Deacon had made a good trade. Although I had an extra pair of his coveralls, he had my race car and was running in fifth place with only a few laps to go.

"How come he's back in fifth place?" I asked.

"If you really want to know," said Cotton Henning, "it's all your fault. If you weren't so damn small, Deacon would be out in front right now.

"He couldn't get into the cockpit," Henning continued, "until we had torn out all of the upholstering. While we were doing that, the engine quit. It took us ten minutes to get it started again."

"Has it been running all right since then?" I said.

"Sure it has, or he wouldn't be up where he is now," replied Cotton.

"Well, if it's any news to you," I exclaimed, "I've been gassed and I want to find out what's wrong with it when the race is finished."

We examined the car together as soon as Litz rolled to a stop and discovered that a stud had backed out of the supercharger, releasing a constant stream of gasoline vapor under pressure into the cockpit. Because of my small stature, I was filling my lungs with those fumes every time I took a breath. Because Deacon was so much larger, his head stuck up in the air above the cowling where he could get a normal supply of oxygen.

That was the end of the 1929 championship trail. Despite the fact I had not been permitted to race at Indianapolis, I was third in the point standing which determined the National driving championship.

Under the present scoring system, I would have been the undisputed winner of the title, but the AAA had some peculiar rules in 1929. Promoters were required to pay a certain fee for AAA sanction of any event. If the promoter wished to advertise the race as a championship affair, however, he had to pay an additional fee. In most cases, the same drivers participated, regardless of whether or not the event was a championship or non-championship race. But points were awarded only when the extra "championship" fee was paid. I didn't receive a single point for the two victories at Toledo, the two at Bridgeville and the one at Cleveland.

There was some consolation, however, in the recognition which Haresnape gave me in an article he wrote that Fall for Motor Magazine. In his capacity as secretary of the Contest Board, Val said: "On performance and consistency alone Wilbur Shaw might well be named the year's champion."

CHAPTER 13

WITH money in the bank and no definite plans until the following spring I welcomed a suggestion by Boots that we take a belated honeymoon.

"How about Niagara?" I suggested. "We might just as well do it in the customary manner."

That idea met with instant approval and we started almost immediately in order to enjoy the trip before winter arrived. Because the United States still was in the shackles of the Volstead Act at that time, I wired ahead for reservations at a hotel on the Canadian side. This was to be a celebration and I was determined that everything would be "first class" with champagne and all of the trimmings. It was late when we arrived and I asked the bellboy, who showed us to our rooms, to hurry back with a menu because we wanted dinner in our suite.

"And bring a bottle of champagne with you," I ordered.

"I'm sorry, sir," he replied, "but hotels in Canada are not permitted to sell champagne. If you want champagne with your dinner, you'll have to go back on the United States side. There are several places which serve it over there.

"I'll be off duty in a few minutes," he added, "and I'll be glad to take you to a quiet place where you can get good food and anything you want to drink."

We washed up quickly, ordered the Speedster brought to the entrance and picked him up at the end of the driveway. He showed us the way to his favorite speakeasy and we enjoyed an excellent steak dinner with three bottles of champagne—on the American side of Niagara Falls, where champagne was illegal at any time, day or night. Then we went back to the Canadian side, took him home and returned to our hotel.

The following day, Boots and I went over to look at the majestic avalanche of water and she insisted on taking the tour underneath the falls. It was the silliest thing I'd ever heard of. Other people could take chances like that—thousands of them did, every day—but I didn't want any part of it. Later in the afternoon we interrupted our sight-seeing in favor of a sandwich and Boots applied a generous coating of English mustard to hers, not knowing what it was like. The first bite almost blew the top of her head off and brought tears to her eyes.

After returning to Indianapolis for a few days, we decided Florida would be a wonderful place during the winter months and it wasn't long until we were headed South. Our plans were rather indefinite, because I had so many friends in that area. One of them, Frank Swain, operated a filling station in Daytona and that was our first stop. He was a bridegroom, too, and I felt sure we would have a lot of fun together.

It was about his normal closing time when we pulled up alongside one of his gas pumps, but no one came out to service our car. I got out to see what was causing the delay and there was Frank, pounding on the glass door while a cute little blonde stood outside of it and laughed at him. After considerable confusion, with Frank shouting introductions through the door, it turned out that the blonde was his bride. She had dropped by to pick up her husband at closing time and finally got tired of waiting for him to check out. She had waited so long for him that she had decided he could wait just as long for her—so she had locked him in.

That night we slept in a hotel on the beach so Boots could hear the waves breaking. She had never seen an ocean before and was absolutely entranced as she watched the sun rise "out of the water" the following morning. Before breakfast, we walked down to the water's edge and I made her taste it to prove it was salty. The Swains had been living in a hotel, too, but all four of us thought it would be a lot of fun being together in a house of our own so that we could do as we pleased. Before the day was over we had rented a furnished house and moved in immediately. Fred made arrangements for extra help at the service station and, for a while, we played all night and slept most of the day.

One morning I was awakened early, however, by a familiar sound. It came from at least a mile away, but there was no mistaking the roar of a 151-inch Miller Marine Engine, such as I had used in my race car. I dressed quickly, jumped in the Speedster and followed my ears until I reached the bay just in time to see a speedboat glide up to the dock. It was Chris Rip's Miss Daytona. Among the spectators on the dock were several acquaintances and one of them introduced me to Chris. He had heard of my success with a Miller engine on the race track and asked if I would like to take a ride in his boat to see how well it handled.

"I don't know anything about racing hydroplanes," I said. "I know I would get a big kick out of the experience, but it looks like a rather expensive piece of equipment for anyone to fool with unless he knows all of the answers."

"There's nothing to it," replied Chris. "All you have to do is give her as much power as you feel you can handle and steer her where you want to go. You can see the buoys that mark the course from here."

I didn't need any additional urging, but I really gave myself a good scare when I took off. The throttle on Miss Daytona was as sensitive as any I had ever felt. I shoved it only about half way down, but the front end of the boat seemed to rear

103

straight up out of the water and at the same time I got a face full of sand. For an instant I couldn't see anything. And when I could see, I was sure the boat was going to do a back somersault and land on top of me. The sand worried me, too, but I learned later that the wind had blown it on top of the hull while the boat was moored at the dock. The sudden start had tossed it into my eyes when the boat reared up so quickly.

I gave the engine a little more throttle until the boat had leveled off. Then I increased the power gradually until she was up on the step. It handled so well that I had it wide open after running three or four laps and there was a big grin on my face when I returned to the dock.

Chris was grinning, too.

"How would you like to drive that boat for me at Miami in a couple of weeks?" he asked.

"You mean race her?" I exclaimed, with considerable surprise.

"I certainly do," he said.

"I never was in a racing boat until now," I answered. "I don't know anything about 'em."

"The hell you don't," he said. "No one has ever driven this one any faster than you just did. Honestly, I think you can win with her. I've already signed up a driver for the Palm Beach race next week," he explained, "and you can watch how he does it. The Miami race isn't until the following week and you'll have time to get in a little practice."

Boots and I met the whole regatta crowd at Palm Beach— Pop Hammond, Gib Bradfield, Jim Booth, Elmer Johnson and all of the rest of them. It was a clannish, close-knit group; but we were accepted with open arms after a little preliminary hazing. For a few days they seemed to take great delight in proving that the "Indianapolis Speedway pro" didn't know much about boat racing. Because of my inexperience in this type of competition, they were able to pocket me frequently and wet me down with all of the spray they could throw. I caught on to their tactics quickly, however, and soon was able to take good care of myself.

Johnson and Hammond—an unforgettable white-haired,

104

sixty-year-old individualist who wore a bat wing collar even while racing—had Miller engines in their boats, also. Bradfield was using an eight-cylinder Duesenberg engine of approximately the same size. Booth (now chief engineer of Thompson Products, Inc., Michigan Division) had been associated with Fred and Augie Duesenberg for several years. Bradfield owned race cars as well as speedboats; and Booth's particular responsibility was to see that all of them ran well.

I didn't get to see much of the Palm Beach race because Miss Daytona developed engine trouble almost immediately and I was busy trying to help the crew get her in condition for at least one heat.

We had her running well for the Miami event, however, and I wasted no time displaying my lack of knowledge about speedboat racing technique. While I was tearing up a lot of water in the bay, Miss Daytona started to slip sideways with me on a right turn. In order to avoid plowing into an island, I made a sharp left turn without thinking anything about it. The boat came around beautifully. But when I got back to the dock, everyone on hand wanted to know why I had tried such a "crazy stunt."

"Don't you know these racing boats usually turn over if a wave catches them at the wrong angle on such a sharp turn at high speed?" they demanded.

"You might get by with such tactics once or twice," Chris said. "But don't press your luck too far."

When the race finally got under way, I quickly found myself running in last place because of my lack of experience in maneuvering for a good position on the flying start. The four ahead of me had done a thorough job of cutting up the water around the first buoy and I thought Miss Daytona would shake herself apart before we could get out of their wake. It was smoother on the backstretch and we were running second to Bradfield on the No. 2 turn. He made the mistake of giving me an opening when he swung a little bit wide around the third buoy, however. I shot Miss Daytona into the gap and wet down Bradfield's boat, Buckeye, so completely that his engine

105

quit. I was out in front despite my poor start. But as I opened the throttle wide again on the straightaway, there was a loud "pop." I had blown the head out of a piston and the safety hose off the supercharger.

Strangely, Chris didn't seem to be discouraged.

"How would you like to help make the necessary repairs and take her to Cuba for the President's Trophy Race?" he asked.

"I'd love it," I said, "if I can get the engine in condition to stay together long enough to have a chance of winning."

"Take over, then," he instructed. "Do anything you think is necessary. The sky's the limit."

It was very evident that he meant exactly what he said and he enjoyed the financial stature to back up his instructions, so I walked into the boat house and phoned Harry Miller in Los Angeles. By the time two sets of pistons and a camshaft had arrived by air, we had torn down the engine and were ready to put it together again. I also had obtained an extra supply of Ethyl fluid from the corporation's representative in that area. We had the engine running like a clock when we shipped for Cuba and this time we meant business.

Up to that time, our trip had been one continuous party. But automobile racing had taught me that my own physical condition was just as important as the mechanical condition of my car. So Boots and I began to keep regular hours and on the night before the race we slipped away by ourselves for a quiet dinner before retiring early. That was our intention, at least. Before we had finished eating, half of the regatta crown was in the same restaurant and most of the group was gathered around our table to talk about the race. It developed into quite a clambake and no one succeeded in getting to bed until long after midnight.

By the following morning, however, the wind was blowing with almost hurricane force. The water between the dock and Morro Castle was about as rough as it ever gets. The only logical thing for the officials to do was order a postponement. But Bill Suerro, brother of the Havana Yacht Club's Commodore, declared he was ready to race. If it wasn't too rough for him, it wasn't too rough for me. We ordered out our boats and Bill's Miss Havana was lowered into the water first by the big crane.

Five seconds after the slings had been loosened, a huge wave sent her straight to the bottom. Bill made one desperate and unsuccessful dive to grab one of the Havana's mooring ropes before scrambling out of the shark-infested water. According to legend, the "man eaters" had continued to inhabit this particular area since the bodies of political prisoners in Morro Castle had been fed to the fishes instead of being buried.

As soon as the crane operator had lowered Miss Havana—and while she was sinking—he had swung the big iron hook toward my boat. Above the hook was a huge metal ball, which had been attached to the cable in order to make it easier to manipulate. Thinking I could be of some help to Suerro, I jumped on the hook, got a firm grip on the cable with one hand and signaled to the operator that I desired for him to lower me to the water level. Maybe his foot slipped. Or maybe he thought I wanted him to lower me to the deck of the boat resting on the bottom of the channel. Whatever his intentions, the brake was released immediately. Clinging to the hook and cable, I hit the water with a big splash and was headed straight for the bottom before he realized his mistake. He got me out of there mighty quick, but to this day I've never found a quicker cure for a hangover.

With Miss Havana gone, officials immediately postponed the race and I headed back toward town in one of the ancient American touring cars which were the only taxi cabs used in Cuba. We were cruising down a narrow street when I recognized one of the race mechanics walking ahead of us. Thinking it would be fun to scoop him up like a sack of mail hanging alongside a railroad track, I took a firm hold on one of the cross-members supporting the top of the taxi and grabbed him as we passed. We were traveling faster than I realized. His weight almost dislocated my shoulder and I felt a sharp pain in my forearm. But I didn't dare let go for fear he might get a leg under the rear wheel of the cab.

Finally he got his feet on the running board and a grip on

the top of the car. When I tried to remove my arm from around his waist, however, it felt as if it were strapped there. I took a look and saw that a screwdriver, which he had been carrying in his hip pocket, had run clear through my arm. The next stop was an apothecary shop, where the druggist swabbed the wound with iodine and bandaged it as well as he could.

After we had baths and put on clean clothes, the weather looked as if it would be days before we would be able to race, so we rejoined the regatta crowd which had decided to rendez-vous at Sloppy Joe's. Business was so good that I even helped tend bar for a while—until the proprietor discovered I was giving away his miniature bottles of whiskey with each sale. He voiced his displeasure so loudly, in fact, that Boots and I decided to leave.

As we reached the street, a Cuban began grinding out a tune from the biggest music box I had ever seen on wheels—an old player piano. A cute little monkey was dancing to this accompaniment and it was evident the monk had never attended one of Arthur Murray's schools. I proceeded to assume the job of instructor and everyone in Sloppy Joe's came out to watch the fun. In less than five minutes we had traffic blocked completely and the local gendarmes were beating on the sidewalk with their night sticks in an effort to get enough reinforcements to "break it up."

Bradfield had the monkey's tambourine and was passing it among the onlookers in order to get a little money for the organ grinder. The cops had considerable trouble getting it away from him, but they finally succeeded and all of us decided to call it a night.

With little chance of racing weather on the morrow, we didn't leave a call at the desk; but I awakened a few minutes before ten o'clock with sunlight streaming in the window. The wind had abated to a great extent and there certainly was no reason we couldn't race. Starting time had been announced as ten o'clock "on the first day suitable for racing" and we jumped into our clothes like a couple of firemen answering the bell.

Luckily, a cab was unloading some new arrivals at the entrance to the hotel. We climbed in, shouting instructions to the driver to take us to the wharf where the boat races were to start. Apparently he didn't understand English, because he seemed to be somewhat puzzled.

"To the wharf, to the boat races," I shouted. "Hurry."

He got the cab into motion quickly, even though I was fairly certain he did not understand what I had said. It seemed to me that he was headed in the wrong direction, but I wasn't sure. It turned out that he was just cruising until he could find a fellow cab driver who spoke English. We found one who straightened out the situation immediately, impressing the necessity for haste on our own driver, and I've never had a worse ride in my life than from that point to the the dock.

When we arrived, there wasn't a person in sight or a single boat on the water. By sign language, I tried to find out from our driver whether he knew where they had taken the boats. I might just as well have asked the nearest telephone pole. The only thing to do was drive back into town where we found another interpreter who said the races sometimes were held inside the bay, so we headed in that direction and found all of the other boats in the water awaiting the starting bomb.

Miss Daytona still was hanging in the slings. I scrambled aboard, signaled the crane operator and had the engine running almost as soon as the boat touched the water. Every second was important, because it was necessary for me to change spark plugs before I could run fast. I had tuned the engine so perfectly that I had to start it on "warm" plugs and then put in "cold" ones. I made the change as quickly as possible and headed for the starting line, but I still was at least a hundred yards away when the cannon was fired. Not knowing where the buoys were on this course, which I had never seen until then, I swung in behind them and took up the chase. It required all of the first lap for me to get within shouting distance.

Empty bottles, bobbing in the choppy water, provided an extra hazard which required a lot of attention. At that speed, any boat which came in contact with a bottle was a dead duck. The mahogany hulls were so thin a bottle would come right on through. It reminded me of an obstacle race. On the second lap I overtook the other boats, one by one—all except Johnson's Sparrow. Although he was reported to have said he would not race against "that screwball Shaw," he apparently had put his boat in the water when it looked as if I would not arrive in time to compete. I wasn't more than ten feet behind him as the third lap started and he swung wide around the next buoy. Using the same tactics as at Miami, I headed for the inside opening and cut diagonally across his wake.

Miss Daytona jumped into the air as she hit his waves and then landed almost on her side—smack against the Sparrow. Johnson veered off course and I went on to win easily.

After a brief rest, while the first heat of a cruiser class race was being run, we came back for the final test. All I needed to win the President's Trophy for Chris was third place or better. The Meadowmere, which placed second in the first heat, had finished with a hole in her bottom and already was up on the dock. This time I got away to a good start. It looked as if it would be a breeze, if I could only stay clear of the bottles, which seemed to be getting more numerous. Bradfield already had hit one, and was out of the race.

I concentrated more than ever on the bottle situation as I started the third lap, without looking far enough ahead to locate the next buoy, and when I finally glanced up I couldn't see it anywhere in that choppy water. I held my course until I thought I surely had gone beyond it, before making the turn for home. It wasn't until the officials failed to fire the gun as I crossed the finish line, however, that I realized I had gone inside the marker. Even then I still had a chance.

Only two other boats were running and—because of my first heat victory—the cup would be mine if I did no more than finish the course. But as I made my turn to begin the extra lap, a huge wave caught me on the port bow. The engine coughed and died. The cockpit was almost full of water. The only thing to do was signal for help and a Cuban navy cruiser dragged Miss Daytona back to the barge. Getting credit for second

110

place provided no more satisfaction than winning first prize in a shaggy dog contest.

That night the Havana Yacht Club was the scene of as lavish a party as I have ever attended anywhere. All of our newly-made friends except Bradfield were on hand and dressed to their eye teeth.

We were beginning to worry about what might have happened to Bradfield when in he came, still wearing his racing togs. At the conclusion of the day's program, he had stopped for a drink or two on his way to his hotel to change clothes. At the bar he had encountered one of his gendarme friends of the previous evening and renewed the argument. The result was a trip to the bastille and Commodore Suerro's intervention had been necessary in order to obtain his release.

His arrival made the party complete. Before it ended, I became an uninvited member of the orchestra, hitting one fish bone against another to create a rhythmic *click . . . click . . . click*. I heard "The Peanut Vender" song that night for the first time, two or three years before it—or the rumba—became popular in the United States. There was an entertainer, too, who could make smoke come out of his ears—one of the few tricks I've ever seen that I haven't been able to duplicate. Quite a place, Havana!

The boat ride back to Miami wasn't as pleasant. It was late in the season. The crew on our boat was making the trip for the last time and celebrating by doing too much drinking. The service was terrible. It seemed as if we waited for hours after ordering dinner. When the waiter finally brought it, he slammed it on the table and said, "I'm sorry, folks, but there's a helluva fight going on in the kitchen and I have to hurry back to help my pals."

He never did bring the wine we had ordered. As a memento of our Havana visit, however, Commodore McHugh of the Cincinnati Yacht Club had given Boots a bottle of very rare champagne with instructions not to open it until we were within the three-mile limit—when it would be impossible for us to buy ad-

111

ditional alcoholic beverages. I went to our room to get it and when I returned Boots was beginning to get seasick.

She excused herself almost immediately, with instructions to save the champagne until she could get back to the table.

"Don't even touch it," she said, "because I want to be here when you pop the cork."

I had good intentions of complying with her wishes. I turned my head to talk with someone in our party, however, and one of my other pals had the bottle open before I knew what was happening. He suggested a toast and all of us joined him. When Boots returned a couple of minutes later, there wasn't a drop left.

Miami was a welcome sight. We had been playing at a mighty fast clip and were worn out. Even though I had enjoyed every minute of my boat racing, it wasn't the sport for me. Frankly, I couldn't afford it. For more than a month I had worked almost as hard as if I had been participating in important automobile races involving several thousands of dollars in prize money. But the only tangible thing I had to show for all that effort was a Cuban newspaper clipping of a photo of myself at the wheel of Miss Daytona under the caption, "Sharo Suprema Categoría."

CHAPTER *14*

DURING the winter, Smith had sold the Whippet Special to Caroll Hall, a broker of Jamestown, N. Y., and the name of the car had been changed to correspond with that of Hall's speedboat, the Empire State. Smith had been retained as mechanic on the car and I was to drive it.

I had every reason to expect another successful season, such as I had enjoyed the previous summer. But Smith had failed to devote as much attention to the body of the car as he had to the engine. It began to come apart in my first race of the year at Langhorne on May 3. By the end of fifty laps my right hip and thigh were raw and bleeding from contact with ragged edges of aluminum which cut through my trousers each time I negotiated a turn or hit a hole—and holes were plentiful.

Running well up with the leaders, I stuck with the car for another thirty-five laps before the physical punishment became so great that I couldn't stand it any longer. Several members of my crew lifted me from the car when I came into the pits for relief and there was a roar from the crowd as the fans got a good look at me. From the waist down, I was almost naked. Louie Schneider had been showing considerable animosity toward me for more than a year, but he grabbed a coat and wrapped it around me—fast. Then he jumped into the cockpit and finished the car in seventh place. That night he rode back to Indianapolis with Boots and me and the breach between us apparently was healed—at least temporarily. Three weeks later I won second money in another 100-miler at Toledo, Ohio, to wind up the brief pre-Indianapolis campaign.

Because of the drastic changes in the rules for the annual "500" that year, I was slated to drive a new and larger Empire State Special. The formula of the previous year, calling for single-seated 91½-inch cars, had been abandoned completely. Larger bodies, with room for riding mechanics, were mandatory. Engines up to 366 inches were acceptable and provisions had been made for a starting field of forty-two cars, instead of the traditional thirty-three. Thirty-eight finally qualified.

Except for our quick trips to Langhorne and Toledo, Smith and I had been working on the new car every day and most of every night for many weeks. I wanted to use the old 151-inch engine in which I had unlimited confidence. Hall had purchased a 183-inch Miller for the Indianapolis event, however. It seemed silly to use something new, which hadn't been thoroughly tested, as a replacement for equipment which had been

113

performing perfectly. But I finally agreed with considerable reluctance.

My fears in regard to the new engine appeared to be groundless as the car ran well in practice. I also turned in the fifth fastest qualifying time to earn a starting position near the head of the pack, but I had completed only fifty-four laps when a wrist pin broke while I was battling with Louie Schneider for third place, behind Billy Arnold and Shorty Cantlon.

No one ever has dominated an Indianapolis race to the extent Arnold did that year. He took the lead on the third lap and added to his advantage all of the way to win by a margin of more than seven minutes over Cantlon, with Schneider, Meyer and Wild Bill Cummings next in order.

One of the most spectacular accidents in Speedway history occurred soon after the start. DePaolo's car wasn't handling properly and he came into the pit after running only twenty miles. Red Roberts relieved him at the wheel and hadn't completed more than a dozen more laps when he lost control on the north turn. Stapp was unable to avoid hitting the skidding car. Deacon Litz, Marion Trexler, Johnny Seymour and Jimmy Gleason all crashed into the wreckage and Lou Moore hit the wall in preference to piling up with the others. There were no serious injuries. But another accident a few minutes later claimed the life of Paul Marshall, a mechanic riding in a Duesenberg Special with his brother, Cy.

The following day we tore out the "183" and began installation of the "151." One week later I won the Detroit 100-mile championship race with Russ Snowberger, Bill Cummings, Ernie Triplett and Chet Miller finishing in that order behind me.

Altoona was the next stop on the circuit, June 14, and I went on ahead with Boots for a couple of days of relaxation. Smith remained in Detroit to check the car and change the gear ratio for the board track, where top speed was more important than quick acceleration. Floyd called me at the hotel when he arrived, and I drove out to the track for a few practice laps.

The moment I fired up the car I knew something was terribly wrong. The engine sounded entirely different from the

114

one we had been using. I didn't say anything because there were too many railbirds around the car. But I motioned for Floyd to move down to the West end of the home stretch, away from the other cars and drivers. I drove on ahead and then waited for him to join me after I had cut the switch.

"You've got a 16-valve 4-cylinder engine in this car instead of the one we've been using, haven't you?" I asked. "Why did you make the change without talking to me about it?"

"This is the one you helped me build for Pop Hammond's boat," he replied. "We don't have to deliver it until next week, so I thought we'd use it today and see how it runs. Sounds swell, doesn't it?"

"Certainly it sounds swell," I said; "but in case you don't know it, the rules for tomorrow's race stipulate that no engine may have more than two valves per cylinder. That leaves us sitting it out, unless we can figure some way to get our regular cylinder block back into the car in time. Where is it?"

"Still in Detroit," he said.

"All right," I said. "Get it; and don't do any talking, either. If anyone finds out about it, we'd have a helluva time convincing them we're not awfully stupid or downright dishonest."

Floyd started to say something else, but he didn't have time. Several drivers and car owners were walking toward us with Eric Von Hambach of the AAA staff. They already had heard the sound of the engine just long enough to arouse their suspicions.

"Go get your car and a tow rope," I said to Floyd, loud enough for the approaching "delegation" to hear me.

"We'd like to take a look at that engine," said Eric.

"What do you mean, you'd like to take a look at it?" Floyd asked.

"Well, we'd like for you to pull the manifolds off so we can take a look at it," Eric answered.

"I'm sorry, fellows," I said, "but we don't have enough time to do it now. I think I heard a rod rattle. We're going to have to pull the engine clear down to check it. We don't have too much time to get the job done and we're not going to waste

115

any of it pulling off the manifolds. You can look at it after we qualify, if you want to."

As soon as Floyd returned with his car, we slipped a rope around the front axle and towed the Empire State Special out to the airport. On the way, I managed to attract the attention of Deacon Litz, who had flown his own plane to Altoona, and asked him to follow us. Deacon arrived as we completed arrangements to store the car in one corner of the hangar and I asked him how much he would charge to fly Floyd to Detroit to get some spare parts.

"I'll do it for practically nothing," he said, "if you'll tell me what's cooking."

So I laid my cards right on the table and told him what Floyd had done; and that the 8-valve block and cam shafts were in the garage in Detroit.

"Boy, you are in a spot," he replied, "and I'll help you all I can. But that single engine plane of mine doesn't go very good at night. It will be almost dark when we get there and we'll have to wait until morning to come back."

Within thirty minutes they were on their way. After making arrangements with the man at the airport to keep everyone out of the hangar until I returned, I took off for the Penn Alto hotel to have dinner with Boots and the gang.

I tried to be as nonchalant as possible at dinner, but everyone knew something funny had happened and I like to think they realized I was a victim of circumstances. About 9:15, Boots and I sallied out of the hotel as though we were going to take a walk. Instead, we went around the block, climbed into our car and headed for the airport. By midnight I had that baby completely torn down, cleaned up and ready for Floyd to drop in the other block the moment he returned.

After a restless night, with little sleep, wondering how this embarrassing situation would turn out, Boots and I sailed into the coffee shop the following morning as if everything was perfectly normal. The place was "jumping" with race drivers, car owners, mechanics and fans. All of them were discussing the fatal accident involving Major Segrave, who had been killed a

116

few hours earlier while attempting to set a new world's speedboat record on Lake Windemere in England.

Into my mind, instantly, flashed the picture of the palm-reading session conducted two years earlier at Daytona Beach by Mrs. Art Means. I hadn't seen her since that day. Art had been laid up the previous season because of a broken leg and she had not been on hand at any of our recent races. As I glanced around the room to say hello to a lot of my friends, however, there was Mrs. Means sitting by herself in a nearby booth.

I grabbed Boots by the arm and said, "Come over here, Baby, here's a gal I want you to meet. She's the most terrific fortune teller in the world."

After introducing the "gals" and inquiring about Art's health, I told Boots how Mrs. Means had predicted the deaths of Lockhart and Segrave.

"She certainly hit the nail on the head two times out of three," I added. "If she hadn't missed on me she would have a perfect batting average."

"Do you remember what I told you?" asked Mrs. Means.

"Certainly," I answered. "You told me I couldn't possibly live more than a couple of years. But I fooled you, didn't I?"

"That isn't quite correct," she replied. "When I said 'two or three years,' you asked me to be more specific. I told you I couldn't possibly give you the exact date, but that it would be prior to June fifteenth, 1930. I sincerely hope you do fool me," she continued, "but it won't be June fifteenth until tomorrow."

"Well, of all things!" interrupted Boots, who hadn't said a word since acknowledging the introductions.

Then and there, right quickly, I learned for the first time that my wife really had a temper—and a vocabulary. With fists clenched and eyes flashing, she used a few hundred well chosen words to take Mrs. Means apart in a matter of sixty seconds.

With icicles hanging on each word, she concluded the sudden tirade by saying, "I think that's the most inconsiderate thing you possibly could have said or done, especially at a time

117

like this on the day of a race, and if you'll excuse us now, I think we'll go."

I mumbled something to the effect that "she doesn't understand race people yet" and caught up with her at the door.

Boots had lost all interest in breakfast, so we headed straight for the airport while she proceeded to let me know exactly how she felt about the incident.

"If that's the way the members of the racing fraternity are," she said, "I'm not going to like any of them."

We had been married only a year and this was a rather rough initiation for her. I tried to explain Mrs. Means had meant no harm, that she was doing nothing but "calling the turn" exactly as she saw it and shouldn't be blamed for the discussion because I had brought up the subject in the first place.

It wasn't difficult to see Boots's point of view, however. The incident in the coffee shop, coming on top of a night of work and worry caused by the episode of the "illegitimate" engine, would have been unnerving to almost anyone except the initiated.

By the time we reached the airport, we had agreed to quit talking about the matter because there were more important things to occupy our attention. Deac's Pitcairn was tied down near the hangar and Floyd already had the cylinder block in place, ready to install the two cam shafts. The four little cams on each shaft were a pleasant sight. Now, I thought, we'd have a chance to win. But I noticed very quickly that they were the old sharp-nosed cams we had bought from Miller instead of the broad-nosed cams with which we had been racing.

"Why those? Where are our good cams?" I demanded.

"I loaned them to Hammond to use in his boat while we were using his engine," Floyd explained, "and I can't get them back until next week."

That was the last straw. I glared at him for a full thirty seconds and then blew my top completely.

"Of all the damn fool stunts you've ever pulled, this is it," I exploded. "If you can get the engine together in time, bring it

118

to the track. If you don't it's all right with me. I don't give a damn whether I race today or not."

Boots and I drove on out to the track. The time trials already had started; and as I watched the early qualifiers I cared even less about my chances of earning a starting position.

The old board track finally had reached that point of deterioration where the rotten timbers were beginning to give way under the tremendous vibration set up by the cars. It was necessary to interrupt the qualifying runs several times to make repairs. Owing to these delays, the trials still were in progress when Floyd finally arrived with the car. We fired it up immediately and I managed to get it into the starting field even though it wasn't running well.

The usual drivers' meeting was held as soon as the trials had been concluded. Then the cars were rolled to their respective starting positions. As I started to climb into my car, however, I stepped on another rotten timber and almost fell through the hole in the track. A crew of repairmen worked frantically for twenty minutes, tearing out a strip of track fifteen feet long and three feet wide before finding solid timbers strong enough to serve as a foundation for the big patch.

Never had I experienced a more hectic 24-hour period prior to any race. When it finally got under way, my heart wasn't in it, and I believe it was the only event in which I ever participated that I felt beaten before I started.

During the early part of the race I was running right behind Lou Moore and Jimmy Gleason. The air was filled with splinters of all sizes as the track continued to disintegrate. It was like driving in a hail storm. All of us crouched low over our steering wheels to get as much protection as possible from the cowling. But it was impossible to drive without letting our elbows stick out from the sides of the tiny cockpits. There was a tingling sensation as the little splinters penetrated the skin and I felt sure that it was only a question of time until the larger fragments of the track would begin to tear into the flesh.

To make matters worse, from a psychological standpoint, several boys had eluded the guards and crawled under the

119

track. Then they had climbed up the supporting timbers to the holes in the track on the outside of the groove we were following. They were sticking their heads up through the holes in order to see the race. A driver usually got accustomed to almost anything in those early days of racing. But this was almost more than I could take. Even though they were in no great danger as long as all of us kept our cars in the groove, there always was a chance that some one would lose control momentarily and cause a terrible catastrophe.

The fans had paid to see a race, however, and unless the officials stopped us, there was nothing to do except put on the best possible show under the circumstances and hope that the guards would take care of the hazardous situation quickly.

On the 22nd lap, I noticed an almost imperceptible loss of power. I began to pay closer attention to the instrument panel for additional signs of trouble and it wasn't long until the heat indicator began to move up. Two or three laps later I heard the first faint taps which indicate connecting rod failure. Kicking out the clutch, I hit the switch and coasted into the pit, glad to have a legitimate reason for giving up the chase. It was a tremendous relief to climb out of the car and become a spectator instead of a contestant. I waved at Boots and grinned. She nodded and smiled. Both of us actually were happy about what we normally would have regarded as bad luck. As a fortune teller, Mrs. Means still was only 66 2/3 per cent right.

CHAPTER 15

ALTHOUGH anxious to sever my connection with Floyd, I already was committed to drive the car in two more races. It was impossible to get our good cams back from Hammond in time for the 100-mile event at Akron, Ohio, on June 22—and I finished seventh. We were able to make the change in time for the Bridgeville race on July 4, however, and I duplicated my Detroit victory of the previous month.

At all of the tracks during that summer of 1930, no "bull session" was complete until after the California drivers had taken advantage of an opportunity to rave about the terrific competition on tap at the Ascot track in Los Angeles during the coming winter.

During one of these sessions, and without any preliminaries whatsoever, someone standing behind me said, "Wilbur, why don't you take my little red car out to Ascot and win some money for both of us?" It was Johnny Vance of Dayton, Ohio, whom I had known for several years.

"I don't know anything about your car, Johnny," I replied, "but if it will run, it sounds like a good idea."

"It's hot," he said. "I've got four carburetors on it and it'll run as fast as any of them. Why don't you drive it next week at Langhorne and see how you like it?"

That suited me fine and the car was just as fast as Johnny said it was. In fact, it was too hot. I qualified it in the front row and was running away from the field when the engine tore itself apart after only three laps.

"There goes my trip to California," I thought, but Johnny didn't seem to be the least bit discouraged. He was fairly well fixed, financially, and offered to get it into good running condition again, immediately, if I felt like I could do any good with it on the coast.

The car was painted fire engine red and Johnny called it Red Pete. He used a 16-valve double overhead camshaft Fronty head on a Ford block with a Ford crankshaft and special rods. I couldn't see any reason for undue mechanical failure if it was put together again right. He had offered me an unusually attractive deal, too—50 per cent of the winnings. It was too good to turn down, so I agreed.

When the car was ready, Johnny called me from Dayton and I went over to pick it up. He asked if I'd mind taking

121

a couple of his friends to California with me. I told him I would be glad to. He made a phone call and in a few minutes I was shaking hands with Mauri Rose for the first time. He and his companion, Frank Tobias, helped us get Vance's car on the trailer. Tobias, a former motorcycle racer and mechanic on Red Pete, was going to California to live. Rose regarded the trip as a vacation jaunt, but was hopeful of getting into a race or two while on the coast. We stopped in Indianapolis later the same afternoon to pick up Boots and were on our way to the Far West.

We talked about racing all of the way to California. Mauri spent almost all of the time telling me what a wonderful driver he was. According to him, no one else knew half as much about racing as he did and this was particularly irritating to me, because I was equally certain I was the best in the business. Frankly, I've never known any top-ranking driver who didn't have such an opinion of himself—apparently it's a prerequisite to success—but Mauri had not yet learned to voice such thoughts with a proper amount of restraint. By the time we reached Los Angeles, I was sure of one thing. If I never saw Mauri again, it would be too soon. But our paths were destined to cross many times and our mutual friendship, as well as my respect for his ability as a race driver, increased steadily.

Harlan Fengler, the "boy wonder" among the race drivers of the early 1920s, had brought the Ascot track under the AAA banner and it was being operated in 1930 by the Glendale Post of the American Legion, which held weekly races with Dr. Fred Loring as chairman of the race committee.

On our way to the coast, we had burned out a wheel bearing near Trinidad, Colorado. But I wired my entry ahead for the 100-lap Fall Classic on November 9 and we arrived with twenty-four hours to spare. Boots found an attractive apartment for us in a new development at LaBrea and Wilshire, almost next door to the Gilmore Ranch, which at that time was still operating as such—complete with oil wells. In later years, the odor of raw oil was to become a part of the West we loved, but it took us all winter to become accustomed to it. Ernie and

Yvonne Olson, Ralph and Sparky Hepburn, and Tony and Marie Gulotta all lived within a block of us.

I qualified on the following day for the No. 5 position in the starting field and charged toward the front the instant the flag dropped. By the end of the second lap I had taken the lead from Stubby Stubblefield, surprising a lot of the railbirds who seemed to think the California drivers were invincible. Five minutes later a piston let go, just as it had at Langhorne, and I was through for the day.

Two weeks later, after wiring Vance for new parts, I tried again in a 50-lap event. This time I was battling Ernie Triplett and Francis Quinn for the lead when I lost a wheel. It bounced and rolled in almost every direction, like a football. How they managed to miss it, I'll never know. But they got by it safely and Triplett won by a margin of about fifteen yards over Quinn, who already had clinched the 1930 Pacific Coast championship.

During the month of December, while Shorty Cantlon was winning three races in a row, I ran into so much piston trouble I couldn't even qualify for a race.

I tore Red Pete down completely and double-checked everything, getting it back together again in time for a race at El Centro, near the Mexican border. This event was on a mile dirt track, so I also had to change the gears in the rear end and adjust the carburetors for a richer mixture. Because the constant mechanical trouble was becoming quite costly, I decided to change my tactics, too. This time I would let some one else set the pace during the early laps and then make my bid right at the finish. For seventy-five miles, the plan worked perfectly. I had stayed within a few seconds of the leaders without difficulty. It was time to move out in front and I opened her up full bore. Two laps later it was all over. Another broken piston.

We located a Western Union office and sent my stock telegram to Vance: "Send better pistons immediately." Then Boots and I drove across the border for some Mexican beer and a quail dinner.

The following morning Boots washed her hair while I tore

the engine down for the third time in as many weeks. By noon I had parts scattered all over the place and just about that time El Centro was hit by the worst dust storm I've ever witnessed.

I closed all of the doors and windows as tight as possible, wrapped the engine parts in newspaper and joined Boots to wait for the big blow to subside. She was thoroughly disgusted. The water in that area was so hard she had purchased bottled water to use on her hair. It had been an expensive job and the dust storm hit before her hair had dried. She looked as if she had given herself a mud pack instead of a shampoo. The storm didn't let up until the next day. Sand was everywhere—in our hair and eyes and mouth, in our food and water, even in our beds and inside our clothing. It was a perfectly dreadful situation. I don't know to this day whether it was the rhubarb or the worry about the sand in the engine that gave me an acute case of diarrhea. But something did and I wished I was dead.

I don't believe I've ever tackled a meaner job in my life than getting all the sand out of that engine. It was inside of everything and all over every part, despite the care I had taken with the newspaper wrappings. It took me two days to get it cleaned and back together before taking off for Phoenix. It was the same old story again, only worse. A broken wrist pin tore the cylinder block all to pieces.

Completely broken hearted—and almost broke financially— we loaded the car on the trailer and headed for Los Angeles. Triplett, Stubblefield, Al Gordon and some of the other boys were beginning to call me "Lucky." That didn't help my disposition any. But I managed to make the necessary repairs in time to race at Ascot the following week end and finished fourth. Although the $400 I earned wasn't much at the rate we had been spending it, the experience was good for my morale because it was the first money I had collected since coming to California.

Encouraged by the way the little car had held together, I gave it a lot of throttle on my qualifying trial a week later. I wanted a starting position near the head of the pack, but the engine blew up again on the first lap.

I was sure I finally had had enough as I coasted back to the pits. With only one small chunk of prize money to show for all of my time and effort, I was about as discouraged as any human could be. Before I could climb out of the cockpit, however, Babe Stapp walked up to me with sympathy written all over his face.

"Look, Bub," he said. "You're a long way from home and what you have been doing is expensive. But it can't go on forever. If you run out of dough, come and see me."

It was just the kind of medicine I needed to turn the lights on again and keep me from giving up. With a fresh supply of pistons and a new cylinder block, I put Red Pete's engine together exactly as it had been for the one Ascot race I had finished two weeks earlier. No one ever took greater pains with a job than I did on this occasion. Then I took the car out for a practice run and tested it with the throttle wide open. Everything stayed together and it sounded absolutely perfect. But in the very first heat on race day, I broke the right rear axle. Because I had a spare handy, it was possible for me to replace it in time for one of the later events on the same program. Again I worked my way to the head of the pack and stayed there for twelve laps—enjoying every second of it—with my engine running beautifully. Then the left rear axle broke. That night I wired Johnny: "What shall I do with it? Please advise."

He wasted no time coming to California himself, to look over the situation. I explained in detail what had happened and how much money already had been spent on repairs.

"Well, let's get rid of it," he said.

That was all right with me, because Art Sparks had offered me a ride in his new car and I was anxious to accept in the hope that I could change my luck with different equipment. I did too. I ran into even more and different trouble.

After qualifying for the outside position in the front row, and leading the race for a number of laps, my right front tire developed into a "sneaker." That's a tire that loses its pressure slowly. Without realizing the tire was low, I roared down the home stretch and started to turn left as usual. Instead of responding, the car went straight ahead toward the wall.

That was my first and last experience with a safety belt, which Art had insisted that I wear because some of the boys had been thrown from their cars in recent accidents. The belt kept me from "getting down in the basement" to minimize the possibility of injury in a head-on crash such as I was about to experience. I had no choice but to sit up straight and take it. I pushed on the steering wheel as hard as I could with both arms in an effort to avoid being thrown against the wheel. But the force of the impact was too great.

The lower part of my chest hit the wheel with terrific force. Every bit of wind was forced from my lungs and for a moment or two I didn't know whether or not I'd ever get it back. When I finally was able to gulp some air again, my broken ribs served notice they were completely out of position. I waved to show my friends I was all right and then concentrated on the job of getting my breath in little bitty pants in order to keep from puncturing a lung.

It was necessary for officials to stop the race so that the wreckage could be removed from the course. Boots was able to cross the track in time to join me at the first aid tent in the infield and she was really frightened because it was the first time she ever had seen me banged up. She sat on one cot while the doctors examined me on another. It didn't take them long to decide that my broken ribs required hospital attention. When this verdict was pronounced, Ivy Overholtzer introduced himself to Boots and offered to make the necessary ambulance arrangements. He had been one of the most helpful men in the tent during the entire incident and it was only a matter of minutes until he was helping Boots make me comfortable for the ride. Finally we were all set.

"If I can be of any further assistance at all, just call me," he said, handing her his card. She thanked him, but didn't take time to glance at the card until the ambulance was in motion. Then she lost her temper.

"He's got a lot of nerve," she exclaimed. "Do you know what this card says? Ivy Overholtzer, undertaker."

She laughs about it, now. But it took a while for her to get over the shock and learn, eventually, that Ivy was one of the best friends any member of the racing fraternity ever had. He really was a race fan and he'd send his ambulance anywhere in California, without charge, to bring the boys home when they were injured.

At the hospital they wrapped me with three-inch tape so tight I could hardly breathe and then sent me home. With each hour I became more uncomfortable. I couldn't sleep at all. Every breath required more effort than the last one. By midnight I was convinced that I'd never live until morning unless I got rid of that tape. Although it was somewhat of a tussle, Boots—protesting all of the time—finally wrestled enough of it off me so that I could get some relief. Consequently, I still have one V-shaped rib where the bones didn't knit properly.

While I was shopping around for a new car, without much success, Rose finished second to Cantlon in another 100-lap race at Ascot.

Good cars were extremely scarce. Every fast car already had a regular driver. After having driven the Vance and Sparks cars, getting into one of the few second-rate cars available was like climbing off a race horse and straddling a billy goat. Early in February, however, I had a chance to drive Stubby Stubblefield's car in a special East-West match race with Wild Bill Cummings as my partner. We won from Francis Quinn and Walt May, but I didn't have any luck in the main event.

The outlook on the coast wasn't very bright, with many more drivers than there were cars. It was about time, too, to make some plans for the "500." According to the "grapevine," Augie Duesenberg was building a new car for the Indianapolis event and I wanted the privilege of driving it. I talked things over with Boots that night and a couple of days later we were on our way home.

My "conquest" of Ascot would have to wait until some other time. But we had made some wonderful friends and renewed

127

many old acquaintances, including Dr. and Mrs. Russell Wilcox and their son, Russ. I had known Russ a long time. He had become a devoted race fan while living in Minneapolis and had been a regular at all of the mid-west events. He and his wife, Betty, were to become our inseparable friends and their home was our home-away-from-home for many years. Through the Wilcoxes, we also met Chick and Shorty Bangs, with whom we have had a lot of fun down through the years.

CHAPTER 16

THE Duesenberg brothers, Fred and Augie, had enjoyed exceptional success at the Indianapolis track ever since World War I. Because of the 1929 economic depression, however, they no longer worked as a team. Fred still was president of the financially-harassed Duesenberg Automobile Company, but Augie had severed his connections with the firm and opened a shop of his own in an old brick stable across the road from his brother's plant.

Although both were extremely capable engineers, they had different ideas concerning the type of car best suited to win at Indianapolis. Fred favored the non-supercharged engine with maximum piston displacement and was preparing two entries of this kind for Jimmy Gleason and Phil Pardee. Augie placed his confidence in a small, compact supercharged engine.

When I reached Augie's shop for my first glance at the new car, there was little to see. Except for a front axle and four wheels, Augie's proposed creation was little more than a twinkle in his eye. The task of building it had hardly begun and the race was only three months away.

128

I didn't waste a minute telling Augie I wanted to drive for him and he came right back at me with a proposition that probably would have stopped anyone without the tremendous amount of enthusiasm I had generated simply thinking about the prospect of driving one of the famous Duesenberg cars.

"If you want to help build it," he said, "you can have the first chance to drive it. But I can't pay you for your time."

This was opportunity knocking its loudest, as far as I was concerned. In addition to all of the pleasure I would get out of helping to build a really fine race car, I'd also have the enviable privilege of working with one of the automotive industry's master designers.

Augie's son, Fritz, and two mechanics joined us on the job, working a schedule which had become commonly known as a "Duesenberg day." We'd report for duty early each morning, take time off for hamburgers and coffee late in the afternoon and then rush back to the shop to start the night shift. About two or three o'clock Augie would put his tools aside and say, "Well, boys, let's knock off and get a good night's sleep. Be back about seven-thirty in the morning."

None of us ever objected. Being a part of such a creative team was a wonderful feeling. Watching a thoroughbred race car take form under our own hands occupied so much of our attention that we seldom even thought of food and drink and rest.

Word soon got around that we were building something "awfully hot" and Terry Curley came out to the shop to apply for a job as my riding mechanic. In those days, for some unknown reason, riding mechanics were mandatory at the Indianapolis track. Theoretically, they were supposed to keep the driver informed about cars moving up from the rear. Actually, they were about as useful as cigar store Indians.

I don't know of a single instance in which a mechanic prevented an accident. Their presence in the car served only to lengthen the casualty list whenever trouble was encountered, because two people instead of one usually were injured. Almost invariably, it was the mechanic who got the worst of it.

They were "excess baggage" in a sport where weight is important. In addition, it was customary to put them on the payroll.

But Terry was a natural as far as I was concerned. He had the greatest smile of anyone on earth and invariably was ready with it when the going was roughest. His vocabulary apparently was limited to a single word, "Okeedokee," and he seldom used it except to acknowledge instructions when he was told to do something. He was a flyweight prize fighter, who didn't weigh more than 115 pounds soaking wet. Like me, he was willing to work for nothing more than a chance to share in the prize money. His only stipulation was that I advance him enough money so he could eat regularly until race day.

That was a satisfactory arrangement, as far as I was concerned, and we put Terry to work running Augie's "German milling machine," which was nothing more than a dignified name for a common hack saw. The finish on a cut by a German milling machine always was done with a file and we had plenty of work to keep Terry busy.

He never did learn that he couldn't exceed a certain rhythmic speed and still keep the teeth in the blade. He insisted on trying to make his cuts too fast. Our bill for hacksaw blades was terrific, but gradually the car began to take shape.

After almost two months of "Duesenberg days," the little beauty was about ready for a shakedown run. At the same time, Augie ran out of money, but this wasn't as serious as it might have been. Usually the Duesenbergs ran out of time as well as money. More factory-built Duesenbergs have shown up at the Indianapolis Speedway without paint than all other makes of cars combined. We still had time to finish this job, if we hurried, and I was hopeful that my own small bankroll would be sufficient to pay for the few additional parts we needed.

But the tension was beginning to mount, as it always does as race day approaches. We didn't have time for visitors or interruptions of any kind, when in walked three strangers. They cornered Augie and spent about thirty valuable minutes talking to him while the rest of us went on working. I couldn't hear

130

well above all the noise we were making, but gradually I realized that they were seeking a contribution for the American Red Cross drive under way at that time.

Augie was trying to tell them, in a nice way, that he wasn't interested in making a contribution at the present time. But they wouldn't take no for an answer. I stood it as long as I could, growing more irritated with each succeeding minute. Finally I walked over to the foursome and said, "Why don't you fellows wake up to the fact that this man is fresh out of money and get the hell out of here so we can get some work done on this car?" Admittedly, it was a rough way to treat a good cause. But by that time we were getting somewhat desperate—at least I was—because a lot of work would still have to be done after we finally tested the car.

About three weeks before race day, the little job was ready for a shakedown run. Upholstering and paint still were lacking, but that made no difference to us because we were extremely eager to see how the car would perform in comparison with the larger cars permitted under the rules governing that year's event.

Our engine was a straight eight, supercharged, with a piston displacement of 156 cubic inches. The wheelbase was 104 inches and the car weighed only 1,600 pounds dry (without fuel, oil and water). To us, she was the most beautiful thing in the world despite an inter-cooler which gave it a lop-sided appearance. The inter-cooler, located between the supercharger and the intake ports of the carburetor, emerged from the side of the car and stuck straight up into the air. We had to cool the air coming out of the supercharger before it got into the engine and the most practical way to do it was to put the inter-cooler out in the open where a cooling job could be done best.

With this arrangement, we believed our little engine would develop just as much power as—or more than—the larger non-supercharged engines ranging in size up to 366 cubic inches.

We towed the car to the track and warmed her up at about 2,000 to 2,500 revolutions per minute, which was in the neigh-

131

borhood of seventy-five to eighty miles an hour. A quick examination of the sparkplugs indicated the carburetion was almost satisfactory and we turned a few more laps at about 110 miles an hour. Another check of the plugs revealed a smooth light brown color indicative of perfection (light specks on the porcelain would have meant the mixture was too lean and a darker brown color would have been evidence of a mixture too rich).

We finally were ready for a high-speed test.

Everyone in the pit area had his stop watch on us as we went back out to cut a couple of fast ones. The blackboard showed 112, then 115. Heading down the backstretch I really "stood on it" and the car leaped forward with a terrific surge. Then I could feel the engine begin to falter and I reached desperately for the cutout switch as I kicked in the clutch simultaneously. But I was a split-second too late. We had burned a piston and dumped a lot of aluminum into the crankcase.

Sick at heart, we put a rope around the front axle and towed the car back to the shop. It was a silent two-mile journey, which seemed to take hours. A thorough inspection revealed the damage was even worse than we had feared. The melted aluminum had gone through everything, requiring a complete tear-down.

Morale was mighty low that night when we headed home. But a little sleep revived the never-say-die attitude of all of us. Four days later we were ready for another test. With high-speed jets set a little richer, in the hope of avoiding more piston trouble, we went through the same routine. Again the engine faltered at about 116 miles an hour. But this time I was prepared for what might happen and I hit the button instantly.

The plugs looked good and the tops of the pistons were wet, as they should be. But the fact remained that the engine had lost power suddenly and the only thing to do was to tear it down again to see why.

Some one could make a fortune by designing a zipper for an American racing engine. If an engine doesn't run well, you tear it down to see why. If it seems to run perfectly, you tear it down to make sure that no part is showing signs of undue wear which might cause trouble in the late stages of a race. And even when you finally get the engine running superbly, with no indication of any excessive strain on any part, you tear it down to see if you haven't overlooked some little adjustment which might make it perform even better.

This time we found the skirt of a piston had started to gall a little bit because the water jacket was not cooling it properly. To correct the situation, we enlarged the port of the water manifold at this point and put everything back together carefully.

Four days before the race, with the qualifying trials already under way, we were back at the track for another test run. With time running out on us, we all kept our fingers crossed, and the little supercharged engine sang the most beautiful song anyone can imagine. So, strange as it may seem, we took it back to the shop and tore it down anyway. We wanted to be absolutely certain there were no signs of high spots on bearings and pistons, which would develop excess heat before the end of a race as gruelling as the "500."

Time trials were scheduled to end two days before the race and we could have met the deadline without too much trouble. But in order to give us ample opportunity to do the job well— and also to get some paint on the car—all of the other fellows agreed to give us an extra twenty-four hours. That's one of the wonderful things about the racing fraternity. Everyone will do anything he possibly can to help the other fellow get in the race. I know of no other professional sport where this camaraderie and desire to be helpful to your rival exists to such an extent. It is the perfect example of American sportsmanship and fair play.

We got the car all buttoned up about noon on May 29 and towed it out to the track with supreme confidence that qualifying would be just a breeze. All of us were equally certain of hitting the jackpot the following day. We warmed up the engine carefully and when I passed the pit on the fourth or fifth lap Augie nodded. That meant it's all right to open it up and I really jumped on the throttle. It was perfectly wonderful the way the little engine responded with a new note of authority in its voice. The tachometer showed 6,800 revolutions per minute before I buttoned it on the backstretch and coasted into the pit. A look at the plugs showed that everything appeared to be perfect.

Then, as if we still had all of the time in the world to get ready for the race, Augie said: "There's no time like the present. Let's go."

We pushed it back to the starting line and told the AAA officials we were ready to qualify. They took their posts as we started the engine again. After one lap at moderate speed, I opened it up on the backstretch and came flying around the north turn with the engine singing a song which was the most beautiful music my ears had ever heard. With the engine turning 6,800 revolutions per minute, the supercharger was turning almost 38,000 rpm's and making more noise than a room full of women screaming at the top of their voices.

I stuck up my hand to call for the green flag and was on my way. The tires screamed going through the south turn and we hit the backstretch with everything tied down. Then, half way down that long straight-away, all hell broke loose.

Never have I seen or felt a race car buck and pitch the way that one did. It rolled and tossed and almost stood on its nose, with the engine making the most expensive noises I had ever heard. I reached for the button and kicked at the clutch pedal, but there wasn't any clutch pedal. The brakes didn't work, either. We still were rolling at terrific speed, but all sound had ceased and I thought I had lost my hearing. It was about as weird a ride as anyone ever has experienced until we finally coasted to a stop.

I unbuckled the hood straps to see how much damage had been done to the engine and there wasn't anything there. It had been broken into a million pieces and scattered half way around the Speedway. We finally found all of the crankshaft, which had broken into three pieces and then we were able to determine what had happened. The largest section of it,

134

about two feet long, had cut the engine completely in two. One half of the engine—and then the other half—had fallen out and passed under the car, which had a clearance of only five inches. It was easy to see what had caused it to buck and pitch.

The fact that I hadn't been hurt didn't enter my mind. I wasn't concerned, either, about the weeks of work and the amount of my own money invested in the car. But I was out of the race, even before it had started. To a professional race driver May 30 is Christmas, birthday and all of the other nice days rolled into one. If you get into the Indianapolis "500," no matter what the outcome, you feel amply repaid for a year of work. You've had your chance. When you fail to start, for any reason, it seems as if the whole year has been wasted.

I felt like going downtown and jumping off the top of the monument. Instead, I walked back to Gasoline Alley and flopped down on a stool in the corner of our little garage. Some of the fellows came in to tell me how sorry they were, but I was too despondent to pay much attention to what they said because I was feeling as sorry for Augie as I was for myself.

Out of this blur of faces and voices, however, one question finally penetrated my numb brain. I thought I heard someone ask, "How would you like to drive one of my cars?"

I looked up, and there was Fred Duesenberg, Augie's brother.

I said, "I beg your pardon," and Fred repeated the question, "How would you like to drive one of my cars?"

The saying that "hope springs eternal" certainly is true in the racing business. My pulse started to beat again and I felt certain that this was as fate had planned it. All spring I had felt that this was to be my year and here was the answer to my troubles. I still was going to win the race.

My next thought was for Terry and I asked Fred if the little guy could ride with me.

"That wouldn't be fair to Otto," Fred explained. "Otto has worked on the car all year and he rode with Pardee when they qualified it last week. I can't ask him to give up his seat." He was referring to Walter Hannowsky, who was called Otto by all of his friends. He had been with the Duesenberg brothers since 1925 and had ridden in the 1930 race with Pete DePaolo.

Here was another problem. I wasn't greatly concerned about Terry, because I knew I'd be able to get a ride for him in some other car. But the rules governing the 500-mile race specified that a driver who qualified a car for the race must start that car in the race.

"Since Pardee already has qualified the car, how are you going to get permission for me to drive it?" I asked.

"You can't start it," he said. "But after he drives the first lap, there is nothing in the world to prevent you from driving the other hundred and ninety-nine. Phil hasn't shown any tendency to be in much of a hurry out there during practice. He says he doesn't feel comfortable in the car," Fred added, "and when we talked things over last night he agreed to turn the car over to someone else right after the start of the race. If you want it, you can have it."

Anyone who isn't in a hurry doesn't belong on the Indianapolis Speedway on May 30. Not only would he be a hazard to other drivers, he might even get run over.

"It sounds like a good deal to me," I said. "Roll it out and I'll take a few practice laps to get used to it."

"You can't do that because the track is closed until starting time tomorrow," Fred pointed out. "You won't have any trouble. Go on home and get a good night's sleep."

I found Terry a ride with Red Shafer, who said his mechanic would rather stay in the pit anyway, and then made the rounds to tell some of my friends the good news.

Terry's parting shot that night, along with his big wonderful grin, was "I'll see you in the morning, pardner, and after you've won the race I'll help you celebrate."

The funny thing was that I was completely confident he knew what he was talking about!

After a bath and dinner that night, I hit the pillow and died. The worry and strain wrapped up in the little car—and then its failure—had used up all the stuff I had, including the re-

136

serve. But the next morning found me feeling like an entirely new person.

It's wonderful to be young and cocky. Every step I got nearer the track that morning, I was more sure it was my day. I was confident the best race driver in the world was on his way to the Indianapolis Speedway to win a 500-mile race. It was going to be a breeze. All I had to do was wait until Pardee brought the car into the pit after the first lap. Then I'd jump into it, overtake the leaders in a few laps and coast under the checkered flag about five hours later.

I went straight to the Duesenberg pit, where Fred and his crew were making a thorough check of both his big Model A "Duesies." Gleason was fiddling around the cockpit of the No. 33 he was to drive and four legs were sticking out of the cockpit of the No. 32 which Pardee was to turn over to me. I strolled over to get a better look at what they were doing and it seemed as if I were walking up to the side of a locomotive. Those big Model A Duesies were almost twice the size of my little job and they certainly looked like a lot of race car.

I wanted to get behind the wheel to get the feel of the car I was going to drive, but the mechanics were too busy to be disturbed. They were putting some Duesenberg hose clamps (baling wire wrapped around a hose connection and then twisted) on the line to the oil pressure gauge. By the time they crawled out, it was time to push the car to its starting position and I didn't even have a chance to sit in it.

Drivers and mechanics gathered at the starting line for the traditional picture and I lined up with them. It wouldn't be right, I thought, for the cameraman to get a picture which didn't include the ultimate winner! Then, as they walked back to their cars to await the starting signal, I headed for the pit so that I would be sure to be ready when Pardee came in after the pace lap.

Seconds seemed like hours, but finally the beautiful Cadillac pace car, with Big Boy Raeder at the wheel, pulled away from the starting line. Stragglers moved into their proper positions as the field rounded the first turn and you could hear the roar of the engines as the pace gradually was increased on the back-stretch. Then out of the north turn they came with a tremendous surge to sweep by the pit area in a cloud of dust sucked up from the tiny crevices between the bricks.

By the time I could see again, the whole pack was back, but Pardee turned a few more laps to let the traffic thin out a little. I was beginning to get impatient, and swearing a little under my breath, when he held up one finger to indicate he'd come in after another lap. He braked to a stop and jumped out. Before his feet hit the ground I had jumped in. And I really mean IN. I went clear out of sight. The car definitely had been built for a man of more than average size, instead of a fellow like me. The seat was so low I couldn't possibly see over the cowling. The steering wheel felt as if it was three feet in diameter. The only way I could reach the foot accelerator was by sliding sideways on the seat and sitting on the left cheek of my rear end. But it was too late to worry about things not fitting. By leaning out the left side of the cockpit I discovered that I could see ahead and we took off.

I shifted into high gear about half way through the No. 2 turn and stepped on it. Nothing seemed to happen. I might just as well have stepped into a fresh cow-pie. A questioning glance at Otto didn't tell me a thing. He seemed quite content. We cruised the full length of the backstretch and through the north turn without anyone passing us, but it seemed to me as if we still must be running in second gear.

As we headed down the main stretch I put my hand on the gear shift lever, nudged Otto and gave him another questioning look. I was asking, "Is this big brute in high gear?"

He nodded "Yes."

By the time we had finished this little bit of silent conversation we were heading into the south turn again and I had to give it my full attention. This time, as soon as we were on the backstretch, I squirmed to the very edge of the seat and put every ounce of weight I had on the throttle to make sure it was wide open. Sure enough, it was.

My bobber went clear under. Apparently this big new Due-

138

senberg was just another bag of bolts that wouldn't even run 100 miles an hour. I wondered how Pardee had managed to qualify it and it was easy to see why he had been so willing to turn it over to me.

What I had failed to take into consideration was that my "yardstick" was gone. Race cars do not have speedometers to show their rate of speed. Instead, they have tachometers to show how fast the engine is turning. And a tachometer doesn't tell you much about your speed unless you know the gear ratio in the rear end and the distance the rear wheels travel with each revolution. As you get to know the car you are driving, you gauge your speed mostly by the sound of your engine, the force of the wind in your face and the feeling in the seat of your pants.

This car, weighing almost 2,400 pounds, rode like a baby buggy. Its 243 cubic inch non-supercharged engine wasn't making any noise in comparison with the mechanical shriek of my smaller job with the blower on it. And certainly no wind could get to me in that deep cockpit. I felt as if we were out for a Sunday afternoon pleasure jaunt.

As I passed my pit for the third or fourth time I executed a French wave of my shoulders, which meant "I'm sorry, gentlemen, but this is as fast as the old goat will go."

I thought maybe they would call me in to see what was wrong. On the next trip around I did the same thing, but Fred Duesenberg did nothing but clasp his hands above his head and give me the OK sign. The thought flashed through my mind that he was congratulating me on taking it easy until I had learned some of the car's peculiarities. And here I was, driving it just as hard as it would go. I wondered what his reaction would be when he gave me the "Go" sign later in the race without getting any visible increase in speed. When we got on the backstretch again, I nudged Otto and pointed to the tachometer, which was showing a little better than 3,900 rpm's. Then I turned the palm of my hand up and moved it up and down, asking him, "Is that all this thing can do?"

He grinned and nodded "Yes."

139

We had passed a few cars, but I'd been too concerned with getting more speed out of my own car to notice which ones we had overtaken. I had taken for granted that they were some of the dogs which invariably seem to get into every race almost by accident. But the next time we moved up in the field I noticed we were passing a pretty good car. And in another minute we passed a damn good car.

The old optimism began to come back. This wasn't going to be as bad as I feared.

"If we can just keep running the way we are," I thought to myself, "we'll make some money after all because most of the other fellows seem to be having some trouble, too."

The track was getting slicker every minute. In 1931 there were no regulations regarding the amount of oil a car could use. We didn't worry about oil leaks, because we could always get more oil when we stopped for tires. And with everyone following this practice, it didn't take long for the track to get well coated with it. When that happened, the only thing to do was to "wish" the car around the track. When you were on the home stretch, you wished you were on the backstretch, where your friends couldn't see you if you started to lose control and did a little fishtailing. And when you were on the backstretch, you wished you were on the home stretch so you could learn if anyone else was having enough trouble to force him into the pits.

I was so busy getting the big "blimp" through the slick turns that I didn't pay much attention to the pit, because it was too near the south turn for me to take more than a very quick look without running the chance of getting into trouble. Every time I looked at Otto, however, he grinned and nodded. I wasn't too concerned with pit signs, anyway, because by this time I had made up my mind to keep on driving as fast as the car would go and to hell with everything else.

Then it happened. As we slid out of the south turn on to the backstretch, four cars were immediately ahead of us. Like a bunch of Sunday drivers on a busy highway, they were running nose to tail and I was crawling a little closer to them with

140

each revolution of my rear wheels. I had the choice of easing up on the throttle or going on around, but I couldn't pass them one at a time. It was either all or none, so I stood on it as hard as I could.

We didn't pass 'em like an express train going by a slow freight, but we did move up steadily. First I got Shorty Cantlon. Then Red Shafer—and I wondered who Terry was pulling for in this little skirmish. Then I caught up with Freddie Winnai and was just moving alongside Ralph Hepburn when I suddenly realized we were almost at the end of the straightaway.

When you are doing your observing with one eye around the edge of your cowling, you can't concentrate on too many things, so I concentrated on Hep's right front wheel. I felt sure he would use good judgment in determining when it was time to ease off the throttle a bit in order to get into the turn properly. If I stayed on it a split-second longer than he did, I might be able to give him an eighth-of-an-inch or so for clearance and get back into the groove ahead of him. But it didn't work out that way.

He wasn't willing to give an inch. Not knowing that I couldn't ease off and drop into the groove behind him—because Winnai and Cantlon were using that particular part of the track—he was determined to hang on as long as I did. When I finally pulled ahead of him and took a quick glance to see what I had to do about getting into the turn it was too late. The turn had started some place back of us and I was much too high on the bank for safety.

Before I could coax it back into the groove leading to the short north straightaway I heard the "eee . . . eee . . . eee" of the tires as they began to lose their grip on the bricks.

The car made three or four little prancing sidesteps and then traded ends as it went into a spin like a top.

Regardless of what any driver may tell you about how he brought a car out of a spin at racing speed, there's only one intelligent thing to do. I don't mean that a driver should give up whenever he gets into trouble. Stay with it as long as you

141

have a chance and give it everything you've got. But when it finally trades ends it's time to get down in the basement as far as you can and push up on the steering wheel. Then look up into the heavens and say "Okay, God, You've got it." Most certainly you don't have it yourself, and if He isn't taking care of the situation you're in a bad fix.

I headed for the basement in a hurry and Otto already was there. While I had been watching Hep's right front wheel he had been looking ahead. He knew, long before I realized it, that we never would negotiate the turn at that speed without being in the groove and was ready for the worst long before I started down.

Usually, by the time you get in the basement, you don't have to wait long for something violent to occur. With four cars right behind us and no place for them to go except through us, I was fairly certain of quick action in this particular instance, but it seemed as if we had been there for several minutes without the anticipated result. So I took a peek over the edge of the cowling, wishing there was an eye on the end of my finger so I could stick it up instead of my head.

The outlook wasn't too bad. The track appeared to be coming around just right so that I might be able to hit the throttle and come out of the spin. But the track didn't give me its full cooperation. It didn't get around in time and we headed straight for the wall, nose first.

At that time the outer retaining wall was perpendicular to the ground, instead of at right angles to the slope of the track; and at this particular spot the wall had sunk a couple of feet, forming more of a ramp than a barrier. The front wheels hit with a thud and we took off into space. Then the rear wheels went bump-bump and it felt as if the car was trying to do a somersault.

With both of us huddled on the floor, the car sailed through the air for twenty-five or thirty feet, tore down the telephone wires strung along the outside of the track and landed on all four wheels. The sound of torn and twisted metal was terrible. Then everything was deathly silent until we heard the siren on

142

the "meat wagon" coming around to see what they could salvage.

They got me out first and everything seemed to be hanging together in good shape. Otto was lucky, too, although his forehead was badly lacerated. They loaded both of us into the ambulance—along with Winnai, who had hit the wall a few feet from the spot we had sailed over it—and then darn near killed us as they tried to set a new record for the trip to the emergency hospital over some of the roughest terrain ever navigated by a four-wheel vehicle.

The doctors went to work on the other two casualties immediately, because they seemed to be hurt more seriously than I. As soon as they decided they were going to make it all right, however, they turned their hungry eyes on me. A little blood was running down over one shoe, so they tossed me up on one of their work benches and slit my pants leg up above my knee with a pair of scissors. This drew fire, of course, because I couldn't see any reason for cutting up a perfectly good pair of pants when I could have stepped out of them with no trouble at all.

I was bleeding where some of the meat had been scraped off my shin bone. They put some ointment on the wound, wrapped it with gauze, and then began to look elsewhere for additional damage. I had lost a little hide in fifteen or twenty different places, which looked almost like floor burns, and the docs poured iodine on every spot. It burned like sin and I was glad to get out of the hospital as soon as they let me up from the table.

With my pants leg flapping around my bandaged shin I headed straight through Gasoline Alley so that I could signal to Boots and Mother that I was all right. They gave me an answering wave so that I'd know they were no longer worried and I sauntered down toward the Duesenberg pit. I wasn't in any particular hurry because I wasn't sure what kind of reception I'd get from Mr. Duesenberg.

The last time he had seen the car I was driving for him it was worth about $25,000; now, at the going price of scrap

143

metal, it couldn't have been worth more than $250. He might think those two missing zeros were important—and I couldn't blame him if he did. Having been solely responsible for washing out an investment of that magnitude, I rather imagined I wouldn't be too welcome. But I did owe him the courtesy of a report on what had happened.

Much to my surprise, Fred didn't seem to be concerned about anything except my physical welfare.

"Are you hurt?" he asked.

"No."

"Are you sure?"

"I got a few scratches," I answered, "but the hospital turned me loose after burning me up with a lot of iodine."

"All right," he said. "Get your helmet and goggles on. We'll call Gleason in and put you in the other car."

I couldn't have been more surprised if he had handed me title to the entire Duesenberg plant. For an instant, I couldn't even believe my own ears. But Fred already had turned away from me and was busy putting a big STOP on Gleason's board.

They gave him the sign on his next lap and by the time he came sliding into the pit I had pulled my helmet over the goose eggs on my head and had my gloves and goggles on. While Jimmy was climbing out of the cockpit, they filled the fuel tank, dumped in about ten more gallons of oil and changed a right rear tire which was beginning to show signs of wear.

I jumped in and promptly went out of sight again in the big cockpit. I must have looked like a pea in a bucket, but by this time I knew the combination. I squirmed into position to reach the things I needed to reach, stuck my head out the left side and took off. At the time, I probably was in a state of shock without realizing it. But after a couple of laps I began to do a little thinking and then I started talking to myself.

"You've just let one of these big Duesies get away from you," I told myself. "Now you're in another one, just like the first one, and if you're real smart you'll take care of it."

I decided to take it easy for awhile. But after a few laps I

144

punched a little harder on the throttle as I came out of the turn and discovered I'd been running wide open all of the time.

I remember, distinctly, thinking: "Gosh, this one won't run, either."

We headed into the backstretch and there they were, almost like they were before, with only Winnai's car missing.

"Well, we'll try it again," I said to myself. And this time things were different—strangely different.

As I pulled alongside of Cantlon he glanced over at me and promptly closed his throttle. Shafer did likewise. When I finally pulled up even with Hepburn, he did the same thing and I began to think there must be something terribly wrong with my own car to make all three of the fellows give so much racing room for no apparent reason. I didn't realize at the time that they must have thought they were seeing a ghost. Except for the numbers, 32 and 33, the two Duesenbergs were identical.

But I did realize we were almost at the end of the straightaway again and for the second time that day I was going into the turn too high. I punched it hard to take advantage of the room Hep was trying to give me. But the track was slicker than ever and I did a very unworkmanlike job of trying to get back into the groove. The tires started that "eeee . . . eee . . . eee" business again and I was resigned to a repetition of my former experience.

This time, however, the back end didn't get all the way around. I managed to get it straightened out with at least a quarter-of-an-inch to spare between the right rear wing nut and the wall. But I was too busy to take a deep breath until we had turned into the home stretch. Then I glanced at the lad who had been riding with Gleason before I took over the car. Honestly, you could have knocked his eyes off with a stick. They were bugged out as if they were ready to pop.

"If you had seen what I did on that turn thirty minutes ago, you'd have jumped," I exclaimed, even though I knew he couldn't hear me above the noise of the engine.

There wasn't much excitement during the remainder of the

145

race. We moved up into sixth place, but were too far back of the No. 5 spot to improve our position unless one of the leaders broke down. We weren't threatened seriously from behind so I began to take things easy with the intention of making sure to keep this car in one piece. Each time I passed the pit I could see Gleason hanging over the wall, watching me as if I had his best girl friend out for a buggy ride. At last it dawned on me that he wanted the fun of finishing in it even if he didn't have a chance of preventing Louis Schneider from winning. With only a few laps to go I slid into the pit unannounced and relinquished the wheel to Jimmy.

After the race I was sitting in the garage, feeling good about the whole situation and pressing on my sore shin with both hands in a vain attempt to ease the pain, when Terry walked in. His priceless grin was gone and I don't believe I ever saw him with a more worried look on his face.

I said, "Hi, pardner, what's the matter?"

"Boy, I'm going nuts," he answered.

My first thought was, "Well, he's finally found out," because any mechanic who rides in a race car has to be nuts. But instead of saying so, I said, "What do you mean?"

"Well," he answered, "Red and I were sailing along the backstretch and I'll swear that I saw you come by in that big Duesie and suck us under and then do three or four gilhoolies in the north turn and take off like a bird and sail right out over the wall." The words came tumbling out like a stream going over a waterfall. "Then, while I was sitting there wondering how badly you were hurt and worrying about you," he added, "you come up from behind and suck us under in the same spot and almost hit the wall again and I'm going nuts trying to figure out who in the hell went over the wall if it wasn't you."

"I'm the guy who went over the wall, all right," I said.

"Are you kidding me?" he asked. "You haven't got a scratch on you."

"The hell I haven't. How do you suppose I got all these things?" I replied, showing him my bandaged shin and twelve or fifteen spots covered with iodine.

146

"Well, I'll be damned," he exclaimed. "How did you manage to get the car back on to the track?"

Like most other drivers and mechanics, Terry seldom paid any attention to car numbers. You get in the habit of recognizing cars by their color scheme or some peculiarity in design. Because he had not noticed the numbers he had been fooled by the fact the Duesenbergs were exact twins.

I explained that I was driving Gleason's car when Terry saw me the second time and he said "Thank God, I'm not completely nuts, anyway."

Terry no sooner had walked out of the door than in came Cantlon.

"Hello, you lucky stiff," he said. "How're you doing?"

"Not too badly," I replied. "At least, I made a little money today and I'm still able to navigate under my own steam even if I am skinned up in a couple of dozen places."

"Say, did you have that St. Christopher's medal with you today?" he asked.

A couple of weeks prior to the race the Runt, as we called Cantlon, had been with me when a feminine fan who was as cute as a speckled pup, had given me such a medal. I'm not a Catholic, but I always have had a healthy respect for everyone's personal religious beliefs and I had promised her I would carry it.

"Certainly I had it with me," I replied. "Why?"

"I thought so, you old hypocrite!" Shorty exclaimed.

"Why shouldn't I carry it?" I asked. "If it takes care of you guys, why shouldn't it help me a little bit, too, when I need it? And I certainly needed all the help I could get today."

"Well, Buddy," said Shorty, "I was one of the fellows you passed on the backstretch in such a hurry right before you failed to make the turn. And I was one of the fellows you passed on the backstretch a little later when you damn near failed to make the turn. But if I were you, I wouldn't take advantage of old Chris too often, because I don't know how much he'll stand for."

CHAPTER 17

DURING the summer of 1931, I continued to drive for the Duesenbergs in the 100-mile championship events scheduled throughout the middle west. But I didn't have much success after finishing third at Altoona in a July 4 race won by Lou Moore. Mechanical trouble knocked me out of three straight races late in the season and the approach of cold weather made me think again of California.

Boots and I reached Los Angeles in time for me to drive in a 100-lap event at Ascot on the last Sunday of October and my luck was still bad. Francis Quinn, Babe Stapp, Ernie Triplett, Arval Brunmier and I were running well bunched at the head of the pack and trying to lap the field when Carl Ryder's car broke an oil line. Art Pillsbury of the AAA staff gave him the signal to "come in" immediately. Ryder ignored it (and later was suspended) long enough to spray several gallons of oil on the track.

Brunmier hit one of the slick spots and spun. Stapp swerved his car to miss Brunmier. Triplett sideswiped Stapp. I had to bounce off the fence in order to get by the wreckage. But Quinn didn't touch a thing and the remainder of the field was able to reduce speed sufficiently to avoid trouble also. After a quick inspection of my car in the pits, AAA officials permitted me to continue. The stop cost me a couple of laps, however, and I couldn't do anything but chase the other fellows across the finish line for ninth place, with Quinn winning.

For a couple of months, I hopped from one car to another in an effort to finally win an Ascot main event. The best I could do was a second and two thirds.

On January 24, 1932, I climbed back into Red Pete, which

148

had changed hands a couple of times since Vance had sold it the previous year. The name had been changed to the Durkee Motors Special No. 44 and it still was a mighty hot car. This time it held together for 100 laps. I took the lead from Babe Stapp on the twelfth trip around the course and nosed out Wild Bill Cummings for my first important California victory.

While I was waiting to collect my prize money after the race, Earl Haskell and Fred Blauvelt called me aside.

"We've just made a deal with Harry Miller," said Earl, "for a new car which should be the fastest thing on the coast. How would you like to drive for us?"

Despite my success that day, all of the previous trouble I'd had with the Vance car flashed into my mind. Without a moment's hesitation, I accepted Earl's offer and on the last Sunday of February the car was ready for me.

It was sponsored by the Gilmore Oil Company and was called the Blu-Green Special in order to attract attention to the particular brand of gasoline which Gilmore was selling at that time. I finished second to Cummings in the race that day and won the next two Ascot main events without difficulty.

Gilmore officials wanted us to try for the world record for four-cylinder non-supercharged cars of not more than 305 cubic inch piston displacement. Kaye Don had set the existing record of 136.980 miles an hour.

With the right gear in the car, and disc wheels on the rear, all of us thought the record was within our reach and late in March we took the car up to Muroc Dry Lake, about a hundred miles north of Los Angeles. With Pillsbury and other AAA officials supervising the record run, we managed to beat Don's mark by a fraction of a mile an hour with an average of 137.252.

Gilmore officials were jubilant. Their trademark was a replica of a lion's head and a week later they presented me with a live lion cub. Colonel Roscoe Turner, the flyer, had one as a mascot, too. I believe his cub was named Gilmore I and mine Gilmore II. Both of them would answer to the name of Hannibal— whenever they were willing to respond at all—and we had a

149

lot of fun with them when they were in a playful mood. When they didn't want to play, it was advisable to give them a wide berth. If you didn't, they could make deep incisions in your arm or face right quick with their claws.

The Gilmore company took care of the cubs most of the time, but we usually took one of them to every race as a promotion stunt—until one night when we were staying in a San Francisco hotel. When Hannibal was exercising, he would leap against a wall, land in the center of the room, leap against another wall and keep this up until he finally used up all of his excess energy. On this particular occasion, we were in a hotel room which had draw curtains across the windows. We had left the window open, when we closed the curtains, and Hannibal apparently thought it was a solid wall. Before we realized what was happening, he had jumped against the curtains in front of a window and sailed right through the screen —falling several floors to his death. He'd given us a lot of laughs, but a lot of trouble, too, and we weren't interested in Gilmore's offer to replace him.

I was at the top of the list in the Pacific Coast point standing when the lion cub was presented to me; and on the same day I received a crash helmet which had been worn by England's famous H. O. D. Segrave, the first man to drive an automobile more than 200 miles an hour. Barney Oldfield made the presentation and I started to wear the helmet immediately. All of us had been wearing cloth helmets up to that time, and the other fellows gave me a terrible ribbing. Newspapers even ran cartoons, showing me wearing a "thundermug," because that's what the helmet resembled. But, with the accident rate as high as it was at Ascot, the crash helmet seemed like a sensible piece of equipment to me and I wore it religiously despite all of the ridicule. Three years later, crash helmets were made mandatory for all AAA drivers.

Another memorable incident at Ascot was the day I won my first helmet dash. Usually a glamorous screen star presented the trophy and bestowed a big kiss on the winner of such an event. I was looking forward to that experience with a great

150

deal of pleasure as I completed the extra lap and coasted back toward the starting line in front of the grandstand. I wondered who the gorgeous movie queen would be. Instead, I found an all-male reception committee awaiting me; and out of the group stepped Jim Jeffries, former heavyweight boxing champion of the world, to make the presentation. Under ordinary conditions, I would have been extremely happy to meet him. That afternoon, however, he was a poor substitute for the shapely individual I expected to embrace.

The first night race of the season at Ascot was scheduled on April 20 and it resulted in one of the most unusual finishes I have ever seen at any track. I went out of the race early, because of magneto trouble, and had a "ringside seat" near the finish line so that I could see exactly what happened. Arval Brunmier had a lead of almost a lap on the field. He came out of the No. 4 turn at full speed on his final lap, headed for the checkered flag, when Al Gordon's car spun in front of him. Brunmier hit it head-on, virtually demolishing it, and bashing in the front end of his own car to such an extent that oil and water streamed from under the hood.

Brunmier's engine didn't stall, however, and the force of the collision had knocked Gordon's car out of the way. With the frame of his car broken and the front wheels pointing at different angles toward either side of the track, Brunmier gave the car full throttle again. The engine still was able to deliver enough power to the rear wheels to force the crippled car slowly toward the finish line, with the front wheels sliding along the track surface, almost at right angles to the direction the car was going. The car couldn't have been moving more than five miles an hour as it crossed the finish line and stalled in the middle of the track, but the effort was enough to give Brunmier credit for winning the race.

One week later I finished second to Chet Gardner in another Ascot race which resulted in an injury to Babe Stapp. He broke his arm when his car spun on a spot of oil and had to remain behind when the rest of us headed for Indianapolis to take another crack at winning the "500."

CHAPTER 18

ON NEW YEAR'S DAY during that winter of 1931–32, while Southern California was defeating Tulane in the Rose Bowl football game, the racing fraternity had moved up to Oakland for a 100-mile championship event.

Ralph Hepburn was one of the favorites in the same big Miller Special he planned to drive at Indianapolis. He was well up with the leaders, too, when a right front tire failed on the 34th lap. The car did a mid-air flip and landed on top of him. Hep was seriously injured and the car appeared to be a complete wreck.

The weather had been threatening all day and as the remainder of the field reached the half-way mark the track was drenched by a sudden shower. Before everyone was able to get his car under control for the slippery going, Bryan Salspaugh looped on the main straightaway.

At Art Pillsbury's suggestion, a new judges' stand had been built at Oakland that year on the inside of the track at the starting line. In order to give the officials a good view of what was happening at all parts of the track, the stand had been erected on 14-foot "stilts." Fred Wagner, George Theobald, Hal Weller, Bert Dingley and Les Manning occupied it during the race with Pillsbury working on the track in front of it.

After looping, Salspaugh's car "broad-sided" straight toward the stand and knocked over the two front supports as if they were match sticks. Pillsbury jumped out of danger, but the stand came crashing down, officials and all. The only thing to do was "call" the race the next time the leader came around the track and Babe Stapp was flagged as the winner. Wild Bill

Cummings finished second, Ernie Triplett third, Louie Meyer fourth and Lou Moore fifth.

Hepburn's injuries were even more critical than first reports indicated. He was going to have to remain in the hospital many weeks. That would be an expensive ordeal and all of us wanted to help in some manner.

Ernie Weil agreed to do most of the work necessary to get his car in running condition again with several of us helping whenever we had a few spare hours. Howard Hawkes provided the money to buy the new parts which were necessary and I promised to drive the car at Indianapolis if it could be repaired in time. Harry Miller placed the facilities of his shop at our disposal and the job finally was completed although the car was late in reaching Indianapolis.

When it arrived, we ran into more trouble because of a bit of thoughtlessness on my part. Help wasn't too plentiful. Almost everyone connected with the rebuilding of the car had his own car to get ready, too. After my first shake-down cruise around the track, I drove up to the garage doors and held the clutch out—with engine running—while someone opened them for me. Usually, all drivers turn off the ignition switch when they reach their garages and push the car through the doors. Because I let the engine run, I burned all of the fillets out of the main bearing. We had to work night and day in order to repair the damage in time to qualify. Actually, my qualifying speed of more than 114 miles an hour would have put me in the No. 1 spot of the second row if I had been ready to run on the first day of time trials, but twenty-one other cars had qualified before I was ready to make my attempt and I wound up in 22nd starting position.

It was a real thrill, during the pre-race period, to spend some time with the No. 1 family of the automotive industry—the Fords. Henry Ford, who had done a great deal to create a demand for his original "Tin Lizzie" by driving the famous Ford "999" to a new world record of 91.370 miles an hour on the frozen surface of Lake St. Clair on January 13, 1904, headed the group. He had been a frequent Speedway visitor in recent years and he always enjoyed talking with the drivers and mechanics in Gasoline Alley. As a concrete example of his sincere interest in the men who risk their lives while pioneering new ideas on the Speedway, he had made personal arrangements for a $10,000 insurance policy on each driver in the 1924 race, when he had served as referee.

Henry's son, Edsel, had been named referee of this 1932 Classic and he also was scheduled to drive the Lincoln pace car. Two of Edsel's sons, Henry II and Benson, were a couple of the most interested spectators who had ever entered the Speedway grounds. Bill, the youngest of Henry's grandsons, had to wait two or three years before he was old enough to get his Speedway "inoculation."

On the day before this 1932 race, the customary $20,000 lap prize fund—assuring the leader of a cash award of $100 for each lap he completed at the head of the pack—was far from subscribed. When Henry learned of this situation, he immediately gave Speedway officials a check for $5,000 to wipe out a big part of the deficiency and I was determined to collect as much of it as I possibly could.

Dean DuChemin, Hepburn's brother-in-law, was my riding mechanic and when the race started we began moving up toward the front of the field immediately. We passed at least a half-dozen cars on the first two laps. Then, right on the main straightaway, as I pulled out to pass another rival, the engine began to "miss" as if I were out of fuel. That couldn't be, so I took a quick glance at the pressure gauge and saw that the needle was flat on the peg. In those days, everyone still used manually-operated fuel pumps. Dean, who had more time to watch the instrument panel than I did, already had noticed the gauge and was pumping like mad. But I didn't realize it.

"Pump, you big lug," I screamed. "What in the hell do you think you're in here for?"

I doubt if he heard me, above the roar of all the engines, and I know I didn't hear his reply. But I also knew the small air lines had filled with fuel, which had backed up all of the way to the check valves. It would require almost a superhuman ef-

154

fort to clear them. Dean did it, however, and we regained racing speed immediately.

Billy Arnold, who had led most of the way in each of the last two previous races, had moved out in front on the second lap and it looked as if he would be hard to catch. But when he hit the wall on the northwest turn on his 58th lap—close to the spot where Al Gordon and Gus Schrader had wrecked a little earlier—the race became a wide open scramble. A terrific battle for first place developed immediately with Bob Carey, Ernie Triplett, Howdy Wilcox II and Ira Hall involved. While they fought it out among themselves, I continued to move up steadily and was sixth at 200 miles. After stopping for fuel and tires, just short of the half-way mark, I began to close in on the leaders again.

Carey spun and lost ten minutes in the pit while changing a damaged wheel. Triplett, Hall, Wilcox and Louie Schneider, who also was ahead of me, made their scheduled pit stops in quick order. When I came shooting down the straightaway on my 116th lap my pit crew had a big "P-1" on the blackboard and I was the happiest guy in the world. For the first time in my life I was out in front of the entire field in a 500-mile race and I didn't know of any reason why I couldn't stay there.

I nudged Dean and made an "OK" sign with my thumb and forefinger.

A few laps later my ear caught the sound of a little grinding noise in the rear end of my car. At first it was almost like a hum. Gradually it became louder and louder, particularly when I stepped on the throttle when coming out of a turn. I started experimenting immediately and discovered that the grinding sound wasn't nearly as evident when I drove at a steady pace. By going through the turns a little faster, to offset my lack of acceleration on the straightaway, I still might be able to go the distance and win. From then on, I drove with my right foot braced in such a manner that the pressure on the throttle didn't vary as much as an ounce at any point on the track.

While I was doing the necessary experimenting, Frame had

155

managed to take the lead away from me. Even this didn't worry me too much, because I knew he would have to make another stop for fuel. He did on the 134th lap and I was back in first place again with my fingers crossed. After completing 152 laps, I was leading by twenty-eight seconds. Whoever beat me to the finish, if I could continue to run, would have to average more than a half-second better than my time on each lap and this didn't seem to be likely. I hadn't figured, however, on the added strain placed on my tires because of my increased speed on the turns.

It wasn't long until the breaker strip began to show on my right rear tire. Frame zoomed by while my crew was giving me new rubber. Even then I wasn't too discouraged. There still was a good chance that I could salvage second or third place and there always was the chance that my chief rivals also would run into some bad luck of their own.

The boys had me ready to go again in a hurry. I put the car in gear and started out of the pit very carefully with the crew giving me a little push to ease the strain on the rear end. But I hadn't moved two feet when the ring gear failed. There was simply no way to get power to the rear axle. All I could do was sit there, mad and discouraged.

Frame went on to win easily with a new track record of better than 104 miles an hour. Wilcox, Bergere and Carey also bettered Pete DePaolo's former mark. Russ Snowberger, Zeke Meyer, Ira Hall, Fred Winnai, Billy Winn and Joe Huff followed in order to earn the remainder of the prize money.

It certainly was a blue Monday for me. I was disappointed for Hep's sake as well as my own. But Leon Duray dispelled part of the gloom by asking if I would like to drive his Ascot and dirt track car during the remainder of the year. I raced at Detroit the following week, without much success, and then returned to California with Leon. Louis Bromme was working for Duray at the time and it looked as if the three of us would form a very compatible owner-driver-mechanic team. After we arrived on the coast, however, Duray decided that he wanted to drive his own car in a few races and I managed to get a ride in my former Blu-Green Special.

I scored a second, a third and two fourths in my first five races—losing out in the other event when a right rear tire failed. In the first night race of the summer at Ascot, on August 3, I drove the No. 5 Gilmore Special to victory, setting a new 100-lap record of 46 minutes and 21 seconds to beat Ernie Triplett by three-fourths of a lap. Mel McKee blew a tire right in front of me during this event and you couldn't have got a sheet of paper between the two cars as I managed to slip by without touching him.

A week later I was running second to Les Spangler, with Ernie Triplett third, when Les spun in some oil from Chet Gardner's car. It had broken a connecting rod. I stalled my car to keep from hitting Spangler and officials decided to halt the race temporarily until the track could be cleared. At about the same instant, Triplett passed me. I pushed my car back to the pits and got the engine running again before the race was re-started from the point at which it had been suspended. At the end of 100 laps, I was flagged as the winner with Triplett second. He protested immediately, on the grounds that I had stalled before the race actually was halted—claiming that I should be penalized a lap for having pushed my car back to the pits—and his protest was upheld the next day. It seemed like an unfair ruling to me, but there was nothing I could do about it.

I still hadn't driven Leon Duray's car in actual competition, although I had spent a lot of time working on it because he was counting on me to drive it in an Italian race that Fall at Monza, with Vincenzo Florio as the promoter.

He had a 4-cylinder 220-inch Offenhauser engine in a 91-inch Miller chassis which had been shortened with a cross spring in the rear. It was a fine little automobile, even though it was hard on tires, and we kept making one adjustment after another on the chassis in an effort to correct this condition.

We built dual wheels for the right rear axle, but they failed to stand up under the strain. We tried tires with extra wide

157

tread without success. For one race we removed the rear brake drums to lighten the unsprung weight of the car, relying only on front brakes, but even this drastic experiment didn't help much.

Leon always was trying to outsmart the other boys in some department, however, and he managed to obtain a trick fuel which he called "mazolum." It was a concoction, I think, similar to the present-day nitro fuels. The car had a lot of "go" with this stuff in it and he was reasonably successful after working out the best possible distribution of weight to reduce tire wear.

After one more race at Ascot, on August 17, we were scheduled to head for New York and sail on the Italian steamer Roma for Genoa. During the time trials for the Ascot event, my No. 5 Gilmore Special broke a crank-shaft. Leon immediately turned his Miller over to me for the day and I was leading the field when a right rear tire blew out, putting me into the fence.

Instead of spinning or going end over end, as in most accidents, the little Miller did a side roll and sailed through the air for several feet—belly up—before landing hard on its side. I was pretty well banged up as a result of this jerking around and the car was damaged so badly that our trip to Europe seemed out of the question.

Leon hauled the wreckage out to Harry Miller's plant, however, and a crew worked night and day for almost a week to complete repairs. He also canceled our passage on the Roma and succeeded in getting accommodations on the Ile de France at a later date. All of this time I spent in bed, trying to get healed up. When I finally did show up at Miller's plant, most of the work was done. The truck was being loaded with spare racing parts and the 91½-inch engine, which Duray had used to establish a qualifying record of 124 miles an hour at Indianapolis in 1928, was being installed as a replacement for the damaged "220."

"Go right back home and go to bed," said Leon. "Tomorrow you'll have to shove off for New York with the truck. I'm going to catch a train right now."

158

CHAPTER *19*

I CALLED Boots, explaining that I would have to drive the truck straight through to the East Coast, and she elected to ride with as far as Indianapolis rather than remain in California during my absence. It was a good thing she did, too. I doubt if I could have made it in time without her help. We alternated with the driving chore, catching what sleep we could in the bumpy cab between shifts behind the wheel. The accelerator seldom was off the floor except when we eased off to change gears or stopped for gasoline and coffee.

It was a dangerous trip at high speed. Spare parts consumed every inch of space in the truck which was not occupied by the race car. We were so heavily loaded that I told Boots never to swerve the truck quickly because such a maneuver probably would overturn it. She followed instructions as though she had been driving one all her life. I know of no one who could possibly have done a better job.

As we made one stop on that first night, however, after I had been asleep for an hour or so, I noticed Boots was emotionally upset.

"What's the matter, honey?" I asked.

"You're going to have to take it for awhile," she said. "I hit a dog about two miles back and I feel sick all over."

She told me she had been coming down a long hill, where there was a service station on each side of the road. The little dog had decided to cross at just the wrong time and she didn't have a chance to miss it without taking a chance of wrecking our overloaded truck.

I slid behind the wheel again and drove until dawn while she curled up on the seat beside me and slept.

159

Sunrise in the mountains, coming with a dazzling suddenness which took my breath away and blinded me with its brilliant beauty, was something I'll never forget.

As I reached the summit, after the truck had labored up one of the steep Western slopes, the sun's sharp rays were like thousands of tiny needles piercing my eyeballs. The actual physical pain was so intense that it lasted for several seconds even after I had pulled to an immediate stop and thrown a protective arm in front of my face with my eyes clamped shut.

The sudden halt awakened Boots. Gradually our eyes adjusted themselves to the situation and we sat there for several minutes, completely enthralled by the grandeur. Then, with a final glance at the silvery outline of towering peaks ahead of us, we started down toward the still-dark valley below.

We pulled into Indianapolis on a Thursday morning, after two days and three nights of constant pounding. I took time for a quick bath and four hours of sleep. That was all I could afford. The Ile de France was scheduled to sail at noon on Saturday.

My hazy recollection of that solo trip from Indianapolis to New York seems more like a bad dream than an actual experience. It was agony. In order to stay awake I drove with all of the windows and ventilators open despite the chilly fall weather. I whistled and sang. On two or three occasions, as a last resort, I pulled over to the side of the highway and ran down the road and back for fifty or a hundred yards in order to get wide awake.

Crawling up some of the long hills in the East in low-low gear, at no more than three miles an hour, I was tormented by the thought of arriving too late to catch the boat. It was a dreadful feeling to have the engine running wide open and be moving at such a snail's pace. On the down grades it was almost suicidal, because I let the truck run as fast as it would go, hoping to make up lost time and still get around the next turn successfully.

It was about eight o'clock in the morning when I reached our designated meeting place in New York.

160

"Where in the world have you been?" asked Leon, as though I had taken a short pleasure trip for an hour or so.

Since then I've thought of a hundred different clever replies I might have made, but at the time I was too tired to do anything except glare at him.

He hadn't been idle himself, however. Somehow or other he had managed to make all of the necessary passport and visa arrangements for me—except actually sitting for my official "portrait." I took care of that chore immediately. I also stayed awake long enough to watch a crew of stevedores slip a net under the big truck and swing it aboard the ship.

Then I found our cabin and went to sleep. I slept through the afternoon and night, as well as the next day and night, before I awakened. Even then I didn't want to get out of bed. But Leon insisted that I get up and eat something. After a shower and a good meal, I began to feel like a human being again. By the time we docked at Havre, I was back to normal and looking forward to letting Leon show me a bit of Paris en route to Italy.

Our first disappointment came as we assembled all of our equipment on the dock. French custom officials said we had failed to declare any of our spare parts and that they would have to take them away from us. They did, too—even confiscating our last pair of pliers and plug wrench, as well as the spare tires and wheels for the race car. We got in touch with Mr. Bradley, who was the AAA representative in France at that time, and he advised us to go on to Paris while he put the necessary wheels in motion to obtain the release of our equipment.

We started, with Leon driving. It got dark on us before we reached Paris, however, and Leon ran over one of the sharp stone curbs which marked the side of the road. The outside tire on the right rear dual wheels was cut in two. When we started to change tires, we discovered we had no jack and no wrench. They had been taken out at Miller's factory in Los Angeles. Boots and I had crossed the entire country without tire trouble. Otherwise we probably would have been delayed to such an extent that I wouldn't have made the boat at all.

We limped into Paris, with a single right rear tire under the heavy load, and got situated in a hotel for the night. Leon had been billed all over the United States as a French driver. Although I knew his correct name was James Stewart, I thought he could speak the language fluently. When I discovered that the only French he knew was "oui" I kidded him unmercifully. I had managed to pick up quite a few French words and was able to get along better than he did.

Early the next morning we purchased a jack and had a wrench made to fit our wheel lugs. Then we changed tires and started a tour of Paris. We paid no attention to the signs which informed us that trucks were not permitted on the boulevards. I think every gendarme in Paris whistled us to a stop and gave us the devil at least once. Each time we would pull into a side street as directed. Then we would drive around the block and get right back on the same boulevard. It was a barrel of fun, with everyone honking their horns and hollering at us. But we saw Paris, nevertheless.

We ate and drank in the sidewalk cafés, learning quickly that we had to cut down on the original size of our gratuities to the beggars, because Paris was full of them. That night we went to the show that is synonymous with Paris, the Folies Bergère, and came away disappointed—like most Americans, I suspect. In the morning we headed toward the Alps and on down into Italy.

The French countryside was beautiful, without a single piece of mechanized equipment in evidence to detract from its venerable appearance. Little stacks of hay dotted the fields, like tiny native huts made of straw. Peasants worked alongside horses or oxen, putting their shoulders to the wheel whenever necessary.

Every road was lined soldily on both sides by trees to provide shade for the traveler and cover for the movement of troops in time of war. We didn't pass more than fifty cars all day. But pedestrians and two-wheel carts prevented us from

162

making good time even though the gravel roads were in excellent condition. The only paved stretches were the cobblestone streets in the towns.

In order to eliminate all unnecessary stops, we had agreed to take turns driving the truck. This would enable each of us to get a little sleep between tricks at the wheel. But the scenery was too enchanting for us to close our eyes while the sun still was in the sky.

When darkness finally overtook us, it was my turn to drive. I let Leon sleep until I couldn't keep my own eyes open any longer and then gave him an elbow in the ribs to awaken him. It was almost midnight and his first thoughts were of food and coffee. That sounded good to me, too, and I managed to stay awake until we pulled into a tiny village where a single dim light was gleaming from the window of what proved to be a little restaurant.

The chairs were piled high on the tables and the proprietor, or porter, went right on scrubbing the tile floor without paying the least bit of attention to us when we entered. I was so tired I didn't care whether or not we ever got any service, but I helped Leon clear the chairs from one table so that we could sit down. Then I leaned forward on the table, with my head on my arms, and proceeded to go to sleep. The next thing I remember was Leon kicking me.

"All right, Frenchy," said Leon, when I looked up, "tell him what you want." So help me, I couldn't even think of the words for ham and eggs.

"To heck with the French language," I said. "Just get us something to eat." Then I collapsed on the table and went back to sleep. I don't know what kind of sign language Leon used, but we ended up with eggs, toast and coffee. With this "fuel," we resumed the trip and I slept while Leon drove. It was dawn when the combination of a sudden stop and a torrent of Leon's superb profanity awakened me abruptly. We had just rounded a sharp bend while climbing one of the long grades in the Alps. Ahead of us was the most thrilling sight I believe I have ever seen.

A sheep herder had chosen that particular hour to move his flock to new grazing ground. He was wearing a cocky little tyrolean hat and short leather pants held up by bright suspenders. Sheep filled every inch of the narrow road. In the background were the most beautiful mountains in the world, every foot of them terraced and cultivated, in sharp contrast to the rugged Rockies of America.

Ohhing and ahhing like a schoolboy, I whipped out a little camera I had brought with me and snapped pictures until Leon broke the spell.

"Get behind the wheel, Sonnyboy," he said. "The sheep are your problem. It's my turn to sleep."

With the help of the sheep herder, we nudged our way through the sea of wool at the rate of about a half-mile an hour and finally reached the border at the top of the mountain. It must have been near a point where Italy and Switzerland both adjoined France, because customs men from all three nations examined our passports. The race car attracted a great deal of attention and caused a lot of comment. Languages were flying all over the place with everyone trying to talk at the same time until they realized we understood nothing but English.

While going through our belongings thoroughly, one of the inspectors suddenly asked if we had any cameras with us and I said no. I got hot and cold all over when I told that little white lie. I realized I was taking a chance of getting us into a lot of trouble. But I had no intention of giving up the pictures I had snapped earlier that morning and, fortunately, the little camera fit into my shirt pocket, where it was at the time. As we proceeded on our way, we realized quickly why cameras were forbidden. Army engineers were fortifying the entire mountain area. But I snapped a few pictures as we rolled along, simply because I knew we were not supposed to take them.

One thing reassuring about the roads through that part of Italy—unlike France—was that we couldn't possibly get lost. As long as we were sure we were on the right road when we left each village, we were certain to reach the next one on our route because there were no places to turn off. The entrance to

164

each town was guarded by impressive, old, armored portals, towers and abutments which had been erected centuries earlier. I took more pictures of these beautiful gate houses than anything else we saw during our entire trip.

It was late in the afternoon, exactly one week prior to race day, when we reached Milano and we drove immediately to Monza, about twenty kilometers from town. We wanted to see the track and get as much information as possible about our missing equipment. But among all of the European racing fraternity on hand to greet us, there wasn't a single person who spoke English. One pleasant Italian fellow, who seemed to be in charge of things, did his best to help us. But our sign language was entirely inadequate for all but the most simple questions.

First, he showed us to a garage and helped us unload the truck. Then he climbed into the cab of the truck with us and pointed the way to a huge house only a short distance from the track. Several mechanics and some of the usual hangers-on, always found around race tracks, also were quartered there. They seemed genuinely pleased to meet us when the introductions were made by our escort. Their friendly smiles and constant chatter made us feel at home, even though we couldn't understand a word they said. But our bare, cold rooms, with tile floor and high ceiling, were absolutely dismal.

The first thing I wanted was a bath. And what an experience that was! The tub was a huge metal affair with a wood stove built right into a special compartment at one end of it. A maid lighted the fire and turned on the water as soon as the tub began to get warm. Apparently it would be a little while before my bath was ready. So I went into the bedroom, undressed and stretched out for some rest while she completed the preparations. About thirty minutes later I went in to see what progress had been made and she indicated that everything was ready.

I said "Okay" and waited for her to leave the room, but she just stood there. I stood there too, for a few minutes, with my robe on, wondering if she intended to watch me bathe. Then I remembered reading about men and women bathing together

165

in the Orient as a matter of course and I thought possibly it was customary in Italy for the maids to remain in attendance. It should have been evident to her that I was ready to get in the tub. And it seemed very evident to me that she had no intention of leaving. Finally I shrugged my shoulders, peeled off my robe and stepped into the lukewarm water. She gave a little scream and jumped out of the bathroom without even looking back.

We were able to understand each other better at the dinner table, however. After Leon and I had stuffed ourselves with salami, cheese and spaghetti—because we didn't know that a meat course was included on the menu—she brought in big steaks with the blood still oozing out of them. They were much too rare for us and Leon tried in several ways, without success, to get across the idea that we would like to have them cooked a little more. I waited until he had given up in disgust. Then I speared my steak with a fork, held it above my plate and lit a match under it.

"Ah! Bien qui," she giggled; and took them out to the kitchen. When she brought them back, they were done to perfection.

Early the next morning we returned to the track with the hope of getting some information about the tools and spare parts which the French customs officials had confiscated at Havre. We didn't even have a sparkplug wrench with which to install the plugs so that we could fire up the engine. Italian wrenches didn't fit our equipment and the 91-cubic-inch engines, such as we had, were very critical on plugs.

Owing to the language problem, it was almost impossible for us to make the Italians understand our questions and we had even greater difficulty understanding their answers. The one word they seemed to use more than any other was *domani*. Everything was "tomorrow, tomorrow" until we became sick and tired of hearing it.

Apparently there was nothing for us to do but wait and it was two days later before we got our first good break since leaving New York. A well-groomed, young Frenchman walked

166

into our garage and, in perfect English, said, "Good afternoon, how are you doing?"

I didn't even ask him his name, or his connection with the race, or anything. I simply jumped up, threw both arms around him to make sure he didn't get away and exclaimed, "My friend, from now on you are my interpreter."

I told him all about our troubles, immediately, and he promised to help. It wasn't until after he had left that I realized I didn't know his name or how to get in touch with him if he didn't return. But while we were eating dinner that evening on the spacious porch of our rooming house, he walked in with quite a crew and sat down at the far end of the huge table. An instant later a hard roll landed right in the middle of my plate. When I looked up quickly, everyone except the Frenchman was grinning at me. It was very evident who had thrown the roll. I acted as if nothing had happened until he became busily engaged, eating and talking at the same time. Then I fired one back at him and hit him right on the chest.

He joined in the laughter at his own expense and as soon as we had finished dinner, Johnny Bugatti—the son of the famous Antole Bugatti, manufacturer of the most expensive and popular car made in France at that time—and I became fast friends. He was the crown prince of the automobile industry in France and truly a prince of a fellow.

"I haven't found any trace of your equipment," said Johnny. "But if you want to ride into Milano with me I'll send some telegrams which might bring good results."

Leon wasn't feeling well, so we went off without him. Johnny insisted on driving his own car, instead of riding in the truck, and it was the most beautiful automotive creation I had ever seen. Low and rakish, it had room for two people in the front seat and another person sitting sideways in the rear. No one else, to date, has designed a coupé as clever as that one, although the basic lines of the Lincoln Continental a few years later were somewhat comparable.

The following afternoon we received word that our equipment had been located and would be rushed to Monza as quickly as possible. Leon, however, was very much under the weather with a severe attack of influenza. While he followed the doctor's orders and remained in bed for the next two days, I kept a lonely vigil at the track for the spare parts which failed to arrive. On the third day, Leon felt well enough to sit out in the sun on a folding chair which had been provided for him. But he was back in bed, looking about as pitiful as anyone could possibly look, when I returned that evening. The huge brown eyes in his bulldog face seemed to reprimand me for not taking better care of him.

Before I could ask any questions, he pulled his huge ham of a hand out from under the covers and said "Look, Sonnyboy, what they did to me." The tip of the small finger on this huge hand was as flat as a spatula. I don't believe I have a distorted sense of humor, but I couldn't keep myself from laughing until I cried in spite of the intense pain which I knew he was suffering. This huge hulk of a man, who had been banged up in more than one race accident without ever whimpering, reminded me for all the world of a little boy with a stubbed toe seeking sympathy from his mother. While shifting position in an effort to get more comfortable in the folding chair, it had collapsed with him and caught his little finger between the rails on the side. Trapped by his own weight, he had been unable to get up or make himself understood. The women folk around the place finally had extricated him and helped him back to bed. My job was to put the finger back into shape, which I did by pressing on the sides and massaging it as gently as possible. I could tell he was well on his way to recovery from the "flu" by the way he yelled as I worked on him. Only a pretty healthy guy could make that much noise.

On the morning before the race, one of those huge two-wheeled carts, pulled by the smallest donkey I have ever seen, rolled up to our garage with all of our tools and spare parts. But by that time we had lost all interest in their whereabouts. While watching the other cars and drivers during their preparatory runs I had learned the *La Pista,* which was the speedway at Monza, was only a small part of the course over which

168

the race was to be run. The rest of the circuit was a road course which rambled through the adjoining countryside. Sharp turns made good brakes and sturdy transmissions absolutely necessary—and we had neither.

Although we had known the two courses adjoined each other, and could be used separately or together, we had been under the impression all along that only the *La Pista* would be used for the race. Our car was designed strictly for speedway use. We had brakes on it only because they were required by American racing specifications. They certainly were not built for heavy duty work. And we couldn't use the braking power of our engine, by shifting from high to a lower gear when approaching the turns, because such a strain on our transmission at high speed would dump everything right in the bottom of the pan.

The arrival of our equipment snapped Leon out of his doldrums, however, and it wasn't long until we were ready to fire up the engine for my first trip around the course. Then I got another shock.

"I'll drive it myself," said Leon. "There's no reason for you to go out and kill yourself just to show everybody how fast this car is. And that's exactly what would happen. You'd come whizzing down that long straightaway with the rest of them, or maybe a little faster, and suddenly discover you didn't have good enough brakes to get into the turn safely."

He must have been a mind reader, because I certainly had been thinking about how much fun it would be to suck a couple of their champions under in front of the grandstand, even if I didn't have any chance to match their speed on other parts of the course. But with no hope of actually winning, it didn't matter much to me whether I drove or not.

During the afternoon we managed to get the car running perfectly and that evening we mapped our strategy so that Leon could give at least one demonstration that we hadn't brought a baby buggy to Italy—that we really had a pretty hot automobile.

We'd had just enough running time to learn how long it

169

would take for Leon to make a lap at reasonably safe speed and we had clocked the other cars and drivers enough to find out how fast they probably would lap it in competition. Leon, of course, would be trailing the leaders from the start. After five or six trips around the circuit, they would be about ready to lap him. If we figured exactly right, Leon could be on the turn leading into the long straightaway when they overtook him. He would be only a few feet behind them when they hit the top of the stretch. Then he could jump on it for a burst of speed which would give them a good sucking under right in front of the grandstand before slowing down for the turn.

The pits at Monza resembled little summer houses, with roofs, and they all looked alike. Leon had not done enough running to get the location of our pit impressed in his memory and he almost wrecked the car on the first lap while looking for my sign. The Italians had installed large wooden pylons to separate the main straightaway of the speedway from the home stretch of the road course, which paralleled it. As he swept past the pits, Leon was devoting more attention to looking for me than he was to his driving. He veered just enough off course to hit one of the pylons with his right front wheel. The spectators laughed, thinking he had lost his way right on the main straightaway. It really was a most embarrassing experience. But, fortunately, no damage was done except to the pylon, which was completely shattered. The wheel and tire still were intact.

A couple of laps later the leaders picked him up from behind on schedule, about midway of the backstretch. As they zoomed by him, Leon stepped on the throttle in order to remain on their tail for the turn into the home stretch. But the engine balked. Unless the powerful little 91-inch jobs are run at high speed constantly, they have a tendency to choke up and not fire on all cylinders. That had to happen, of course, right at the psychological moment for Leon to start his grandstand play. The job of cleaning out the engine, with rapid manipulation of the clutch and throttle, required only a few seconds. But by that time Leon had a lot of ground to make up if his show was

170

to come off as scheduled. He stood on it as hard as he could in an effort to close the gap on the turn.

Standing in the pit, waiting for the pack to come into view, I was as tense and excited as at any time in my life. I knew exactly what was going to happen, I thought, and I was cocked and primed to enjoy every second of the performance. When the foreign cars swung into the main stretch, I was all set to let go with a wild yell as Leon charged around them in full view of the huge crowd. But nothing happened for a full second—or maybe two. Then Leon's car came into view, tail first and skidding toward the outer edge of the course. It picked out a nice sturdy tree and wrapped itself around the trunk.

Fortunately, Leon wasn't seriously hurt, except pridewise. But we weren't allowed to move the car until after the race was over, with Rudi Caracciola the winner in an Italian Alfa Romeo.

The job of loading the wreckage on the truck could wait until after we collected the $4,000 appearance money we had been promised. Mr. Florio, however, was not to be found. The only answer I could get from any of his associates was *domani* and I was beginning to detest the word more and more every time I heard it. We really needed the money. We hadn't received a dime prior to the race and the supply of American cash we had brought with us was almost exhausted.

While I was still hunting for Florio, a Pirelli representative came up to me. With some talk and a lot of sign language, he offered to trade a rain-resistant racing suit made by Pirelli for one of our Firestone tires. He was quite interested in finding out what kind of tire could withstand such a smack as Leon had given it against that pylon without blowing out or suffering any apparent damage. Under ordinary circumstances I'm sure I would have been more generous. But, since we were short on money, I told him it would take at least $250 if he wanted to examine one of them.

Once again I heard that damn word, *domani,* and I was sure I would never see him again. Early the next morning, however, he returned with a bundle of two hundred and fifty old-fashioned large dollar bills—almost enough to paper one entire side of our garage if we had wanted to use them for that purpose. I gladly gave him a tire and both of us were well pleased with the transaction. After closing that deal and loading our equipment, I went in search of Florio again. They told me he had gone to Rome. I tried to find out who might have our $4,000. But the only answer I could get was "Florio." Johnny Bugatti also had left Monza and Leon agreed that our best bet was to go some place where English was spoken. We moved into a little hotel on the square at Milano and finally located a sympathetic Italian connected with the American attaché's office. The American attaché wasn't much help. He shrugged us off as a bad deal and I had visions of selling pencils on the Milano square to keep from starving. The Italian, however, succeeded in arranging second-class passage for us on the Roma, as wards of the state. With the $250 from Pirelli, we had a whale of a time on the homeward journey before going broke. But it was a rather inglorious climax to a foreign invasion such as we had planned.

I was anxious to get back to California with the hope of winning enough races during the remainder of the 1932 season to regain first place in the Pacific Coast point standing. By the time we reached Los Angeles, however, the situation looked almost hopeless from my standpoint. I'd missed seven races and Ernie Triplett was well on his way to his second straight championship. Five other drivers also had moved ahead of me while I was in Europe.

I closed in on the leaders by finishing fifth or better in four of the next five races, without winning any of them, and had a good chance to take second place as we headed into the December stretch. I was driving the Gilmore Red Lion Special and I set a new world record of 102.098 miles an hour for a one-mile circular dirt track while qualifying for a race at Oakland. The car was performing perfectly and I felt confident of winning the 100-mile event without trouble, but rain washed out the program.

Two weeks later at Ascot, with another chance to take sec-

172

ond place in the point standing, I was far ahead of everybody at the three-quarters post of a 200-lap race. I was moving up to lap Al Gordon and Triplett when Gordon spun. Triplett avoided hitting Gordon's car and went on to win, but I hooked Al's rear wheel with my left front wheel and was through for the day, although neither of us was hurt. In the final 1932 Pacific Coast standing I was third, 23 points behind Spangler.

CHAPTER **20**

HOWARD HAWKES, the famous movie director, was among the regular fans at Ascot. He seldom missed a race, and during the winter of 1932–33 his tremendous interest finally culminated in the filming of a race picture called "The Crowd Roars." It starred Jimmy Cagney and Joan Blondell, with most of the racing fraternity participating in various capacities. Harry Hartz was the technical director. My particular role was to drive a race car through a wall of gasoline flames during one of the crash sequences. Working under Hawkes's direction was an inspiring experience. An even greater thrill came when he invited me to his studio during the latter part of February.

After a little conversation about movies and racing he exclaimed, "I want to enter a car in the next Indianapolis race. I want you to help design and build it. And I want you to drive it."

If there ever was a time when I thought the world was my oyster, it was right then. Cost was not to be a factor in the construction of the car—within reason, of course—and I was to have a free hand in selecting my helpers. Before sundown,

Riley Brett was at work on plans for the engine. Myron Stevens was ready to start on the body as soon as we could get the necessary material. All three of us were close friends and I knew we would be able to work in complete harmony to create the finest race car any man had ever seen.

By the first of March all of us had "cleared the decks" for two months of intensive round-the-clock work in order to get the job done. Then, like a bolt from the blue, came the bank holiday proclaimed by President Roosevelt. Regardless of how much money a man had on deposit, or invested in gilt-edged securities, the only cash at his disposal was what he happened to have in his pocket.

I phoned Hawkes as soon as I saw the morning papers and held my breath while the connection was being completed. My spirits soared immediately when I heard his calm voice say "Hello, Wilbur," as if he didn't have a worry in the world.

Without any preliminaries I said, "Howard, what does this bank holiday do to us?"

"I'm afraid it kills the whole thing," he replied. "I'm terribly sorry, but everything is at a standstill as far as finances are concerned. The Lord only knows what will happen."

I don't remember how the conversation ended. I felt as if someone had hit me over the head with an axe.

The word got around quickly that I needed a ride at Indianapolis, however, and I accepted an invitation to drive Duray's Mallory Special.

Racing continued at Ascot that spring, too, and early in April I was involved in what probably was my worst accident in California. For several laps I had been chasing Al Gordon, the early leader, before moving up on the outside in an effort to pass him on the main straightaway. From that position I was confident I could get into the next turn faster than he could. I gave my car every possible inch of throttle and waited for him to "back off" as we neared the turn.

Al wasn't willing to concede a thing. He had a certain psychological advantage and was ready to use it regardless of the consequences. From his inside position, he was almost sure to

174

spin if he went into the turn as fast as I did. If he spun, the chances were better than even that I would be pinched off between his car and the outside rail unless I dropped back to stay out of trouble. He knew exactly what his chances were and was willing to gamble that I wouldn't run the risk of such a crash. I was equally certain that, at the last instant, he'd realize the gamble was too big to take.

Together, we came down the straightaway, hub to hub and running wide open. I watched him out of the corner of my eye, waiting for the first opportunity to cut in front of him. And I could see him watching me out of the corner of his eye, ready to ease off as soon as I gave any indication of abandoning my attempt to pass him—in the interest of self preservation. But, like most race drivers, neither of us was willing to let the other fellow get away with such a bluff.

Bill White, a mutual friend, told us afterwards that both of us acted as if we were running on a mile straightaway—instead of on a closed course with a sharp left turn coming up in only a fraction of a second. Nothing but disaster, of course, could come from such foolhardiness.

As we hit the turn, the rear end of Al's car started to come around and it glanced off of the side of mine. It was a miracle that the cars did not lock wheels and go end over end. But the impact served to help Al straighten out and regain control as my car was thrown hard against the outer guard rail. It did a full spin and a half before making two complete rolls and dumping me out on the track. Almost all of my clothes were ripped off—and a lot of skin, too—as I slid along the macadamized surface. Examination at the hospital revealed that I also had torn a deep hole in my left arm.

Doctors and nurses still were painting my wounds with iodine when the ambulance pulled up to the hospital entrance with another victim. It was Gordon. After escaping unscratched from our crash, without losing the lead, Al had hit the rail when he missed a turn all by himself a few laps later.

If we had not been such close friends, I probably would

have been more sympathetic. One look at him, however, assured me that he wasn't hurt any worse than I was.

"Pour the rest of the iodine on that big so and so," I exclaimed, "and let him burn for a while."

A couple of nurses started to work on him as one of the doctors rolled me over on my stomach and said, "I think we'd better give you a shot of anti-tetanus."

I told him I didn't want any, but Al spoke up quickly from his cot a few feet away.

"He certainly needs it. Go right ahead."

I had a lot of trouble talking them out of following Al's advice, at least temporarily, as we continued to "crack off" at each other while the medical staff completed its work. There were no broken bones, but I had lost most of the skin off one arm and there was one spot that looked awful. Apparently a sliver of the track surface had penetrated my flesh to a considerable depth and then disintegrated into dozens of tiny particles—bits of crushed stone and grains of asphalt. Using a slender probe, soaked in iodine, they dug out the larger particles and all of the smaller pieces they could locate before releasing me.

Russ Wilcox had come in to see how I was getting along and to drive me home. Instead of taking me straight home, however, he took me to a doctor's office and informed me that now I was going to get an anti-tetanus shot whether I liked it or not. He literally dragged me into the room, with me protesting every step of the way. He stayed with me every instant until the doctor had given me a shot in the left cheek of my posterior. Then he took me home and turned me over to another close friend of ours, Florence Parke, who was a graduate nurse. Almost every day, for almost a month, she applied the necessary medication and redressed my injured arm and countless "floor burns" to make sure the wounds did not become infected. I was to be reminded of the accident at regular intervals for many months after the arm had healed, however. Each tiny piece the doctor had missed would work its way up through the flesh and form an irritating pimple-like bump under my skin. When I couldn't stand the itching any longer,

I'd scratch the pimple and out would come another little particle of the Ascot track.

I also started flying again. I'd had some preliminary instruction—and finally had "soloed" in 1930—as a member of the 424th squadron of the United States Army Air Reserve at Schoen Field, near Indianapolis, with Gene Genaro as the lieutenant in charge. But I don't believe I had flown a plane since that first solo flight and I hadn't even thought about flying since I'd got into the habit of spending my winters in California. Bob Blair, however, was operating several planes out of the Los Angeles (Mines Field) Municipal Airport during this spring of 1933. He also served as an honorary official at some of the Ascot races and he was talking with Riley Brett about some of the movie stars who were taking instruction under his direction when I strolled up to ask Riley when he planned to head for Indianapolis.

He told me and then said, "Why don't you learn to fly while you're out here, Wilbur? It's a lot of fun."

"How long will it take me?" I asked, without saying anything about my earlier instruction.

"You should be able to solo after five or six hours," said Bob.

"I'll be out in the morning," I promised. "And I'll bet I'll solo quicker than that."

I'd had very little experience in the air to begin with and I knew I was so rusty that I might just as well start from scratch if I ever was to become much of a flyer. I never did tell Bob about my Air Reserve record, but in three hours I was on my own again and I've had a lot of enjoyment out of flying down through the years. I've got more real thrill out of one fast lap around the Speedway than out of my thousands of hours in the air, but I always have felt that flying gives every pilot a certain sense of superiority over material things that can't be experienced in any other manner.

Jimmy Stewart, Brian Aherne, Jimmie Dunn, Henry Fonda and Ruth Chatterton were some of the movie stars who were taking flying lessons at the same time. Often we compared notes on our experiences. Bob Blair and I became close friends, as did Boots and Bob's wife, Maggie. Later in the year we went on several hunting trips together and the following fall, Bob and I became business partners in the operating of a charter plane service.

Soon after I had earned my pilot's license under Bob's instruction, I also made my first—and only—parachute jump, because I didn't ever want to find myself in a spot where I had to jump without having gone through that experience at least once, voluntarily. Russ Hankforth took me up to about 3,000 feet and I bailed out above the airport with Jimmie Dunn and some of the other Hollywood personalities watching. It was a perfectly marvelous sensation, drifting along with the breeze, in complete silence. By manipulating the cords which connected my harness to the 'chute, I could float to the left or right, as I desired. I got a terrific kick out of the experience. But the 'chute did give me somewhat of a rough time by dragging me along the ground when I landed, and it left me with no desire to make a career of such stunt work.

A few weeks later Boots and I experienced our first earthquake. I was in the air when it started and I landed while it still was in progress. The planes in the hangar actually were waving their wings. The damage had been considerable in the Long Beach area, according to first reports, and my first concern was for Boots. At that time our home was a small apartment in a house on top of a mountain which was part of a restricted area called Hollywoodland.

I did a lot of worrying while waiting for her to answer the phone, but the sound of her voice was wonderful and she assured me immediately that she was all right.

"It was the strangest experience," she said. "Before I had even felt the first shock, I heard a noise which sounded like a truck on the road above. I stopped what I was doing, to listen, because I knew trucks were not allowed in this area. Then the house began shaking. Pictures thumped against the walls. I remembered being told to stand under the arch of a doorway or in some part of the house which had been reinforced in

178

comparable manner," she continued. "So I ran to the archway leading into the dressing room."

"As long as you are all right, it doesn't make any difference now," I said. "But that probably is the only archway in the house that isn't reinforced. They put it there only for appearance."

While we were talking, both of us felt a few of the earthquake's after-shocks and I decided the smart thing for me to do was hurry home. The after-shocks continued, so I rigged up an old Chinese gong, which was a part of our interior decorating scheme, with some string to create a makeshift seismograph in order to keep track of them. Bosworth and Florence Parke had joined us for the evening and none of us went to bed all night. There was too much excitement, listening to the reports from Long Beach and waiting for the Chinese gong to register the next tremor.

Originally, the apartment had been a laundry room in the home of Mr. and Mrs. J. E. Peverill and their daughter, Wilma. He was a retired Packard distributor from Waterloo, Iowa, who had been told he had only one year to live. He felt certain he could make a liar out of his doctor—and did—by getting a lot of sunshine, fresh air and moderate exercise. Being a thrifty mid-westerner, he also had converted the laundry room into one of the most attractive little apartments I had ever seen.

He was almost twice my age. But, for exercise, he would fill a wheelbarrow full of dirt and dump it on the other side of the road. For more exercise the next day, he would shovel the dirt back into the wheelbarrow and return it to the spot from which he had taken it. To pass the time away, he even had dug a cave—as a quick refuge while sun bathing—in the jungle-like area of Griffith park, which was just across the road. Boots often joined him for long walks in the evening, while waiting for me to return from the airport. One night I brought home an Irish Setter, wondering what his reaction might be to having a dog on the premises. When I awakened the next morning, Mr. Peverill already was at work on the project of constructing a suitable runway outside our patio in the only small, flat area available on the mountain side. But by the time he had finished the job a few days later, we no longer had the dog. I had taken it to the Gilmore Ranch to shoot dove and see how it acted in the field and it had run away.

I didn't have too much time to devote to flying during that spring of 1933, however, because Duray needed considerable help in getting the Mallory Special ready for the "500." It was somewhat of a freak, as race cars go. The frame was stock Whippet. The front axle and spindles also were stock. In my opinion, it looked more like a flat, ugly mongrel than a thoroughbred race car. But Leon claimed it was easy to handle, with enough horsepower under the hood to win even though it was far from the fastest thing in the field.

Magnetos are used on almost all race cars, instead of battery ignition, because they are more dependable. Duray had made a deal with the Mallory Electric Company, however, to use battery ignition in return for the payment of a sizeable sponsorship fee. I didn't believe there was a battery on the market at that time which could be mounted solidly enough to withstand the tremendous vibration generated during a 500-mile race. Leon wasn't worried. But the first thing I did when we reached Indianapolis was go to the Prest-O-Lite Company in Speedway City and order a special battery. In fact, it was a unit of two eight-volt batteries in a single case. Then I rigged up a switching device of my own design so that I would be using only one battery at the start of the race, with the other held in reserve in case of trouble. We built a special rubber mounting for the battery box and were all set for the start of the race after qualifying without trouble. By that time I had discovered the car was far from being the easy handling thing Leon had described and I was fairly certain it wouldn't hold together long enough for us to finish the race.

Before the event ever got under way, however, the officials and drivers became embroiled in one of the hottest arguments of Speedway history when Dr. Allen—head of the Speedway medical staff at the time—ruled that Howdy Wilcox II was unfit to drive.

180

Howdy was not related to the original Howdy Wilcox, whose 1919 Indianapolis victory had been partly responsible for my decision to become a race driver. The "II" tag on his name had been added by sports writers in order to distinguish him from the 1919 winner.

Most of us had been racing against Howdy for two or three years. We knew he was a diabetic, taking eighteen units of insulin daily, but that never had affected his driving ability. He had finished second the previous year at Indianapolis and had qualified well for this 1933 race.

When the announcement was made on the morning of the race that Howdy would not be permitted to drive, all of us flared up in a hurry. This was cruel and inhuman treatment as far as we were concerned and entirely unnecessary. None of us who were competing against him and risking our own lives in the race had voiced any objection to his participation.

I doubt if any of us would have opposed the ruling if it had been made at the proper time, a couple of weeks earlier. But such a decision, at almost the last minute, seemed extremely unfair after a driver had gone through the ordeal of earning a starting position and had experienced all of the pre-race tension. We were unhappy that year, too, because of the reduction in prize money due to the depression.

Several of us—including Wild Bill Cummings, Babe Stapp and Shorty Cantlon—circulated a written statement which every driver and alternate driver signed. It read:

> "We, the undersigned, refuse to participate in
> the 500-mile Indianapolis race scheduled today
> unless Howard Wilcox is allowed to drive in
> said race."

This was handed to Chief Steward Eddie Edenburn at 9:30 A.M., after the field had been given the signal to line up for the start of the race. Eddie promised to have an answer for us at 9:45, after the official photo of the starting field had been taken. Then he went into a huddle with Captain Eddie Rickenbacker of the Speedway.

181

At the designated time, fifteen minutes before the race was scheduled to get under way, Rick addressed all of the drivers at the starting line and explained why he thought the ruling was necessary.

"I know how all of you feel about Howdy," said Rickenbacker. "I would like to comply with your request because I know it is sincere. But none of us ever would be able to forgive ourselves if Howdy did start this race and then was involved in an accident involving other cars and drivers, due to his physical condition."

The discussion still was raging, hot and heavy, when it became time to start the race at ten o'clock. Someone suggested that Mauri Rose, who had been unable to qualify his own car because of a broken radius rod on the last day of the time trials, was available as a replacement for Howdy. We certainly had no objection to Rose as a driver, but such a change did not eliminate what we believed to be the unjust treatment of Wilcox. It also was pointed out that Rose had never been in the car for even one practice lap.

Harry Hartz answered that objection by suggesting that the Wilcox car be taken out of its scheduled starting position and placed behind the entire field so that Rose would have a chance to get acquainted with it during the early laps, before getting into heavy traffic.

At about ten minutes after ten, with the crowd getting impatient for action, Rick ended the argument after a quick conference with Edenburn.

"The Wilcox car will be moved to the rear of the field immediately," he announced. "Every other car in the starting lineup will move up one position. And this race is going to start in exactly five minutes if there is only one car ready to run at that time and I have to drive it myself."

It was evident he meant exactly what he said. And at 10:15 the race was under way. Rick had not said, specifically, whether Rose or Wilcox would drive. Rose was in the car when it crossed the starting line, however, and all of us knew it before we had gone many miles. During the first fifty miles, he

182

worked his way from last place to sixth position. At 125 miles he was fourth, but mechanical trouble developed a few minutes later and his charge toward the head of the pack ended.

Billy Devore was my riding mechanic and for the first hundred miles we devoted most of our attention to learning how to keep from being tossed out of the car. It bucked like a bronco on the rough brick surface and was almost unmanageable on the turns. I was in no hurry to try to move up near the front too quickly and was not among the first ten at the 100-mile mark. The fellows battling for the lead, however, soon began to experience trouble.

Cummings, the leader for the first thirty-two laps, had the unusual experience of losing his radiator cap. There wasn't another one like it available and it took his crew twelve minutes to improvise a satisfactory substitute. Fred Frame replaced Cummings at the head of the pack, only to have his timing gears fail. Babe Stapp was next to set the pace and he held the lead until it was necessary for him to make his second pit stop after 129 laps. While all of this was going on, I had improved my position steadily and was running next in line behind Louie Meyer when he took command as Stapp was refueling. Meyer and I had made our second stops several minutes earlier.

At this stage of the race, one of the front-drive cars got out of control as it approached the southwest turn. While trying to avoid hitting it, Malcolm Fox cut in front of Les Spangler and both cars crashed into the wall. The yellow caution light was on for approximately fifteen minutes and almost all of us who still had a chance to win, took advantage of the situation to make another pit stop which would enable us to go the remainder of the distance.

Meyer's crew did such a quick job that I didn't have a chance to take the lead away from him and I certainly didn't have a car capable of overtaking him when he was running again. He pulled a little farther ahead on each trip around the course while Devore and I became increasingly worried about whether or not our car would be able to go the distance. Because of mechanical trouble, Stapp no longer was a prominent contender.

Each lap seemed like an eternity. Every instant I expected the engine to lock up with a loud squeal and quit for the day. I eased off the throttle until I was running only a hundred miles an hour, compared to Meyer's 105. If Lou Moore, in third place, had realized my predicament, I'm sure he could have overtaken me or forced me out of the race while I was trying to withstand his challenge. But Moore didn't know what my situation was and apparently was content to protect third place against Chet Gardner's bid.

Meyer had the race all to himself. With two laps to go, he passed me again, giving him a lead of four laps, as I recall it. And as he pulled alongside of my Mallory Special, race fans witnessed one of the strangest incidents which ever happened in a 500-mile race.

Louie lifted his foot from the throttle, cupped his hand to his mouth and shouted, "Are you going to make it?"

Billy Devore grinned and yelled back, "Sure we are."

With all of the worries I had at the time, that was a display of much more optimism than I could stomach.

"Shut up, you damn fool!" I exclaimed. "Do you want to jinx us?"

At the same instant, I gave Billy a good jolt in the ribs with my elbow. Louie had only five more miles to go. We had at least fifteen and we would be the luckiest guys in the world if we made it. But we did, with a margin of almost a half-minute over Moore.

The engine sounded as if it was so close to flying apart that I didn't even run the customary extra lap in case of a scoring error. When I got the checkered flag for second place, I pulled into my pit immediately and Duray was so happy he picked me bodily from the cockpit. Then he gave me a great big kiss in front of everybody and embraced Devore, too.

Instead of returning to California immediately, I decided to remain in the midwest during the summer. With the points won at Indianapolis, I thought I might be able to win the Na-

184

tional AAA driving title by copping a couple of the 100-mile dirt track championship events. The first one, at Detroit on June 11, was a complete "washout" as far as I was concerned. Mechanical trouble ended my chances before we had even reached the half-way mark. Cummings won it. At Milwaukee, on July 18, I led the field home with Chet Gardner, second. But I failed to finish again at Syracuse, and there was no chance of overtaking Louie Meyer in the point standing.

Early in the fall Boots and I headed for Los Angeles again to finish the season at Ascot. By that time I also had dropped back in the Pacific Coast standing and Gordon already had the title clinched. I didn't win a single important Ascot race during the remainder of 1933 although I managed to collect quite a little prize money by running well in most of the events.

I was third in the National AAA championship standing, which gave me No. 3 as my car number for the next twelve months, and I started the new year with my fingers crossed. The only other time I had used No. 3 on my car was in 1930 and I hadn't enjoyed much luck during that season. History began to repeat itself when clutch trouble forced me out of the first important 1934 race at Ascot, on January 7. Bad luck also ended my chances in the next two races. I didn't have much success, either, in my first fling at stock car racing early in February at Mines Field. Consequently, I devoted most of my attention to flying until it was time for another Indianapolis "500."

CHAPTER *21*

DURING the winter I had made a deal to drive the car in which Mauri Rose had done so well during the early stages of the 1933 Classic, after Wilcox had been denied permission to compete. It was a "hot" automobile owned by Joe Marks and his mother-in-law, Mary Falcione. She was a wonderful old lady who was held in high regard by the entire racing fraternity. We all called her Grandma Marks. She operated a grocery and delicatessen in Gary, Indiana, and was a real race fan.

The car definitely was fast enough to win, in my opinion. The only problem we had concerned the new fuel limitations.

Ever since the first automobile race on a closed course, one of the most important hazards had been slick spots on the track caused by oil leaks. For several years, a few of us had been campaigning for regulations which would eliminate that danger. It wasn't unusual for a car to use fifty or sixty gallons of oil in the Indianapolis event and eighty per cent of it was on the track during the late stages of any race. Every time a car stopped for fuel and tires, it also took on another ten or twenty gallons of oil.

To correct this situation in 1933, the entry blank had provided that no car would be permitted to use more than six and a half gallons of oil and that ruling certainly had met with my approval. For the 1934 race, Speedway officials had gone a step farther and announced that each car also would be limited to forty-five gallons of fuel for the five hundred miles. That had a lot of us worried and we were willing to try anything which would give us greater mileage at high speed—so that we would not be in danger of running out of fuel near the finish.

Russ Snowberger was about the only driver who didn't seem to be a bit concerned about the problem. He made no secret of the fact that he had figured out a way to get at least twelve or thirteen miles to the gallon at racing speed, but he wouldn't tell anyone how he was going to do it.

"For fifteen hundred dollars I'll let you in on my secret," said Russ. But I wasn't ready to spend that much money for the information. If he could work out the answer, I thought I ought to be able to do the same thing. For more than a week, I "made like an engine," as the modern-day bee-boppers would say. I tried one idea after another without much success. The

186

answer finally came like a bolt out of the blue, while I was sitting between Louis Schwitzer and Lee Oldfield—and paying no attention to the speaker—at an SAE meeting (Society of Automotive Engineers) a few days before the race.

"I've got it!" I suddenly exclaimed, slapping both of them on the back.

"You've got what?" asked Lee.

"I've got the answer to the fuel problem," I replied. "I'll bet I can average fifteen miles to the gallon at a hundred and fifteen miles an hour."

"How are you going to do it?" asked Louis.

"That's my secret," I answered. "I'm not positive my idea will work, but I think it will. And by this time tomorrow night I'll know for sure."

I glanced around the room until I caught Snowberger's eye and made signs for him to meet me at the door after the meeting broke up.

"Man, I've got it," I said, as soon as we had found a spot where we could talk privately. "Come over to my garage in the morning and I'll show you what I'm going to do if you'll agree—in case I have a satisfactory answer—to show me your system in return. We probably have hit on the same answer, but maybe both of us can benefit by exchanging ideas."

Snowberger had been working behind closed doors, with the windows of his garage covered with newspapers. He wouldn't even let anyone come close to his car unless his carburetors and manifolds were hidden from view. I adopted the same policy the following day and then got together with Russ. It turned out that both of us had come up with the same solution to the problem and we promised each other we would keep the knowledge to ourselves. I didn't even let the members of my crew know what I was doing while I was making the necessary units to install on my car.

With the fuel problem solved, I was sitting on top of the world. The oil limitation hadn't worried me a bit.

The car handled beautifully, too, in contrast to my Mallory Special of the previous year. Otto Wolfer was my riding mechanic and I was able to turn practice laps consistently at 117 miles an hour with my right hand resting on his knee to prove how easy it was.

Like most of the other fellows, we had been using castor oil in the car. When I fired it up to qualify on the first day of the time trials, however, my oil pressure was off almost fifteen pounds. I killed the engine immediately so that the crew could make the necessary adjustments.

"It's all right the way it is," they told me. "The only reason the pressure is down is because we drained out the castor oil today and put in Lion Head mineral oil."

I really hit the ceiling then. The car had been running perfectly on our practice laps and I had no intention of letting anyone change any part of the "combination" at this late hour —even though the car was called the Lion Head Special.

"Push her back to the garage," I ordered, "And take that stuff out. Let me know when you get the castor oil back in and then I'll qualify."

I know I made every member of the crew mad by assuming such a dictatorial attitude. They made the change without too much grumbling, however, and thirty minutes later I qualified for the No. 2 starting position. Otto and I were about as smug as any two people could be because both of us thought we had the race in the bag.

For the first few laps of the race we were busy checking our gauges to be sure everything was functioning properly. Kelly Petillo was setting the pace and we were running third or fourth. On the seventh trip around the course, Kelly eased off the throttle as he neared the pits and it was plainly evident he had an oil leak.

I made another quick check of the instrument panel and nudged Otto.

"Here we go, Boy!" I exclaimed. "It's about time for us to start collecting some lap prize money." I doubt if he could hear me, but he must have gotten the general idea of what I said because he gave me a big grin in reply and we began to move.

188

At the start of the fourteenth lap we closed in on Frank Brisko, who had taken the lead when Petillo stopped. I had good intentions of moving ahead of Brisko on the backstretch. There was a big oil streak "in the groove" on the No. 2 turn, however, and I had to swing out about fifteen inches in order to avoid it.

"Some other unfortunate guy like Petillo will be on the sidelines in another minute or two because of the new oil rule," I thought to myself. At the same time, I decided to wait another lap to pass Brisko, so that I could get into the turn knowing exactly how wide it would be necessary for me to swing in order to keep my wheels out of the oil when I gave 'er the gun to move ahead of him. But when I rounded the same turn on the fifteenth lap, the oil streak had moved out another fifteen inches and was in the exact spot on the track where I had planned to run.

I passed Brisko, anyway. The next thing I remember was seeing the big black tire marks where two drivers, Chet Miller and George Bailey, had skidded in the oil and climbed the outer wall. The entire field reduced speed and I took another look at my instrument panel just in time to see the hand on the oil gauge head for the zero mark.

I hit the "kill" button and kicked the clutch out simultaneously, with the hope of avoiding any damage to the engine.

"Damn it, Otto, it's us," I groaned, as we coasted to the pits.

The oil plug in the bottom of the aluminum sump had worked out and we had pumped every drop of our six and a half gallons of oil on to the race track. As far as I was concerned, the race was over unless I could get back into action as a relief driver. Even that possibility didn't appeal to me at the instant. I was down to rock bottom, emotionally, after enjoying the absolute heights so briefly. I was so low I probably would have jumped off the Brooklyn bridge if it had been handy.

It wasn't long until some one from Lou Moore's pit grabbed my arm, however, and asked if I would drive relief for Lou. I agreed immediately. He had a fine car—the Foreman Axle Special—and was running in sixth place, about two and a half minutes behind the leader, when I took over on the seventy-sixth lap. Cummings was out in front with Brisko, Mauri Rose and Ralph Hepburn right on his tail to make it a four-cornered battle. Cliff Bergere was driving the other car which was ahead of me and I closed in on them steadily.

When I finally had to stop for fuel and tires on the 152nd lap, I had passed all of them but Rose and Cummings, who were about forty-five seconds to the good. Moore climbed back into the car and I started to relax on a stack of tires for a little rest when Duray grabbed me.

"Come on up to my pit," he shouted. "I think Rose is getting tired and I may need you to finish for him."

Having driven the ill-handling Duray car the previous year, I realized how hard Mauri had been working. The fact that he looked tired was no surprise to me. But Mauri had the stamina and determination to finish the job. He was only twenty-seven seconds behind Cummings at the end—with Moore third.

Mr. Foreman, who headed the company which had sponsored the Moore car, walked up to me a few minutes after the race was over.

"I want to thank you for doing such a fine job for us today," he said. "I'm going back to Chicago tonight, but I expect to be back in Indianapolis tomorrow and I want to see you."

"I'll be out here at the track most of the afternoon," I replied.

When he failed to show up the following day, I assumed he had forgotten all about the conversation. In fact, I didn't see him again for almost five years.

The meeting finally occurred in the lobby of a Florida hotel.

"You're Wilbur Shaw, aren't you?" he asked, as I walked up to the desk to register.

"That's right," I said, "And I know I should recognize you. But I can't recall your name."

"I'm Mr. Foreman, formerly of the Foreman Axle Company," he said. "Do you remember when I talked to you after the 1934 race and told you I wanted to see you the following day?"

"I certainly do," I replied. "What was it all about?"

190

"I intended to build you the finest race car anyone had ever put together if you were willing to drive for me," he explained; "but I suffered a serious heart attack which made it necessary to dispose of my business interests. When I was able to be on my feet again, I came to Florida to take things easy. Now I own this hotel and I hope you'll be my guest."

CHAPTER 22

ALTHOUGH Mr. Foreman was unable to keep his appointment with me, I had the good fortune of becoming acquainted with Gil Pirrung of St. Louis a few weeks after the 1934 race. He was a young graduate of Yale who was interested in getting into the race business. He also was interested in some ideas I had concerning a new front-drive car for Indianapolis.

"Get a couple of good men to help you build the kind of a car you want," he said, "and be sure to get the job started early enough so that you won't run out of time."

At last, I was to have the type of car which I felt sure could win the Indianapolis Classic. Roscoe Dunning and Myron Stevens agreed to help me build it and by mid-summer we were on our way back to California to get started on the job. Harry Hartz and I also had accepted an invitation from the Chrysler Corporation to make a series of record attempts in the new Chrysler Airflow on the Bonneville Salt Flats in Utah during the month of August.

As Boots and I were driving across Arizona we overtook two brand new cars going in the same direction. Ralph Hepburn and his wife, Sparky, were in one, and Cliff Bergere was driv-

191

ing the other. Within five minutes, all of us had decided to make a quick detour to Mexicali before going on to Los Angeles. After enjoying an excellent dinner of Mexican food—and a little tequila—we made the rounds of the night spots. Actually, there wasn't much to do except eat, drink and gamble. Boots wasn't very much interested in gambling, but she finally decided she would take five dollars and play roulette until she lost it.

The rest of us devoted our attention to different games of chance and it didn't take me long to lose what cash I had with me. I suppose I should have been worried about the situation. But everyone appeared to be ready to call it a night and I was sure I could cash a check or borrow enough money from Ralph or Cliff to take care of what little expense we would have during the remainder of the trip. Before I had time to see Ralph about a loan the next morning, however, he was knocking at our door.

"Wilbur, could you let me have twenty-five or thirty dollars until we get to Los Angeles?" he asked. "I went broke at that dice table last night."

"I was just coming down to your room to ask the same question," I said. "I don't have anything but a little silver in my pocket. Let's go see Cliff."

He was broke, too. All of us had our hotel bills to pay, we needed fuel for our cars, and we hadn't had breakfast yet, either.

"Go on back to our room with the gals," I said. "I'll go down to the desk and cash a check." But the man on the desk wasn't the least bit obliging and we didn't know a soul in town.

The five of us held an emergency board meeting and pooled our resources. Boots had won about twenty dollars playing roulette while the rest of us were going broke. Sparky had a piggy bank with her, in which she had placed all of the nickels and dimes received in change since she had left California in May. Ralph and Cliff and I emptied the silver out of our pockets while Sparky broke open her piggy bank.

After setting aside as much money as we thought we would

192

W. S. going over the wall at Indianapolis in 1931. Ralph Hepburn's car is at extreme left and Tony Gulotta's and Fred Winnai's cars to the right.

Louie Chevrolet, Harry Miller, Fred and Augie Duesenberg, reading from left to right, pictured at the Roosevelt Raceway, New York, in 1934.

Benson Ford, Henry Ford II, Tony Gulotta, Edsel Ford, Henry Ford, Eddie Rickenbacker and an unidentified cameraman at the Speedway in 1932.

O'Dell & Shields

Frank Hinkley and Jimmy Gleason, the driver, in the Duesenberg which W. S. drove in the 1931 race after going over the wall in another Duesenberg.

The car which W. S. drove over the wall in the 1931 race. Seated in it in this picture are Phil Pardee and Walter Hannowsky.

W. S. presenting the Champion 100 Mile An Hour Club trophy to Col. Roscoe Turner in 1938.

W. S. winning the 1939 Indianapolis race in the Italian-made Maserati.

Another view of W. S. and the Maserati.

Wide World Photo

W. S. being flagged as winner in the annual Indianapolis classic, 1940.

W. S. at the wheel of the Gilmore Special which he designed, built and drove to his first 500-mile victory in 1937.

Henry Ford, Gar Wood and Barney Oldfield, from left to right, at the Speedway for the 1932 race.

From left to right: Harvey Firestone, Jr., Harvey Firestone, Sr., Henry Ford, Edsel Ford, Henry Ford II, and Benson Ford at the Speedway in 1932.

Part of the Speedway's garage area and all that remained of the Miller Special after the fire during the early hours of Race Day, 1941.

The Shaw Special, which W. S. drove to second place in the 1938 Indianapolis race, after winning with it in 1937. It was then called the Gilmore Special.

O'Dell & Shields

Mrs. Shaw and W. S. in "Victory Lane" following his third 500-mile victory in 1940.

Victory smile and wave, 1940, with three fingers raised to emphasize his third victory. Ready to congratulate him are Russell and Leonard Firestone and Harvey Firestone, Jr.

O'Dell & Shields

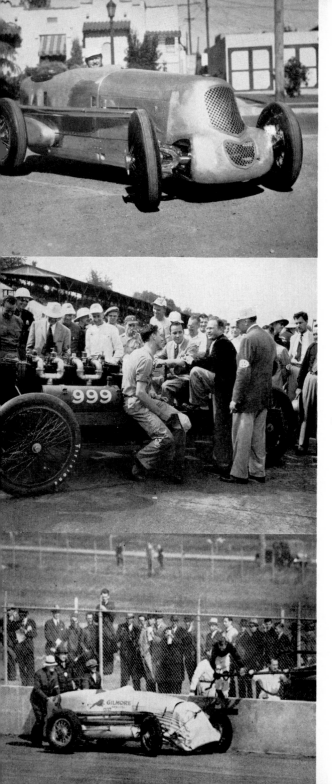

W. S. at the wheel of the front-drive Pirrung Special in 1935.

Wide World Photo

Bill Ford seated in the famous Ford 999 race car. Talking to him are W. S. and Chief Steward Harry McQuinn. 1953.

W. S. was forced out of the 1936 Vanderbilt Cup Race in New York because of a smash-up. His car is shown being removed from the track.

Wide World Photo

W. S. and his mechanic, Gordon Squire, in the Empire State Special. 1930.

O'Dell & Shields

W. S. and the Flying Cloud Special. 1928.

O'Dell & Shields

W. S. with his mechanic, Byron Stevens, at the time of the 1936 Indianapolis race.

O'Dell & Shields

W. S. and the Mallory Special which he drove to second place in the 1933 Indianapolis race. Pictured with him is Bill Devore, riding mechanic

O'Dell & Shield

Myron Stevens, mechanic, pictured with W. S. before the 1935 Indianapolis race.

O'Dell & Shield

The Miller Special with W. S. at the wheel and Dean DuChemin, riding mechanic, beside him 1932.

O'Dell & Shield

W. S. with Otto Wolfer, riding mechanic, before the 1934 Indianapolis race.

Gar Wood, Pop Myers and Edsel Ford, from left to right, at the Speedway in 1932.

Tony Gulotta

Ted Horn

Chet Miller

Doc MacKenzie

Harry McQuinn

Bob Swanson

George Robson

Ray Keech

Kelly Petillo

Shorty Cantlon

Rex Mays

Mauri Rose

Louis Schneider

Louis Meyer

Ralph Hepburn

Fred Frame

Floyd Roberts

Howdy Wilson, II

Billy Arnold

Bill Cummings

Jimmy Snyder

Deacon Litz

George Sauders

Freddy Winnai

Leon Duray

Lou Moore

Babe Stapp

Dave Evans

Cliff Bergere

Russell Snowberger

need for fuel to get our three cars to Los Angeles, there wasn't enough left to pay our hotel bills. Ralph made the suggestion that he could tow Cliff's car in order to cut down the fuel bill and I felt certain that I could get a check cashed somewhere along the way if we needed it. We shuffled our funds again and finally decided we could make it by confining our breakfast expense to coffee and doughnuts. We paid our bill and strolled into the coffee shop for five cups of coffee and two orders of doughnuts. Boots and I split one doughnut so the others could enjoy a whole one. Then we rigged a tow bar on Ralph's car and headed northward. By the time we reached Indio, southeast of Palm Springs, our fuel supply was almost exhausted. But one of the tellers in the bank at Indio finally agreed to take a chance on my personal check to the extent of ten dollars and our worries were over.

The record run on the salt flats, with Hartz, was a memorable experience. The new Chrysler Airflow certainly was equal to the objectives set for it, but tire wear was a major problem. With Firestone tires, I felt certain we would have no difficulty breaking all existing stock car records for the class B division, which included all engines with piston displacements ranging from 305 to 488 cubic inches. Firestone engineers knew how to build tires for high speed driving because of the experience they had gained in designing the tires used by all of the outstanding drivers at the Indianapolis Motor Speedway. Chrysler was using the product of a different tire company on all of its production models at that time, however, and refused to give us permission to change.

The 10-mile circular course, which had been laid out by AAA officials for our use on the record run, was located near Salduro, Utah. Ab Jenkins and his crew had established headquarters at another point on the same course and was getting ready for a record run as soon as Hartz and I were finished. Ab planned to use Firestone tires and several of my friends connected with the Firestone Racing Division were on hand. Every time one of my tires let go I had to drive by the Firestone headquarters while completing the lap before changing it and the boys finally rigged up a special sign for me, calling attention to "Firestone's One-Stop Service."

I was boiling internally about this situation when another tire blew out. This time it was the right front one and all the tread was torn off. It wedged between the brake drum and the frame, tearing the hydraulic brake line loose. With the car completely out of balance as the result of the tire failure, I felt as if a giant had taken hold of the front end and was trying to shake it apart. I pushed the brake pedal all of the way in and kept right on bouncing along at almost a hundred miles an hour. For a second or two, it seemed as if it would be impossible to keep the car from rolling on me. Gradually the car lost momentum and I was able to bring it to a safe stop. Repairs were made quickly. Hartz took over for the next couple of hours and then it was my turn again as darkness began to close in on us.

I doubt if there is any other place in the world that can match the loneliness and eeriness of Utah's great salt flats at night. There isn't a living thing within miles—no animal or insect life, no plant life, not even a single blade of grass. There isn't a sound of any kind, except what sound you make yourself. But the heavens are an awe-inspiring sight, with the stars apparently so close that you feel as if you could reach up and pluck them out of the silent darkness enshrouding the huge plateau located more than 4,300 feet above sea level.

In preparation for the night part of the 24-hour record run, Hartz and I had assembled all of the road flares we could locate. We placed them in position around the inside edge of the course, about three hundred feet apart, and I made sure that all of them were lighted before returning to headquarters to relieve Hartz. I climbed behind the wheel while the crew refueled and changed tires again.

Harry stuck his head through the window before they were finished and said: "I don't think you're going to like those flares out there, Wilbur. They may be a beautiful sight to stand here and look at," he added, "But the smoke forms all kinds of crazy images on the course."

"Either the heat is getting you, or you're getting sleepy," I told him. "What difference does it make if you do see a few images? You know there can't possibly be anything on the course in front of you."

Ten minutes later, I knew I was wrong. The smoke from those flares began to take the strangest forms I had ever seen in my worst nightmares. Images of other cars and trucks—even mountains—suddenly would loom ahead of me. More than once, I thought I was headed straight for a tree, even though I knew there wasn't one within miles of the course. A serious mental hazard began to develop, but I was determined to lick it. When the smoke suddenly took the form of a group of children running across the course, however, I finally admitted to myself that I'd had enough of it.

Time was too precious for me to use up even a few seconds to stop in order to give the necessary instructions for the removal of the flares. But I scribbled a note on a pad, which we kept in the car for such purposes, and tossed it to the crew the next time I passed the starting line. The boys removed the flares as quickly as possible and the remainder of the record run was uneventful, with the moon and stars providing sufficient light until dawn. Our tire trouble was particularly discouraging. One Chrysler dealer in Salt Lake City even took tires off the cars in his show room and rushed them out to the course in order to make sure that we would have enough rubber to finish. But Harry and I managed to keep above ninety-five miles an hour while running—we drove for two-hour shifts—and we covered 2,2056.4 miles in twenty-four hours for a new record of 84.343 miles an hour despite the time lost while changing tires and refueling.

The task of designing the Pirrung car kept me busy during most of the fall. Because I lacked enough mechanical drawing ability to put all of my ideas on paper, I built a chassis of wood and modeled the car in plaster of Paris. We had moved into a little house on Orange Street. Harry and Ann Hartz lived only a few blocks away. Harry often kept me company while I worked on the model and I usually had plaster of Paris all over the living room. Boots never seemed to mind how much mess I made.

Occasionally, for relaxation, Boots and I would rent a Pitcairn and fly down to Ensenada for a Kawamus (sea turtle) barbecue with the Husong boys. Ross and Inez Hadley usually made the trip with us in their own plane, which was much faster. They could fly circles around us—and often did, just for fun. The Husong boys, born in Germany, had been educated in the United States and lived in Mexico. Their Kawamus barbecues were something very special. They would catch one of the big sea turtles and then call Ross on the telephone to say "Better come down, we're having a barbecue."

In order to qualify for the barbecue, every guest was required to drink a full water glass of turtle blood. They made quite a ceremony of it, and it really wasn't bad when fortified with tequila. It was cold and salty and it looked like tomato juice with foam on top. They would take the turtle to their house on the beach and stand the big shells on edge around the fire to roast part of the meat. The remainder would be cooked in Mexican style with beans and other native food.

It was customary for the Husongs' "special guests" in this "Turtle-Blood Drinking Society" to spend the night in the nearby Del Playa Hotel on the beach, although it had been closed officially for some time because of the financial difficulties encountered by the management. There was no electricity or hot water. We even had to climb over the courtyard wall to enter the building. The Husongs always managed to have maid service available, however, with candle light and fresh linen. Their parties really were a lot of fun.

A man of average size wasn't tall enough to reach the propeller of a Pitcairn plane, in order to start the engine, but Jack Reemer always would drive down just to be on hand to help us get started when we were ready to fly back.

A 200-mile AAA championship had been scheduled at Mines Field in mid-December but weather interfered and forced a postponement to December 23. This time we got under way as scheduled and I worked my way up through the field until I had passed everyone except Kelly Petillo at the half way mark. As I closed in on Kelly, a heavy fog closed in on us. We were on the backstretch when it began rolling over the course and we had difficulty finding our way back to the starting line. You couldn't see a hand in front of your face. We had completed only 126 laps, but race officials stopped the event immediately with Petillo still in front. I didn't realize it at the time, but it was an omen of what was to come at Indianapolis.

In February, I entered the 250-mile Gilmore Gold Cup event over the road race course at Los Angeles Municipal Airport but failed to finish because of a broken spindle.

The Pirrung car was occupying most of my time, but I still was doing some charter flying and Herbert Marshall called one afternoon while I was taking time out to help Boots prepare to entertain our "dinner club" on the occasion of our sixth wedding anniversary. Six couples of us had formed this club and we met every two weeks. Marshall wanted me to fly him to Palm Springs immediately. I promised to meet him at the airport and told Boots I'd get back in time to join in the festivities. We reached Palm Springs without trouble, but the weather was turning bad rapidly. Under ordinary conditions, I might have waited for better conditions, spending the night at Palm Springs if necessary. I didn't want to miss our anniversary party, however, so I took off immediately. By the time I reached White Horse Pass I was in the center of one of California's rare thunder storms. Because of the treacherous wind current, even in normal conditions, it was common practice to hug the side of the mountain, letting the wind boil over the top and on out into the valley below. Keeping on an even keel and off the side of the mountain that night was tricky business. I kept thinking the danger would be over as soon as I succeeded in getting through the pass. But the ceiling at Los Angeles was so low that lights on the oil well derricks "flew by me" on both sides as I sneaked under the storm and into the airport.

Until I reached the apartment, everyone was sure I had used good judgment and decided to remain overnight at Palm Springs. I thought I would get a rousing reception. But I've never had so many people mad at me at one time, before or since. Individually and collectively they all proceeded to give me hell for taking such a chance. Bob Blair was particularly outspoken.

"Anyone silly enough to take such a chance hasn't any business flying an airplane," he exclaimed.

"When my time comes," I answered, "I don't believe it will make any difference whether I'm flying an airplane in bad weather or sitting at home in a comfortable easy chair."

Boots ended the argument quickly.

"I'm glad you came back tonight, anyway," she said, giving me a big kiss. "Everyone else is glad to see you, too, even if they do think you shouldn't have taken such a chance. So let's quit talking about it and have fun."

Before heading for Indianapolis, I also teamed with Babe Stapp and Al Gordon for another stock car record assault in a Hudson 8 on Muroc Dry Lake. Because of its smaller piston displacement, in comparison with the Chrysler Airflow, Hudson was in the class C division for cars with a piston displacement of not more than 305 cubic inches. This time, however, we used Firestone tires and actually surpassed some of the records set in the Chrysler. Top speed of the Hudson was approximately three miles an hour less than that of the Chrysler, but better tire wear enabled us to exceed Chrysler's 1,000-mile mark with an average of 85.848 miles an hour.

The Pirrung car was a beauty and when we got back to Indianapolis, I could hardly wait for a chance to cut a few fast laps. When I finally did get it up to "high C," however, I almost nullified our entire year's work. I was heading into the first turn when Maynard Clark spun one of the Thorne Specials right in front of me. With a front-drive car, running as fast as I was running, I didn't dare close the throttle. That would have caused me to loop instantly. I couldn't tell whether his car would spin toward the inside wall or the outside wall—we had both to contend with in those days—although the chances were better than even that he would go one way or the other. With that thought in mind, I headed straight for him and he spun

198

toward the outside wall just in time to let me sneak between his car and the inner barrier. It was a close fit, with not more than an inch to spare on either side, but I didn't even scratch the paint.

After "cooling off" for a little while, I got back on the track at high speed and was swinging through the No. 3 turn when the car suddenly tried to straighten out and head toward the the outer wall of its own accord. I heaved and tugged on the steering wheel with all of my strength to keep from crashing. When I finally rolled to a standstill, the right front wheel wouldn't turn at all. A small sleeve in the hub had collapsed. After making the necessary repairs, everything went smoothly until Race Day.

A few days before the big event, I participated in the formation of what probably is the world's most exclusive club. Only fourteen drivers ever had gone the full five hundred miles without relief on the Indianapolis track at an average speed of more than a hundred miles an hour. Twelve of us still were living. One member of the group was Dave Evans and he conceived the idea of forming a "100-Mile-An-Hour Club." Officials of the Champion Spark Plug Company invited all of us to a dinner party and the Champion 100-Mile-An-Hour Club became a reality. Billy Arnold, first to qualify for the club in 1930, was the only living member unable to be present. Those who attended the dinner with me were Fred Frame, Howdy Wilcox, Cliff Bergere, Russ Snowberger, Louie Meyer, Chet Gardner, Lou Moore, Bill Cummings, Mauri Rose and Evans. Although the speeds have gone up and up at Indianapolis with each succeeding year, it still is mighty difficult to qualify for membership and it is unusual for more than three or four newcomers to make the grade annually. Starting in 1937, the club has made an annual award to some individual who has made an outstanding contribution to racing and two years later it was my pleasure to present such a plaque to Colonel Roscoe Turner.

On the night before that 1935 race, I went over in my mind every bit of work we had done on my car during all of the

199

many weeks of preparation. It took me a long time to find something to worry about, but I finally did. Roscoe Dunning had made the throttle connections out of ⅛ rod and I worked myself up into quite a sweat wondering whether or not they would be strong enough for the race. The following morning, determined to change them, I was out of bed by four o'clock. When I reached the track, Roscoe already was there. He probably had spent the night there. The usual race day tension had been building up for all of us and he wasn't the least bit receptive to my idea that the throttle connections should be changed.

When I insisted, he said, "Change 'em yourself, if you want 'em changed. But the connections are absolutely all right the way they are now." Then all of the color drained out of his face and he collapsed on the floor of the garage in a faint. Like a lot of other fellows in the racing business, he'd been working too hard for too long a time without much sleep. He was completely exhausted and finally had reached the end of his rope. My chief concern, naturally, was getting him back on his feet again. That took a little while and I forgot all about the rods until it was too late to change them. They didn't give us a bit of trouble during the race, however.

Stevens was riding with me and we moved up to fourth place during the first thirty laps while Rex Mays, Tony Gulotta and Babe Stapp were fighting for the lead. After grabbing first place for a few laps, Stapp went out of the race because of mechanical trouble at the 70-lap mark while the rest of us were making our first scheduled pit stop. Some one handed me a quart milk bottle full of ice water and a lot of my friends will always believe the milk bottle kept me from winning the race. Stevens and I each had a drink out of it. Then I poured some of the water on the top of my head and offered him another drink. The work of my crew had been particularly efficient, however, and I suddenly heard Dunning yell, "Okay, go!" The car was in gear, so I stepped on the throttle and started to roll again with the milk bottle still in one hand. I wanted to toss it to some member of my crew, but no one was looking in my direction. I was afraid I would hit some one in the face with it, or smash it against the pit wall, if I simply tossed it in the general direction of my pit. And before I could make up my mind what to do with it, I had killed my engine. It took twenty-five or thirty seconds to get it started again. By that time, Kelly Petillo had moved ahead of me and I was still fourth despite Stapp's bad luck.

Mays and Gulotta both went out of the race, shortly after reaching the half-way mark, and I still was trailing Petillo when it became time for us to make our second pit stop. He coasted in after 139 laps and I was in first place for five trips around the course before I had to stop for fuel and tires also. My crew did the job in almost record time. Petillo had the benefit of equally fine service, however, and when both of us were running again he had a 33-second advantage. With fifty-five laps to go, I still had a chance to catch him and I also was doubtful of his ability to finish. On his first qualifying attempt, Petillo had used too much fuel (we were limited to two and a half gallons for the twenty-five miles). On his second trial, he had torn up an engine. It had been necessary for him to patch it, rather than replace it, and I really had not regarded him as a dangerous rival even after he had made the grade in fast time on his third attempt.

But the weather man gave me the same unkind treatment he had dished out during the winter when fog had made it necessary to halt the 200-mile event at Los Angeles. Rain forced officials to display the yellow caution flag, which made it illegal for any driver to improve his position. Petillo was able to reduce his speed in order to conserve fuel and minimize the danger of engine failure, without worrying about any pressure from behind. Although the weather did protect second place for me, it ended any hope I had of winning and we finished in that order with Bill Cummings third, Floyd Roberts fourth and Hepburn fifth.

Since that day, I've never permitted a glass container of any kind in my pit. An old-fashioned, long-handle sauce pan—the type found in any kitchen—has been much more practical as a receptacle for drinking water.

Promoters of auto racing were having rough sledding during that summer of 1935. Many had gone out of business as the result of the depression and drastic cuts had been made in the prize money for those events which still remained on the schedule.

One of the newcomers in the promotional end of the business was Carl Stockholm of Chicago, a former amateur and professional bike rider of international reputation. While serving with the Army of Occupation, following World War I, he had been shot in the knee by the accidental discharge of a friend's gun. He started riding a bicycle to strengthen the muscles in his injured leg and became so adept at this form of exercise that he won a position on the United States Olympic team for the 1920 games at Antwerp, Belgium. Later he campaigned successfully in the six-day professional bike races.

Carl was a real race fan and in 1935 he tackled the task of restoring the old Roby track to its former status as the hub of racing in the Chicago area. Later, after it became evident the expense of rebuilding the old stands would be too great, he shifted his programs to the Cook County Fair Grounds. All of the drivers were grateful for this added opportunity to compete for regular purses, but we needed a full schedule of 100-mile championship events at other tracks in order to keep busy and continue eating.

Ten of us, who were among the most active at that time, decided the only thing to do was to promote races ourselves. Together, we formed Champion Drivers, Inc., and entered the promotional field to compete for our own prize money against any other drivers who wanted to enter the various events. The original group, which immediately was dubbed "The Big Ten," consisted of Louie Meyer, Fred Frame, Al Gordon, Shorty Cantlon, Bill Cummings, Lou Moore, Deacon Litz, Russ Snowberger, Babe Stapp and I. Each of us put up $500 for original promotional expense and obtained the services of H. Kirby Shellaby of California as general manager.

202

It was a costly experience. Instead of making a profit, we had to put more and more money into the venture every month. The weather was atrocious almost every time we scheduled a race. After postponing one event three times because of rain, we finally had to cancel it without a single penny of income to offset all of our advertising and publicity expense. We finally abandoned the idea and most of us headed for California for the winter season. But public sentiment against racing in that area was growing steadily because of the mounting fatalities. The competition at Ascot was more intense than at any other track in the world. Some drivers took almost unbelievable chances in a desperate effort to win. Twenty-four had lost their lives since 1930.

As far as sudden death was concerned, the racing fraternity was a hardened group. Al Gordon expressed the opinion of most of us when he answered such criticism by saying, "What difference does it make? We all have to die some time."

A few days later, on January 26, it was Gordon's turn during a 200-lap race with the two-man Indianapolis-type cars. Moore, Cantlon, Frame and I had gone out of the race early because of mechanical trouble. Rex Mays and Floyd Roberts were battling for the lead with Gordon in hot pursuit. Spider Matlock was riding with Gordon and their car hit a slick spot on the south turn. It crashed through the outer guard rail, tail first, and hurtled down a 12-foot embankment. Gordon died in the hospital about an hour later while Mays, Meyer, Roberts, Cummings and Chet Gardner led the remainder of the field home in that order. Matlock joined Gordon in death the following day and racing activity in California was doomed for many years to come.

CHAPTER 23

EVEN before the tragic Gordon-Matlock accident, I had made up my mind that the only way to make any money out of racing was to own my own car. After paying all of his expenses, Petillo had banked almost $20,000 as the result of his Indianapolis victory because he hadn't had to share the prize money with a car owner. I felt certain I could do even better than that and I already had sold my interest in the Los Angeles Aircraft Company to Bob Blair in order to get some working capital.

First, I constructed a quarter-scale model of myself, using paralin, the material from which we made windshields for our race cars. I put the little figure together with rivets so that the shoulders, elbows, wrists, hips, knees and ankles all worked. Then, working at home in our little apartment, I designed a car to fit my figure. Although I would have preferred a front-drive car for Indianapolis, they were not practical for any other type of course, and I decided on a rear-drive car so that I could use it in other events, also.

I'd put some lines on the drawing board and then have a conference with Boots and any of our kibitzing friends who happened to be present. Finally, the plans for the body of what we lovingly referred to as the "Pay Car," were complete on paper and I took them to the Gilmore Oil Company in an effort to get some financial help in exchange for putting the Gilmore name on the car.

"If I don't win the Indianapolis race, I'll repay every penny you are willing to advance me to help build the car," I promised Earl Gilmore and Clarence Beesemeyer.

"We won't make a deal like that," said Gilmore, "but we'll go along with you to the extent of fifteen hundred dollars if you'll carry the Gilmore name."

"We'll paint the car for you, too," added Beesemeyer, and we shook hands on it.

Myron Stevens was to be my riding mechanic and he agreed to work with me on the car for fifty dollars a week plus ten per cent of the prize money.

You've never seen two eager beavers tackle a job with more determination than the team of Shaw and Stevens. We worked from seven o'clock in the morning until eleven or twelve o'clock at night.

In order to have the body lines perfectly smooth, I had conceived the idea of turning the frame rails inside out. The only visible part of the frame was the top flange, where the body and underpan joined, and it was the cleanest possible job aerodynamically. We made the front axle out of a piece of chrome-moly tubing obtained from the Douglas Aircraft Company. Riley Brett had given me an idea on the design of the spindles and steering arms; and they were perfectly beautiful. I designed the brakes myself, using Stutz safety drums. The supports I made out of heat-treated chrome-moly flat stock; and it was while making the skeleton anchor plates in the Offenhauser shop that I almost lost my left hand.

In order to get the plates to the shape I desired, it was necessary for me to drill approximately five hundred holes in this extremely hard metal, which should never have been drilled in the first place. It's easy to become careless on such a repetitious task—and that's exactly what happened in my case.

In my hurry to finish the tedious job, with only fifteen or twenty holes to go, I made the mistake of holding the plate with only one hand. It was a stupid thing to do. The drill caught in the hard metal and the plate swung with it. If I had not been wearing a Scottish rite ring on my finger, I probably would have lost most of my hand.

Fortunately, the edge of the plate hit the ring and jumped enough for me to escape any permanent damage. But it dug into the back of my hand, severed an artery and scraped off the flesh clear to the bone, folding it back on my wrist like the top of a convertible. Fred Offenhauser came running over with a bottle of oil-o-salt to pour on the wound and offered to drive me to a doctor's office. But I was so mad at myself because of my carelessness that I wouldn't listen. Instead, I wrapped a towel around the injured hand and resumed drilling.

It was only a matter of minutes until there was so much blood on the floor that I felt as if I was wading in it. Riley Brett finally couldn't stand it any longer. Without any preliminary conversation, he took the drill out of my hand and said: "Come on. Whether you like it or not, you're going to a hospital before you bleed to death."

By that time I was beginning to feel weak. The little industrial clinic near the Offenhauser plant was a welcome sight when we parked in front of it.

I sat on a table while the doctor tied off the bleeders. Then, with a critical eye, I folded the flap of flesh back into its proper position and told him I wanted it sewed back on "without any puckers."

Eddie Demeree, a Los Angeles newspaper man, and his wife came running into the hospital before the job was finished. They had dropped by the shop to see what progress we were making and driven straight to the clinic when they learned what had happened.

"How about a cigarette?" asked Eddie.

"I can use one about now," I answered.

He lit one and offered it to me, but I didn't have enough strength to raise my good hand and take it from him.

"What the hell's the matter with me, Doc?" I asked. "I'm as weak as a cat."

"Young man," he exclaimed, "You have practically bled to death. Another five minutes and it wouldn't have been any use to bring you here. But if you'll drink plenty of liquids and get a good night's sleep you'll feel better in the morning."

Riley took me home and Boots managed to get me into bed without too many objections on my part. But with each succeeding minute, the pain became more intense. In order to stand it at all, I had to hold my hand above my head. Everytime I let it down, even a little bit, the pain was unbearable. Sleep was impossible.

I was at the clinic when it opened the following morning. After examining the wound, the doctor instructed me to soak it in Dakin solution and I followed his advice faithfully for twenty-four hours. I thought the treatment was intended to ease the pain and heal the wound at the same time. But the back of my hand began to turn gray and there was no feeling in the skin at all.

Thoroughly disgusted with the result of the prescribed treatment, I went tearing back to the hospital on the third day.

"Look what the damn Dakin solution is doing to my hand," I exclaimed.

He told me calmly that the only reason he had prescribed the stuff was to dissolve the dead flesh so that the wound could heal properly.

"But the whole back of my hand is dead," I said.

"Certainly it is," he replied. "I could have told you that when you first came here. But you were so determined that I was going to sew the flesh back into place without any puckers that I was afraid to tell you."

"For God's sake, man, get it off of there then," I exploded. "This hand has got to heal up in a hurry."

He started clipping with a little pair of scissors. It was real torture when he hit a nerve which still was alive. I felt sure I could do just as good a job as he was doing, without hurting myself half as much.

"Let me have those scissors," I said, "If you'll hold that dead part up with the tweezers I'll trim it off. I know where those live nerves are."

It took at least thirty minutes, but when all of the dead skin and flesh had been removed, there was a lot of satisfaction in seeing that all of the "control cables" and working parts underneath were in good condition.

I couldn't be of much help to Steve for the next week or ten days, so I "chased parts" with Boots doing the driving and my hand held straight up in the air because that was the only position which seemed to ease the pain. It was during this period that Boots really became a good driver in traffic. We never went on any errand except in a helluva hurry. I made her drive into spots I knew she believed she could never negotiate. But she always squeezed through and gained additional confidence each day until she became as proficient in traffic as I was.

Steve kept reassuring me that everything was being done with the same care I would have taken myself—and I had a tremendous amount of confidence in him—but I tried to inspect each operation as the assembly work progressed. One little detail, however, escaped my careful scrutiny and it developed into one of the most expensive mistakes any race car builder ever made.

During one of my brief periods away from the shop, Steve fitted the hood panels. Usually this is done by mounting them on half hinges bolted or riveted securely to the radiator shell. The hinges then are covered with leather, held in place by little copper split rivets. Apparently Steve placed everything in position to make sure it would fit properly and then inserted the copper rivets—overlooking the fact that he had omitted the important step of first fastening the hinges securely to the radiator shell. Those little copper rivets were all that held the half hinges in place.

With the hinges covered by leather, the error escaped my inspection. Due to my complete confidence in Steve's workmanship, I didn't take the time to examine the installation thoroughly. Besides, at that stage of the job, I was beginning to have financial worries. There wasn't much doubt about it. Unless I stretched the buying power of every dollar to the very limit, I was going to run out of money before I ever got the car to Indianapolis.

Like almost all race car builders, we always had a lot of visitors. One of our steady customers at lunch time was Ross Hadley, and apparently he sensed my problem without my mentioning it at any time. After lunch one day, without pre-

208

liminary conversation of any kind, he laid a check upside down on the work bench.

"What's that for, Ross?" I asked.

"That's just to help along a little bit," he answered. "If you have any financial worries, this ought to ease your pain to some extent."

I picked it up and saw that it was drawn for $1,000. Honestly, I could have cried. The lump in my throat was so big I had to take a couple of deep breaths before I could even talk.

Then I said: "Look, Ross, I think we're going to make it all right; and I don't need this yet, anyway."

"Put it in the bank," he replied. "If you don't need it, all right. But if you do, it will be there. And if it isn't enough there's more where that came from."

As the time approached for the start of our trip to Indianapolis, I checked on shipping costs and discovered it would be much cheaper to build a trailer.

With my Air-Flow DeSoto half full of traveling bags, tools, spare parts and other racing equipment, four of us crowded into the car with the heavy trailer behind. Many close friends were on hand to wish us good luck. Ross and Inez Hadley had brought along a bottle of champagne to "launch" the car properly on its trip to Indianapolis; and I'm sure Inez never knew how Boots and I held our breath when she broke the bottle over the car's nose. But even if the fresh paint had run down the front of the car with the champagne I wouldn't have uttered a word of reproach because of their interest, moral support and financial help. They made our departure somewhat of a ceremony. But it certainly wasn't an auspicious one. We hadn't gone three blocks before a big sedan backed out of a driveway unexpectedly. I had to stop so quickly that the trailer jack-knifed and the trailer hitch was badly bent.

It was almost morning before we finished the task of repairing the damage and installing a special vacuum brake arrangement on the trailer with its control lever attached to the steering post of the DeSoto. Then we went to bed for some much-

209

needed sleep and it was the following noon when we finally hit the road.

The new brake system was perfect. A little experimenting revealed that the vacuum brakes on the trailer worked so well it was not necessary to use the foot brakes on the DeSoto. With the air-intake and exhaust gauges on the control panel, it was like playing engineer on a railroad and the entire trip to Indianapolis was a pleasant one.

On the way, I heard an expression which tickled my insides and came to be one of my favorites. We had pulled into a little desert town, Victorville, to spend the night. The only garage where we could get our "pride and joy" in out of the weather, was a small one full of posts used to separate the stalls for ordinary cars. In order to get both the DeSoto and trailer under the roof and out of the way, I had to back into the garage. It requires considerable skill to back a trailer, because almost every movement is exactly the opposite as in backing a single car. This was my first attempt and it took quite a bit of maneuvering on my part to park it neatly between two posts. An old westerner—complete with high-heeled boots, 10-gallon hat and a big chew of tobacco—was in charge of the garage. He watched the entire procedure without offering a single word of advice. As I turned off the ignition and climbed out of the car, however, he drawled, "Partner, you sure got a nice scald on her that time." Having grown up with a knowledge of butchering from my uncle down in Shelbyville, I knew exactly what he meant and it was the finest compliment he could have paid me.

We arrived at the speedway on the evening of the third day and the race car immediately attracted a lot of attention among the racing fraternity, especially from the technical committee. Some predicted the car would be hard to handle because the type of cross members used in the wide frame was so flexible. One expressed the opinion the car would prove to be so unmanageable that it would be necessary to bar it on the grounds it would be a hazard to other competitors. Ironically, as they discussed the potential failure of the car because of its basic

210

design, most of them leaned against the hood, with their hand almost on top of the one weakness which ultimately cost us the race.

Our critics were silenced quickly by the superb performance of the car as soon as we took it out on the track. I could close the throttle at the starting line, coast into the turn before "getting on it" again, and turn a lap as fast as anyone else had ever turned one up to that time. This was due, primarily, to the fact that the lines of the car were so clean aerodynamically. Wind resistance was reduced to almost the absolute minimum. The first time or two it gave me somewhat of a weird feeling, but it was wonderful as soon as I became accustomed to it. The car definitely came up to my fondest expectations and I felt certain I could win with it easily.

After the first thorough test, we checked everything and discovered the left rear hub had a tendency to loosen at high speed. Examination revealed the threads had been cut in the wrong direction. But Offenhauser shipped us a new hub immediately by air. We were back in business within five days. Although we had missed the first day of the time trials because of this delay, ample qualifying time still remained and the car was running perfectly.

With everything ready on the morning of May 17, we strolled down to Tom Beal's stand for a leisurely lunch. I didn't want to make my run until later in the day, when the wind probably would be less of a hazard. After eating, I leaned back with my knee against the counter and swapped stories with some of the boys for almost an hour. When the session finally broke up, my leg buckled under me and a sharp pain shot through the joint as if some one had jabbed an ice pick into it. I doubt if anything ever caused me greater physical suffering. Evidently I had paralyzed a nerve in my right knee as the result of the pressure of my weight against the counter. I couldn't even walk without help, but I borrowed a cane and hobbled around Gasoline Alley with the hope that exercise would abolish the intense pain.

I felt as if I had to qualify that day. There is something

211

about the time trials that creates almost as much tension and anxiety as when you are waiting for the starting signal on race day and wondering whether or not your motor will start. Regardless of how dependable a car he has at his command, every driver is a bundle of nerves until he actually has earned a starting position. Despite my physical condition, I didn't want to wait until a later date, because each day of delay would push me farther toward the rear of the pack. The rules for the "500" provide that all qualifiers line up in the order of their speed ahead of the qualifiers on subsequent days unless they are crowded out of the starting field entirely by faster cars.

Rex Mays, Babe Stapp and Chet Miller already had clinched the front row positions and five others also had qualified on the first day. The best I could hope for, even by running faster than anyone else on this particular day, would be No. 9 position, on the outside of the third row. Seven others already had qualified while I was limping around the garage area and a decision to wait until the morrow would eliminate any chance to be near the front.

It began to cool off in the late afternoon and the wind gradually diminished to make qualifying conditions ideal. I told my crew to push the car up to the starting line and I started to hobble in that direction on my cane. I was half way through the pit area when an automotive accessory manufacturer called me to one side and said, "Wilbur, I'll give you a thousand dollars to put my spark plugs in your engine instead of Champion Plugs before you qualify."

The offer almost took my breath away. I appreciated his confidence and I needed the money at that particular time as much as any healthy man in the entire world needed it. But I didn't take it. I didn't want to make a single change which might disturb the apparently perfect combination we had worked out with Champion Spark Plugs.

As soon as the Firestone crew had checked the tires carefully, Steve and I climbed into the cockpit. The engine roared into life. As usual, all of the drivers and mechanics near the

212

starting line gave each of us a hand shake or a pat on the back to wish us good luck. Chief Steward Charlie Merz and Ted Allen, secretary of the AAA Contest Board, also walked up at this instant and I thought they intended to wish me luck, too. Both were good friends of mine.

But Charlie's first words were, "Where do you think you're going?"

Thinking he was ribbing me, I said, "I'm going to qualify this goat, Brother. Do you want to go for a fast ride?"

"No you're not!" he exclaimed.

"Who's going to keep me from it?" I shouted above the noise of the engine.

"We are," Charlie answered. "Shut her off and I'll tell you about it."

I hit the cut-off button and looked at Charlie and Ted as if they were both crazy. Then, in a kittenish mood, they explained that I—as secretary and treasurer of Champion Drivers —was responsible for fifty dollars owed by this group to the AAA.

"You can't qualify until it's paid," they added.

Following the tragic race at Ascot the previous winter we had abandoned the idea and settled all of our outstanding obligations. Somewhere along the line, however, it seems as if I had inadvertently overlooked payment of one small sanction fee. Allen had picked this particular time to bring it to my attention.

It was apparent that he and Charlie both regarded it as a big joke. They were enjoying the situation immensely. But I was burning to a crisp. I thought it was the most inconsiderate trick any official could pull on a competitor at such a tense moment. Blowing up completely, I told them so in no uncertain words. Even though my leg was killing me, I walked all of the way back to my garage and returned with a personal check for the exact amount.

Then I climbed into the car again, as mad as any one man can be, and started my 10-lap qualifying run. I thought I had kept track of each lap. Because of my anger, however, I ap-

parently miscounted. When they gave me the white flag, signifying that I was starting my tenth lap, I was under the impression that they were giving me the checkered flag which meant
I had completed the required distance. In line with the fuel
limitations for that 1936 race, anyone who used more than two
and a half gallons to qualify was rejected. Consequently, everyone hit the cutoff switch as soon as he had completed the
distance and coasted back to the starting line. I did the same
thing—only I did it one lap too soon. By coasting the tenth lap,
instead of the eleventh lap, my average speed would have
been reduced so greatly that I would not have been one of the
fastest thirty-three cars eligible for starting positions. No car
which completed the full ten laps could be granted a second
chance, and unknowingly I was about to make a spectator of
myself, instead of a contender.

As I came coasting down the main stretch toward the starting line, fully satisfied with my performance, I could see Leon
Duray lumbering toward me and waving his long arms. Apparently he wanted me to stop. I couldn't see any sense in
stopping, because I would have to push my car the rest of the
way, inasmuch as I had shut off the engine. As I started to
swerve around him, I heard him shout: "Stop, you damn fool.
Stop. Don't cross that line."

I still didn't know what all the excitement was about. But
I respected Leon's judgment enough to slam on my brakes.
When he explained things, I was madder than ever—at myself
as well as at the officials. As soon as they could fill my fuel
tank again, I made another qualifying attempt and ran the
full distance this time, at an average of 117.503 for the best
speed of the day.

The following morning we tore the car down completely
and examined every moving part. There wasn't a single thing
which did not appear to be in perfect condition. After reas-
sembling it, we ran some fuel tests to make sure we would not
exceed the race limit of forty-two and a half gallons. We had
more than an ample margin of safety, so we locked up the car
two days before the race to wait for the starting signal. Unless

something unexpected happened, we were sure the race was ours—and a great many other people were of the same opinion.

On the night of May 29, sleep was impossible. Mentally, I went over every nut and bolt and cotter pin I could remember installing. As soon as daylight arrived, I headed for the track. My crew already had moved our equipment and official allotment of fuel into the pit—five 7½ gallon cans filled to the brim and one similar can with exactly five gallons in it. At seven o'clock we pushed the car into our pit and Art Sims practiced a few quick wheel changes while I laced on a very special pair of shoes which always gave me a feeling of complete confidence.

I'm one of those fellows who professes not to be superstitious. But I always had worn this particular pair of dirty, grimy, old bowling shoes in competition since my early racing days. Although stained with oil and grease—and even aluminum from the Golden Egg I had driven on dirt tracks in 1923— they probably had been in and out of more race cars than any pair of shoes in the world. They looked it, too.

At nine o'clock, along with the other crews, we pushed the car to its designated starting position. The next sixty minutes seemed like eternity. There was a lot of conversation, a lot of back slapping and a lot of hand shaking, of course. But it seemed as if time was standing absolutely still. We checked and rechecked little things which we already knew were perfect. We posed for the traditional panoramic picture at the starting line. We watched the finish of the mammoth parade and all of the pageantry which helps make the 500-mile race the world's greatest sports spectacle. Tension mounted with each succeeding second until Starter Seth Klein finally gave the signal for which all of us had been waiting.

The ear-shattering sound of thirty-three engines drowned out every other noise. Tom Milton, first two-time winner of the "500," moved slowly toward the first turn at the wheel of the Packard pace car. For the first time, at his personal insistence, the pace car was to be one of the special awards to the winner and I felt sure that he was driving "my car."

215

We maintained our respective positions behind him—at least all but one of us did—as we gained momentum slowly for the flying start at the end of that first lap, which doesn't count. The exception was Wild Bill Cummings, who had won the race the previous year. The thing every driver fears until he really is rolling—some type of last minute mechanical failure which nullifies month after month of work and worry—had forced him out of the running before he had even crossed the starting line. Because of a sheared clutch shaft, he had moved no more than six inches, and a quick repair job was impossible.

But the rest of us were on our way. For five or six laps I was busy adjusting all of my faculties to the sudden change of tempo. Then I began to move up steadily. At twenty-five miles I was third, thirteen seconds behind the leader. At fifty miles, I was second, only four seconds back (about 225 yards). At seventy-five miles I was right on Babe Stapp's tail with the other boys strung out behind.

At times it's difficult to remember that the race is for five hundred miles. No one ever won it on the tenth lap, or the fiftieth, or the 199th. You've got to go the distance unless you're willing to be satisfied with a little consolation money. But everything was working according to plan. In fact, Stapp wasn't setting quite as fast a pace as I believed would be necessary to win, and I saw no reason to let him continue to collect all of the $100 lap prizes.

On the thirty-first lap, I checked all the gauges on my instrument panel and made sure that everything was functioning perfectly. Then, as we rolled into the backstretch on the next trip around, I nudged Steve with my elbow to let him know this was it. At the same instant I eased down on the throttle and sucked Stapp under. He followed me through the turn as if he intended to do something about the situation. I jumped on it even harder as we hit the home stretch, however, and enjoyed a 50-yard lead as we reached the southwest corner. I did it deliberately, because it's mighty discouraging to have some one run off and hide from you in this manner. I wanted to convince him that he might just as well begin to concentrate

216

on salvaging second place. From then on it was going to be a breeze for us. Even though I eased off the throttle a little, in order to save tires and not strain anything more than necessary, we increased our advantage steadily until we had lapped the entire field at the 200-mile mark.

In fact, we had a lead of more than two full laps on every rival except Stapp and he was eighty-one seconds behind when we made our first scheduled pit stop. He moved back into the lead during the minute and forty seconds required to take on fuel and change a right rear tire, which was beginning to show signs of wear. We knew Stapp would have to make a pit stop himself within twenty miles, and from then on it looked as if we would have clear sailing to the finish without serious pressure from behind. Everything was proceeding beautifully. There wasn't a cloud in our sky.

It happened as we pulled alongside Ralph Hepburn at the head of the home stretch on the eighty-third lap. He glanced over to see who was sucking him under and then gestured frantically toward the front of our car. Steve raised up in the cockpit to take a look and it seemed as if every drop of blood drained from his face. He looked like a ghost as he leaned over and shouted in my ear as loud as he could, "Stop, quick."

I couldn't imagine what had happened, but I knew Steve well enough to realize it was serious. He was really scared. With such little warning, it was all I could do to bring the car to a halt before overshooting the pit, but we made it, and I jumped out to see what all the excitement was about. The hood was almost off. The side panels, to which it had been anchored, were flapping in the breeze. Before the end of another lap it almost certainly would have torn loose and possibly decapitated both of us.

Making repairs was a major problem. There wasn't a single thing sticking out on the car which could be used as an anchor for wire or straps which might hold the hood down. The only solution was to drill holes through the metal and wire the hood into place. Almost seventeen minutes were required to finish the job and we were thirty miles behind the leader before we were rolling again.

We didn't have a chance to collect much more than a little consolation money, but in racing no one ever gives up. You never know what might happen to the other fellow. And there's always a certain amount of satisfaction to be derived from challenging one driver after another for fifteenth place, twelfth place or tenth place—as the case may be. At least we were still in there pitching and adding a little to the show.

With Stapp also encountering unexpected trouble, the battle for first place developed into a duel between Lou Meyer and Ted Horn as we continued to improve our position steadily by overtaking the stragglers. At the finish we were seventh, but I was more convinced than ever that I could beat them the next time I had a chance.

Meyer, scoring his third "500" victory for a record which was going to take me four more years to equal, had completed the distance in 4 hours, 35 minutes and 3.39 seconds. With two minutes and twenty-nine seconds deducted for his pit stops, his actual running time was 4:32:34.39. My official time of 4:47:49.00, less 19:30 in the pit, made my actual running time of 4:28:19.00, four minutes and fifteen seconds faster than his.

Failure to install three cents worth of rivets had cost me more than $30,000 in prize money, plus the satisfaction of winning. It was almost more than I could take. As I pulled up to the garage and shut off the engine, I turned to Steve and looked him straight in the eye. With all of the sarcasm and bitterness at my command I said, "How do you feel?"

It was the meanest thing anyone could have said to him at that particular time. The instant the words were out of my mouth, I could have bit off my tongue. I've been sorry ever since, because he was—and still is—one of the best mechanics in the business.

CHAPTER 24

AFTER I had driven Pirrung's front-drive car to second place the previous year, he had purchased a dirt-track car from Leon Duray. It was the same chassis Leon and I had taken to Italy, but Pirrung had put a 220-inch engine in it. By the summer of 1936, Gil's interest in dirt track racing was waning. I heard the car was for sale and thought it was just the one I needed to win some prize money at Springfield (Ill.) and Milwaukee. It was a hot evening in August when I drove down to his garage on Tenth Street to buy it. When I got there, Joe Thorne already was trying to make a deal for the same car and I didn't want to get into a bidding contest with Joe. As soon as Joe realized I was interested, however, he wanted the car more than ever and he came up with a compromise offer.

"I've already got one dirt track car," he said, "but I want this one, too. Suppose I buy it and let you drive it during the remainder of the season. That way we can both make some money out of the deal." I agreed and took it to Springfield the following week.

Doc MacKenzie, who also had driven for Pirrung at Indianapolis in 1935, was among the entrants. This was to be his first race since an accident a couple of months earlier and he was all "cocked" to show us he hadn't lost any of his desire to win. For more than seventy laps he set a terrific pace, but no driver can stay in top condition without practice and I felt certain he couldn't continue at that speed much longer. When he finally asked for relief after seventy-two laps, I was in position to take command of the race and I won easily with Tony Willman second in MacKenzie's car and Cummings third.

We had to race at Milwaukee the following day, so I proceeded to get the car loaded on the trailer while the officials were figuring the prize money. I was feeling very satisfied with my day's work as I headed for the office. On the way I passed Cotton Henning.

"I did all right today," I exclaimed, with a big grin.

"As far as winning, you did all right," he said. "But you didn't make any money."

"What do you mean?" I demanded.

"Just what I said," he answered. "You didn't make any money. This race today was worth exactly nine hundred dollars to the winner and it shouldn't take you very long to figure how much of that is your personal share."

I grumbled about it all of the way to Milwaukee and Boots did a good job of listening without having very much to say. It was late when we arrived and we got out to the track early the next morning after getting very little sleep. The course was as dusty as any I have ever seen and the start was so ragged that we had to make four trips around it, behind the pace car, before the starter was satisfied with our alignment. Everyone seemed to be jockeying for a little better position than he was entitled to. I was on the inside of the second row with Cummings on my right and the entire field roared into the first turn at full throttle when the green flag finally dropped.

All hell broke loose instantly. It was too dusty for me to see exactly what happened. But I know I hit a lot of things going through the turn and a lot of things hit me. Something shattered my goggles and almost knocked me out of the car. I drove by instinct until I reached the backstretch. The pain in my right eye was so intense I couldn't open it and my left eye was so filled with water that everything seemed to be a blur. I groped my way around the course to the pits and stopped. Someone put a cool, damp bandage over my eyes and rushed me to a hospital.

A doctor was just finishing the job of taking the tiny particles of glass from my eyes and face when a calm, feminine

220

voice said, "Now, have you had enough of this silly dirt track racing?" Without even looking around, I knew it was Boots.

"I certainly have," I said. "But I have to finish the season because I've already promised to drive in most of the races still on the schedule."

A few minutes later we learned that MacKenzie had been killed in the accident and that several of the other fellows had been badly injured. The race was the first of a series of events in rapid-fire order at Milwaukee that week, however, and three days later I was back in action on the same track for a series of 10-lap dashes.

The most important date on the racing calendar that fall was the opening of the new Roosevelt Raceway on Long Island and everyone connected with the sport soon began to converge on New York.

A group of wealthy sportsmen thought the American public would go for the European type of road racing and they were investing a great deal of money in the project. The idea was to combine the best features of speedway and road racing competition in an effort to give the top drivers of each Continent an equal chance to win. As soon as I took one look at the unique course, however, I knew the Europeans had received by far the best part of the bargain.

The turn at the end of the one long straightaway was banked substantially. But the remainder of the course consisted entirely of short stretches and virtually flat turns. As the result of the knowledge gained on my trip to Italy with Leon Duray, several years earlier, I felt certain no American car had the necessary brakes and transmission to make a good showing.

As an example of the tremendous difference in equipment, Tazio Nuvolari was driving a Ferrari-Alfa which developed about 450 horsepower. He had a four-speed transmission which enabled him to use any gear he wanted at any given time for the purpose of utilizing his maximum horsepower constantly. In addition he had marvelous brakes and a beautifully handling chassis. He and most of the other Europeans could outrun us on any of the straightaways, apply those wonderful

221

brakes and ooze through the turns without taking any chances. In some of the turns, our driving technique enabled us to pass the Europeans. The instant they could see their way out of a turn, however, they would punch their throttles and disappear in the distance like the rear end of a Walt Disney cat going over a hill. We had two-speed transmissions and we never used the lower gear ratio at any time except when starting from a stand-still position.

I thought seriously of withdrawing. First, however, I intended to show them I could get around the course as fast as anyone even though I didn't have the necessary equipment to go the full distance. In the time trials, Billy Winn won the pole position and I grabbed the No. 2 spot with Tazio Nuvolari getting the other front row berth in an Italian Alfa Romeo. But I still didn't know what to do about the race. Even though I was skeptical of being able to finish the 300-mile event, it went against the grain to let the Europeans win by default. Finally I took my problem to Pop Myers and Louis Chevrolet. After considering all the angles, Pop made up my mind for me with one simple statement.

"Wilbur," said the grand old guy, "you'll kick yourself all of the way back to Indianapolis if you sit on the sidelines and watch somebody else win it at a much slower average speed than you think will be necessary. A million things could happen which would make you awfully sorry that you hadn't at least tried."

That clinched it and I got busy on the job of figuring how I could improve my chances. Unless I happened to be extremely lucky, there was good reason to believe I would spin and kill my engine somewhere along the route when my brakes started to wear out. If I couldn't get started again, without assistance, I would be out of the race; so I decided to put batteries in the mechanic's seat in preparation for such an emergency. Although compulsory at Indianapolis that year, riding mechanics were not required for the Roosevelt race.

After doing all of my practice with the mechanic's seat empty, however, the added weight of the batteries proved my

222

undoing on race day. It is difficult to describe just what put me into the wall, but the accident happened, actually, because I went into the turn too slowly. In practice, I had been throwing the car into the turn and broadsiding through it by steering with the throttle. Driving more conservatively at the start of the race, in order to take as much strain as possible off of my equipment, I cut my speed to about fifty-five miles an hour for the first turn and tried to steer the car through it with my front wheels. The added weight of the batteries and a full fuel tank, plus the effect of brand new tires, enabled the locked rear end of my car to take complete charge. There wasn't enough weight on the front end to pull the rear end through the turn and the car continued in a straight line for the wall. I went for the brakes instantly, but it already was too late to avoid disaster. The only thing to do was brace myself against the steering wheel in an effort to keep from being crushed by the impact. I had made the steering wheel myself, cutting the spider and rim in one piece out of an Atkins circular saw and using moulded rubber on the rim. A 300-pound man could have stood on it without doing any damage. We hit with such terrific force that the right front wheel was smashed back under my feet and the steering wheel was bent right down to the instrument panel as I held my body away from it with every ounce of my strength.

Although the crash almost jarred my teeth loose, I wasn't hurt a bit.

Boots was sitting with Barney and Mabel Barbin, with whom we were staying, and the Victor Emanuels in a penthouse box on the roof of the grandstand. As soon as I had made a quick inspection of the damage, I joined her and watched the remainder of the crazy-quilt race from that point. As I had feared, the Americans didn't have a chance although Winn stuck close to the leaders until a rear axle broke with five laps to go. Foreign cars took the first five positions. The crowd, expecting much more speed than the course would permit, appeared to be bored to death. When Nuvolari's winning average of 65.99 miles per hour was announced over the public address system,

223

Victor Emanuel turned to me and exclaimed: "Gosh, I drove faster than that coming out here from New York."

CHAPTER 25

THE pay car was in sorry shape. I brought her back to Indianapolis on the trailer and rented space in McCoy's garage for the job of getting her ready to run again in the next "500."

Almost every time I had lost an Indianapolis race because of mechanical trouble—and on many other occasions, too—I had been able to put my finger right on the person who had been responsible for the failure. This time I would be my own mechanic and there would be no one to blame but myself if I failed.

I filled out my set of tools, bought a welding outfit and cut off the frame where it was badly mangled on the right side. When I got it back together, the front end wasn't as smooth and beautiful as when Steve had done the job. It clearly showed the work of an amateur. But one thing I had done was make everything "hell for strong," as Art Chevrolet used to say.

I had taken the engine down to Karl Kizer at his Century Tire Company and we had gone through that baby as though our lives depended upon its performance. The new rules limited fuel strictly to the type of commercial gasoline sold at regular corner service stations and this presented quite a problem. In racing terminology, commercial gasoline is a "hot" fuel. Extreme care had to be taken in order to reduce the possibility of burned pistons and other mechanical trouble likely to develop because of the increased heat generated in the engine

224

at high speed. In all prior races it had been possible for us to use considerable benzol in our fuel mixtures to minimize this danger.

We finally succeeded in getting the engine to run perfectly except when we wanted to shut it off. Then the commercial fuel would pre-ignite because of internal heat. The engine would kick and buck and keep right on trying to run even without any spark. In order to kill it we had to put the car in gear, set the brakes and let out the clutch. Such procedure tears the heart out of a man who really loves engines because he understands the stresses and strains imposed under those conditions. But we had no alternative. And our only consolation was that everyone else was faced with the same problem.

A lot of work remained to be done when I shifted my base of operations to the garage area of the Speedway in May. And the only way to accomplish it was to go on the night shift. During the day, there were too many interruptions by friends and sightseers. I made a practice of working late at night and then not showing up at the track until around noon the next day. I had the best-lighted garage in the world. Gene Genaro of the CAA, had managed to capture an airport beacon light for me and it was so bright you could read a newspaper by it up in the north turn, almost a mile away.

Jigger Johnson, who had ridden in the winning car with Louie Schneider in 1931, was to be my riding mechanic. Jigger was a great guy to have around, because of his terrific sense of humor, but I didn't let even him do any of the work on the car. I had hired a boy for sixteen dollars a week to wash parts. If he washed a part, and I handed it back to him, he was to wash it again without any argument. Under no conditions was he to put any part on the car or even touch it.

I was getting things pretty well organized, but was running out of money a few days before the start of time trials, when Frank White of the Burd Piston Ring Company walked into the garage.

"Do you think you can set a new qualifying record Saturday?" he asked, after the usual preliminaries.

"I know damn well I can if it's not too windy," I replied.

"I believe you'll do it, too," he answered. "And if you do it with Burd rings in the car I'll pay you seven hundred and fifty dollars."

That sounded like a good deal, so I walked over to the work bench and picked up a set of Perfect Circle rings such as I had been using.

"If you've got a set as good as these I'll put 'em in," I said.

He brought them in the following day and as soon as I could get the car back together I started to run some fast practice laps under the tutelage of Leon Duray. The record at which I would be shooting had been set by Leon almost ten years earlier when he had qualified his Miller Special at 122.391 miles an hour for the 1928 race, with one lap at 124.018. Since then, the track had been improved considerably and, after taking his advice to "quit trying so hard and let the car do it," I ran several unofficial laps at 125 and "buttoned it up."

Usually, when qualifying, I waited until late in the day to make my attempt because the wind often subsided at dusk. This time, however, the forecast wasn't particularly favorable for the late afternoon and I was anxious to get my hands on that extra cash. There didn't seem to be any point in waiting until the last minute. As things turned out, it was well that I didn't wait, too.

I signalled for the green flag after two warm-up laps and completed the required twenty-five miles at an average speed of 122.751 without difficulty of any kind. But a few minutes after I had pocketted the $750 check, Wild Bill Cummings broke my new record with an average of 123.445 to win the pole. I didn't even see him do it. By that time, even before my engine had cooled off, I was tearing it down in my garage to make sure everything was all right. I spent the next two nights examining every part of the car, using a magnifying glass on many occasions to look for tiny flaws and little abrasive spots. Then I put her together again and went back out on the

226

track to run a few laps in order to make certain that I still had the perfect combination.

In those days, it wasn't necessary for cars to pull behind the pit wall while making minor adjustments during the practice period. I stopped to check the color of my spark plugs and pulled up immediately behind a car which was being worked on, about a hundred feet south of the entrance from the track to the garage area. I had just unbuckled the hood of my car when someone yelled "look out" and almost everyone tried to scramble over the pit wall.

Car No. 66 (I never did like "upside down numbers" like that, or 88 or 99), with Overton Phillips driving, had broken a crank shaft just north of the starting line and was spinning in our direction—completely out of control. By the time I realized what was happening, I didn't have time to get over the wall if I had tried. But the spinning car missed me and my "pay car" by about six inches, smashing into the one ahead. O. C. Rhode of the Champion Spark Plug Company and Tony Caccia, who had been working on it, were caught in the crash. Rhode and George Warford, a spectator in the pit area, were killed.

It was a horrible experience. Rhode was a close friend of mine and I still can close my eyes and see every detail of that crash exactly as it happened, but no race driver would be in the business very long if he permitted himself to brood over such things.

Race day morning was clear and bright. By eight o'clock, the sun was as warm as it normally is at ten. It was going to be a scorcher. While my crew was getting things arranged in the pit, I started to check the refueling equipment and discovered that we didn't have the right gauge. I had asked my step-father, Charlie Morgan, to bring the gauge from the oxygen tank of my welding outfit. But he had brought the acetylene gauge by mistake. The one I needed was at home, nine or ten miles from the track, with the race scheduled to start in a little more than an hour.

At that moment the top of my head felt as if it was ready to explode. There isn't a good driver in the world who doesn't become extremely tense and irritable as race time approaches. I'm no exception. As soon as Charlie and Art Sims realized what was wrong, they took off while I still was blowing off steam. Even with the help of a sympathetic motorcycle policeman, whom they recruited on the way, it's difficult to understand how they managed to get through all of the race-day traffic and return before the race got under way. But they made it with several minutes to spare and I really breathed a sigh of relief when Art finally got the proper gauge installed. Ford Moyer and Pem Cornelius also deserve a lot of credit for the perfect management of my pit during the race. No one ever kept a driver better informed concerning his relative position than they did that day.

Everyone expected Louie Meyer's race record of 109 miles an hour to be broken. Captain Eddie Rickenbacker was on record in newspaper interviews with a prediction of 112 miles an hour. Some of the more optimistic members of the racing fraternity were talking about 115. After taking every possible factor into consideration, I decided that anyone who could average 113.5 for the full distance should finish in front of the pack. That's the goal I set for myself, which meant that I would have to run at about 116 to offset the time lost on pit stops.

There was good reason to believe Jimmy Snyder and a couple of the other boys would run even faster during the early stages. Snyder, especially, was sure to go like a bomb from the instant the starting flag dropped. He had qualified faster than both Cummings and I, with a brand-new six-cylinder supercharged car designed by Art Sparks for Joe Thorne. He was back in nineteenth position in the starting lineup only because he had not been ready to qualify on either of the first two days of time trials. But he had experienced a lot of piston trouble during the preparatory period and I felt certain he wouldn't be able to go the route.

Herb Ardinger, who had earned the outside position in the front row, jumped into the lead on the first turn. Snyder came charging up through the pack as expected and took the lead

228

during the third lap. Louie Meyer also was running ahead of me. But I overtook Meyer and Ardinger during the first fifty miles and was running in second place—about twenty seconds behind Snyder—when a broken transmission put him on the sidelines for the remainder of the day. That put me in the lead with only twenty-six laps completed (sixty-five miles) and I increased my advantage until I had gained a lead of a full lap or more on everyone except Ralph Hepburn before making my first pit stop at the end of seventy-four laps. Hep zoomed into first place just as I pulled out of the pit but I passed him about ten minutes later to take command again.

The heat of the sun was becoming almost unbearable and I was content to run only fast enough to discourage Hep from making any attempt to challenge me for the lead. He tailed me for more than twenty laps. Then, on the verge of heat exhaustion, and with both hands blistered, he pulled into the pit and turned his car over to Bob Swanson. The change was made swiftly and when I had to make my second pit stop on the 130th lap, Swanson took first place in Hep's car. Ted Horn moved into the No. 2 spot before I was running again. From here on, however, it looked like smooth sailing for me. I had all of the fuel and rubber I needed for the remainder of the afternoon, but Swanson and Horn still had their last pit stops to make.

Horn stopped first, on the 146th lap, and I was in second place. Swanson stopped on the 163rd lap, turning the car back to Hepburn, and I was back in the lead. With only thirty-five laps to go, I had a margin of almost two full minutes on Hep and Horn was twenty-five seconds farther back.

"This time you've got it in the bag," I told myself. "Just take it easy." I backed off the throttle slightly on the backstretch and took a good look at the gauges on my instrument panel. Everything appeared to be all right, but as I went into the next turn I noticed that the oil gauge dropped almost to zero. I eased off immediately and it came back to normal as I straightened out for the main stretch. Then it dropped again on the south turn and I realized suddenly I was almost out of oil. The supply was so negligible that centrifugal force on the turns carried what little oil remained away from the pickup valve. At 5,000 rpm, the engine was making a lot of revolutions on each turn without a drop of lubrication.

I had time for a pit stop without losing the lead, but the rules did not permit adding oil after the race was once under way. The only course open was to try to nurse the car through the last 30-odd laps and I thanked God for the lead I had managed to build up. Hepburn was so far back that he certainly would have no intention of trying to catch me this late in the race, unless he discovered I was in difficulty. I had to alter my driving tactics, however, in order to conserve what little oil remained. Running wide open down both long straightaways and coasting through the turns, I must have looked like a novice. I didn't shut off at the end of the straightaways until the very last second and that caused me to do a lot of "fish-tailing."

The boys in the pits must have thought the sun finally was getting to me, too, because a couple of laps later they put the word FRAME on my blackboard. Thinking that I was near exhaustion, they had lined up Fred Frame to stand by as a relief driver. When I saw the word FRAME, however, the first thing that flashed into my mind was that something was wrong with the frame of my car which I had repaired following the accident at Roosevelt Raceway. I nudged Jigger and pointed toward the right front side of the car, asking him in sign language to take a look. With a puzzled expression on his face, he did nothing but shrug his shoulders and sit there. It was useless to try to make him hear me, so I continued to point in every possible manner. I pointed over the cowling and down toward the right. Then I pointed under the cowling and over toward the right. Suddenly, as I cut off the power to coast through the northeast turn, while still pointing, he grinned and nodded his head as a signal that he understood. At the same instant, before I had any idea of what he intended to do, he grabbed for the hand brake between us and gave it a jerk.

How in the world we managed to get through the turn without cracking up, I'll never be able to tell you. We skittered and slid and broadsided for almost two hundred feet before I was able to release the brake and get the car under control. I gave him a good hard elbow right in the ribs to discourage any further action of that kind and then took a look at my right rear tire. Some of the tread had been torn off and the breaker strip was showing all of the way around.

Now I really was in trouble. I still had twenty laps to go. My oil supply was all but exhausted. My right rear tire was ready to blow at any instant. My tired arms felt as if they were ready to drop off. My right foot was completely numb. I wasn't even sure it still was attached to my body. There was no feeling in it at all. But more important than anything else was the fact that Hep's crew was sure to notice the condition of my tire. For the rest of the race he would be charging at full throttle.

I asked my pit for a position check and they gave it to me on the next lap. The figure 1:54, with an arrow pointing in the opposite way I was travelling, told me I had a lead of exactly 114 seconds—about a lap and a half. Some quick mental arithmetic showed me that I could run approximately six seconds a lap slower than Hep without losing the lead. I quit driving so deep into the turns, in order to relieve the worn tire of as much strain as possible, and Hepburn began to close in immediately. He cut my lead to one full lap, with eleven laps to go, and roared on in an effort to wipe out my rapidly dwindling advantage. As he pulled out of my vision, however, I knew exactly where I stood.

During all of the practice period, Hep never had turned a lap at more than 120 miles an hour. His qualifying average under perfect conditions had been a fraction below 119. Even if he could duplicate that effort for the last eleven laps, I could finish in front by running 111 miles an hour. It worked out perfectly, too.

When I got the white flag, signifying one lap to go, I still had a lead of about two hundred feet. That was enough to permit me to get through the south turn ahead of him. I could

231

run wide open without too much danger on the backstretch and thus postpone the crucial showdown until the very last turn. Coming out of the final turn I swung as wide as possible to ease the pressure on the tire and give the oil a chance to get back to the pickup valve a little quicker. Hep dove for the opening on the rail instantly. I could see the front end of his car out of the corner of my left eye. I think I waited until the oil pressure showed again, but I'm not sure. I do know that I planted the accelerator as far down as it would go and held my breath until we crossed the finish line more than 2,000 feet away.

The official timer's tape showed that I beat Hep to the wire by 2.16 seconds, setting a new race record of 113.580 mph. I closed the throttle immediately to save what was left of the engine if any damage had been done. As I coasted into the south turn, Hep roared by me like a freight train passing a tramp. Then it suddenly dawned on me that he still could win the race if someone had made a mistake and given us the checkered flag too soon. That's the reason every winner runs an extra lap or two and it was evident Hep was hoping for just such an error.

There was no time now to think about oil pressure and worn tires. He already was about a hundred feet ahead and I had my work cut out for me. It seemed to me that he charged into the north turn harder than at any time during the entire race, but I was right on his tail again by that time. Everything held together as we zoomed through the turn, only inches apart, and I sucked him under again on the dash down the home stretch to the finish line. Actually the extra lap had not been necessary. There had been no error in scoring. But I certainly felt better for having made it.

Boots and Mother were on hand to greet me, along with the usual newspaper, radio and newsreel men, when I rolled into the Victory Lane "bull pen." It was customary for the winner to perch on the back of the seat for pictures and interviews. But I was too exhausted to scoot up there. What's more, my right foot hurt like the very blazes of hell and I could hardly move it. Jigger helped me climb up on the back of the seat, however, and I wound up the interviews as quickly as possible while the boys were getting their pictures.

The foot was giving me so much pain that I wanted to get to the field hospital immediately. But when I tried to stand, I knew I never would be able to make the trip alone. A couple of the fellows finally took me there with a "shoulder carry" such as football players use to help their injured team mates off of the gridiron. They lifted me up on one of the examining tables and Dr. Allen removed my right shoe and sock. When he pulled off my sock, some of the meat on the right side of my foot came off with it. The gruff old Doc, wearing a white beret and chewing on a big cigar, looked at it for a full minute in absolute silence.

Then he grunted and said, "Say, you've really got a hell of a looking foot here." With that, the hot ash fell from the tip of his cigar and landed right on the burned flesh. If I hadn't been so damn tired, I probably would have socked him. Actually, I believe I didn't even open my mouth to object. He brushed off the ashes with a piece of cotton, applied some ointment and bandaged it with instructions to stay off of it for several days. The burn was caused by the fact that I had braced my foot against the side of the transmission in order to hold the throttle steady throughout the race. The transmission got as hot as a grill and the side of my foot was cooked as tender as any beefsteak.

I should have gone straight home. But first I wanted to stop at the Gilmore accessory booth in the garage area for a little bit of celebration and refreshment. The boys carried me all of the way and helped me get comfortable on a box by the door. An eight-foot, wire mesh fence with three strands of barbed wire on top, surrounded the area. There wasn't any danger of being bothered by strangers. Before I had time to relax, however, Louie Schneider walked up to the fence, which was about thirty feet away. I couldn't hear exactly what he said. But he made some sneering remark about being a "lucky so-and-so." As far as I was concerned, our earlier feud had been forgotten completely, but Louie apparently still bore a grudge and his "smart crack" touched me off like a skyrocket. I jumped off the box, bad foot and all. I went over the fence like a monkey, landed on the other side of it and hit Louie right on the nose faster than I can tell about it. It would have been a tough job to get over that fence any time, even when in good condition. But the incident provides some idea of how determined and resourceful a person can become as the result of being keyed up for more than four hours of competition such as I had experienced.

When things quieted down a bit, I went back to the hospital for something to stop the pain in my foot. On the way my friends, who were carrying me again, cracked off about my weight. Out of curiosity, I climbed on the hospital scales and they registered only 127 pounds despite the fact I had taken on a considerable amount of liquids during the last thirty minutes. I had started the race weighing 138.

Boots picked me up in the car at the hospital and drove me home. A lot of our friends already were there to offer congratulations and dip their noses into the family cup. But the pain in my foot was almost unbearable by this time. The pills at the hospital hadn't done a bit of good. After I had joined the crowd for one drink, Boots didn't have much trouble convincing me that I belonged in bed. She tucked me in without any argument and the gang was considerate enough to leave very shortly. But even with peace and quiet—as tired as I was—I couldn't get to sleep because of the pain. The bandage seemed to be too tight, so I removed it. That made it worse. Even the light refreshing breeze from the open window seemed to increase the pain. I sat up in bed until after midnight, with my hands cupped around my foot to shield it from every possible source of irritation. I thought I would lose my mind any instant.

About one o'clock in the morning, I happened to think of my old friend, Wayne Eubank. Boots got him on the phone and told him how I was suffering. He climbed out of bed, stopped at his drugstore for some powerful sleeping pills and came out to the house to see what he could do for me. He gave

234

me as many as he thought I could stand and they helped some. Although they never did put me to sleep that night, they enabled me to get a little rest in preparation for the Victory Dinner the following evening.

Each driver had been given two tickets. After winning, I had turned my pair over to Bob and Margaret Blair, who were my guests from California. Surely I could get two more for Boots and Mother, I thought. But the place was packed. There wasn't a spare ticket available at any price. Finally, the management squeezed in a couple of extra chairs and my worries were ended.

As Pop Myers passed out the checks, it was a wonderful feeling to step up and collect prizes totaling more than $35,000. But the one thing about the entire affair which I recall with particular clarity, was the presentation of a beautiful bouquet of roses from the Boy Scouts of Indianapolis. I'll always remember my scouting days with a great deal of pleasure and appreciation.

CHAPTER 26

CARL STOCKHOLM still was promoting races in the Chicago area. Even after my decision of the previous year, to quit dirt track competition entirely, I had promised Carl I would race for him if I ever won "the big one." His next event was scheduled the following week end and I entered as I had promised. I thought surely my foot would heal sufficiently in a few days for me to drive in some of the sprint races on the program, but the doctor refused to give me permission.

235

"If you do anything to cause an infection," he warned, "we probably will have to amputate."

I sent my car up to Chicago anyway, so that someone else could drive it, and Boots drove me up on the day before the race. We had dinner with the Stockholms that evening. His promotional problems, of course, were the chief topic of conversation and his greatest concern seemed to be the selection of an announcer for his public address system to keep the fans informed of what was happening.

"Why don't you handle the mike for me tomorrow?" he asked.

"I don't know anything about the duties of an announcer," I told him.

"That doesn't make any difference," he said. "All you have to do is introduce the drivers and keep the crowd posted as to what position they are running in during the race. That ought to be easy for you."

I finally agreed, rather reluctantly, and had the time of my life the next afternoon. It was fun, kidding the boys over the PA system. I even took a friendly dig at Carl by explaining to the fans that the track was a little dustier than usual because the promoter was in the cleaning business and was trying to get some new customers. During the various sprint races it often was possible for me to tell the fans, in advance, what to watch for and everyone seemed to enjoy my comments. Carl offered me a regular announcer's job and a couple of similar propositions followed from other promoters, but I didn't have time to accept.

Despite the American public's apparent lack of interest in European-type racing, Steve Hannagan and Joe Copps were beating the drums again for a 300-mile event at Roosevelt Raceway on July 3. The course had been altered to make it faster by eliminating some of the turns and I wanted another crack at it even though the European entrants still had a tremendous advantage because of their superior equipment for that type of competition. I was hopeful of getting a ride in one of the better cars from the Continent, so that I could match

236

driving skill with them on an equal basis. With that idea in mind, I left the "pay car" in Indianapolis when Boots and I headed East, but I might as well have wished for the moon.

The Auto-Union and Mercedes-Benz cars from Germany were the class of the field with the Italian Alfa Romeos and Maseratis also rated as far superior to American cars because of better brakes and transmission. All of these factory teams, however, were closed corporations. The Germans didn't even want an American to look under the hood, let alone drive one of the cars. The only European cars available were the older Italian models which had been discarded in favor of new ones.

I was particularly interested in getting a good car because the Roosevelt management had posted a special prize fund for American drivers to encourage their participation. Rex Mays and Joe Thorne had managed to get lined up on two of the 1936 Alfas. The Martin brothers of New York and Enzio Fermonti had purchased a couple of the older Maseratis. I finally got a chance at the Fermonti car when he spun it in practice and decided to pass up the race.

The car was no jewel by any manner of means. In fact, it was almost worn out. But it was faster on that particular course than any of the American cars. The only trouble was that it began to come apart as the race progressed. Finally the exhaust manifold broke. At any other track I would have been through for the day, because AAA rules specified that no car could compete unless its exhaust header was intact and all exhaust fumes carried aft of the cockpit.

I expected to be flagged off the course at the completion of each lap, but nothing happened. Apparently the rules for this event were different. At any rate, I continued to run despite the heat from the engine and the fumes which smelled strong enough to almost push me out of the cockpit. At the finish, I was trailing in eighth position—not very good, but better than I could have done in my own car on that course.

Bernd Rosemeyer was the winner in a German Auto-Union at a speed of 82.25 miles an hour. Dick Seamen, who had been pressing him to the limit before being forced to stop for fuel late in the race, trailed by fifty seconds in a Mercedes-Benz. Rex Mays was third at the wheel of the Italian entry which Nuvolari had driven the previous year. Foreign cars also placed fourth, fifth and sixth.

The day prior to the race, I was sitting inside my garage with several friends when one of the newer Maseratis was pushed into view.

"If I had a car like that," I exclaimed, "even though you may regard it as second-rate in comparison with the German entries here, I'd win the next 500-mile race with it."

Mike Boyle, an auto racing enthusiast of long standing who had owned a number of race cars, spoke up quickly.

"If I can get one, will you drive it for me?" he asked.

"I will if it's half as fast as I think it is," I said.

"I wouldn't want to give up my pay car for something else that isn't as good," I added; "but if I don't like the Maserati, I'll guarantee to get a good man to drive it for you."

Boyle instructed Cotton Henning to see what could be done about buying one of the Italian cars and it was delivered a few months later. I went out to inspect it as soon as it arrived.

There sat the prettiest little car ever entered in a 500-mile race. But it was a 91 cubic-inch job and the bottom dropped out of my hopes as far as winning with it was concerned. It had never entered my mind that the Maserati factory might be building two or three new models that year with engines of different sizes—or that Cotton would even consider a "91." But there it sat, bought and paid for.

In my opinion, it simply wasn't strong enough for an Indianapolis "500." It would be like pitting a middleweight against a heavyweight in a boxing match. But I was willing to withhold judgment until we could give it a thorough test.

After Cotton had checked everything, we fired up the engine for a few warm-up laps. It seemed to be performing perfectly and finally I cut two or three laps at top speed. The best I could do was 118 miles an hour, which would be good enough to get the car into the race, but not enough to win, taking into consideration the usual pit stops and race-day traffic.

Even before the Maserati had been delivered, because of my agreement with Mike, I had obtained assurance from Mauri Rose that he would drive either the Maserati or my "pay car," depending on my own decision. I explained the situation to both of them immediately and Rose was signed on the Boyle car.

During the entire winter of 1937–38, I was like the proverbial kitten on a tin roof. Working for the Perfect Circle and Ethyl Corporations, while trying to get the pay car ready in Ford Moyer's little garage behind the Indianapolis Star building, didn't give me much time for rest or relaxation. Moyer actually did most of the work with considerable assistance from Karl Kizer, whose help had been an important factor in my 1937 victory. Cotton Henning always was willing to lend a hand, too, whenever I called on him.

I fought a cold all winter long and wound up with a good case of the flu in the early spring. By race time I was in sorry shape, physically. Although the spirit was willing the body was a little on the weak side. Even in this condition, however, I felt fairly certain I could win again.

My "board of strategy" consisted of Pem Cornelius, Bill Hunt, Ford Moyer, Kizer and several sports writers familiar with racing problems. The consensus of opinion was that an average speed of 115 miles an hour, including pit stops, would be good enough to lead the field home. That meant an actual racing average of about 117 miles an hour in traffic would be necessary to offset the time lost in the pits.

I doubt if I have ever run any other race as close to the schedule I had set for myself. But it wasn't quite good enough. Rex Mays, Jimmy Snyder and Floyd Roberts waged a terrific battle for the early lead while I stayed within striking distance in the pay car—never in front but always among the first ten. For a while it looked as if my strategy would be successful as Mays and then Snyder dropped out of the running because of supercharger trouble.

I was right on schedule after making my only pit stop at about 300 miles, but still in sixth place. I continued to improve my position steadily and finally moved into the No. 2 spot. Roberts was going like a bomb, however, and it was evident that I didn't have a chance to overtake him unless he ran into trouble, too. That's the way we finished. I did the task I had set for myself, averaging 115.580, but it wasn't good enough. Roberts beat me to the finish line by almost three laps for a well deserved victory with a new race record of 117.200. Chet Miller was a close third with Ted Horn next. Rose, in the little Maserati, failed to finish, despite a superb job of driving which had enabled him to gain fifth place before being forced to the sidelines.

It was a terrible disappointment, but no one ever deserved to win more than Roberts did that year. Financially, because I had driven my own car, I was much better off than if I had won the race for some other car owner. My earnings, combined with the salary I was receiving for my off-the-track activities, would make 1938 a very profitable year.

During the following summer and fall months, the Perfect Circle Corporation kept me as busy as any one man could possibly be. I was working so hard and traveling so much, in fact, that I felt I was about ready to fall apart. I finally reached the point where I couldn't even drink a glass of water without burping. Boots was accompanying me on all of these trips and worrying about my health. One evening, while I was experiencing the usual indigestion symptoms after a dinner in New York, she told me how silly she thought it was for me to continue at such a fast pace. In ten minutes she sold me on the idea of taking a much needed vacation.

We were scheduled to report back to the Perfect Circle factory in Hagerstown, Indiana, a few days later. I explained our plans to the Teeter boys and Theron Bradshaw, my immediate boss. They agreed that a little rest would be good for me, but weren't too happy when I told them I had no idea of when I would be ready to get back on the job.

240

"When I finally relax," I said, "I might enjoy the experience so much that I'll want to stay that way."

"You'll feel better in a few weeks," said Bradshaw. "When you do, let us know."

Boots and I spent several days in Indianapolis with my mother and stepfather before heading for California. Our first stop was Los Angeles, to visit my former business partner, Bob Blair, and his wife, Margaret. Bob and several of my other flying pals were "teed off" about the CAA regulations requiring everyone who flew for hire to have a commercial rating. The examination was reported to be extremely difficult. This was a new challenge, which came as a change of pace for my strenuous activities of recent months, and I decided to try for a commercial license immediately. With an armload of aviation books on aircraft design, engines, navigation, meteorology and CAA regulations, I headed for Palm Springs with Boots.

For three weeks we had a perfectly wonderful time in the sun, chasing jack rabbits on horseback, swimming, diving and playing badminton and deck tennis. In between these various types of physical exertion, I crammed for the CAA exams and presented myself at the administration building in Los Angeles as confident as anyone could possibly be. When I finished, almost four hours later, I was quaking in my boots and not the least bit sure of having passed it.

As I walked out of the building, several Army and Navy officers were watching preparations for the take-off of America's newest light bomber—so new the Douglas Aircraft Corporation had not yet delivered it to the government for official tests. It was a real thrill to watch this marvelous twin-engine creation climb into the heavens with almost unbelievable speed. I suddenly had the urge to go aloft, too, and I borrowed one of Blair's small planes.

While I was getting ready to land, about twenty minutes later, I watched the bomber zoom to 3,000 feet and "buzz" the field at about 100 feet as it pulled out of a power dive. Then, apparently to show the plane's climbing ability at half-power, the pilot—John Cable—shut off one engine as he started to regain altitude. The ringside seat I had for these maneuvers was perfect and I circled once more to watch the demonstration. Suddenly the left wing began to drop. The plane went into a steep vertical bank and then into a flat spin. In a matter of seconds, the plane was going through some of the wildest aerial gyrations I have ever seen. The pilot started his second engine again, but by this time his task was hopeless. At 500 feet he climbed out of the cockpit and jumped. I could see him jerk the rip cord of his parachute, but it failed to open. His body plummeted to earth like a bomb with a white streamer attached to it. The plane crashed into a cluster of unoccupied automobiles in a nearby parking lot and burst into flames. Paul Chenidlin, Cable's only companion on the flight, had been trapped in the cabin. Two mechanics braved the fire, however, and pulled him from the wreckage with no major injuries other than a broken leg.

It was a sickening thing to see. I circled the wreckage a couple of times while regaining control of my emotions and then landed to join the most depressed group of people I had ever encountered in my entire life. Most of them had known the pilot well. During the remainder of the day, no one could think or talk about anything except the accident. Blair even forgot to tell me, until the following morning, that CAA officials had asked him to let me know I had passed the commercial rating examination. All that remained for me to do, in order to get my commercial license, was to prove my ability on a special test flight and this was easy. A couple of weeks later, after getting a letter from Cotton Henning, Boots and I returned to Indianapolis.

CHAPTER **27**

IMMEDIATELY after the 1938 race I had held a "council of war" with Boyle and Henning. The misunderstanding concerning the type of Maserati I wanted for the "500" had been ironed out and Mike had instructed Cotton to go to Italy personally in order to bring back a new 183 cubic-inch car. The letter from Cotton explained that he was on his way. "I'm leaving the truck in New York while I cross the pond," he had written. "As soon as I know the exact date of my arrival back in the States I'll cable you at Indianapolis and you can meet me at the dock." The cable came about a month after I had returned to Indianapolis and I made the trip to New York by plane.

The car he uncovered at Customs was all I had hoped it would be. It looked like it would run forever—and fast. I was so pleased, I probably acted like a little boy with a new red wagon as we loaded the Maserati on the truck. According to Cotton, all I talked about during the first part of the homeward journey was how we were going to annihilate the Indianapolis track. Cotton certainly held up his part of the conversation, however. As I recall it, I didn't have much chance to talk because he was so busy telling me all about his trip and how the Italian workmen did everything.

A little before midnight, we were coasting down one of the long Pennsylvania hills at a pretty good clip. All of a sudden the darndest racket started anyone ever heard. I looked back quickly and saw sparks shooting in all directions. Running as fast as we were, down grade, it took several hundred feet to stop. When we finally had a chance to see what was wrong, the thought of what might have happened gave both of us the cold chills. The truck's spare gasoline tank, full of fuel, had broken from its moorings. Still connected to the truck by the gas line, we had dragged the tank along the highway and it was only a question of a few more seconds before friction would have worn a hole in the metal and set the stage for a really expensive fire. We probably would have been unable to save a thing. It was two very grateful guys who lashed the tank securely into place before proceeding on their way.

Even though the temperature was below freezing, I had hope of fueling the car as soon as we reached Indianapolis and doing a couple of fast practice laps on the Speedway. The newspapers had carried stories about the car on the day it arrived in New York and quite a reception committee was on hand when we pulled up to the garage. Cotton recruited everyone in sight to help us unload and climbed up on the truck with me to supervise the operation. I looked down and noticed the bed of the truck was covered with water.

"Where did that come from?" I demanded; and I could see the color drain from Cotton's face before he answered,

"I don't know, but I'll bet I can make a good guess. Don't say a damn thing more about it until we get rid of everybody."

With as much help as we had, it didn't take long to unload. Apparently no one had heard our little conversation about the water and we didn't have much trouble clearing the garage of onlookers when we told them we had no intention of running the car immediately.

We locked the garage doors as soon as the last of the hangers-on had left. Cotton removed the hood and our worst fears were realized. Both cylinder blocks of the straight-8 engine were cracked. The Maserati mechanics had fired up the engine for Cotton before the car had left the factory—to show him that it was in good running condition. They had neglected to drain the water after the demonstration, however, and it had frozen during the latter part of the voyage or on our cross-country trip from New York.

Although Cotton had ordered spare blocks when he took de-

244

livery of the car, it was unlikely they would arrive for five or six weeks via normal channels. They had to be cast and machined in the Maserati factory before they could be shipped. He cabled Italy immediately, requesting that new blocks be forwarded at the earliest possible moment by plane as well as ship—as a safeguard against any possible disaster which might delay their arrival—and we received them in ample time, thank God. We installed them as quickly as possible and the whole incident was one of the best kept secrets I have ever known. Only our immediate crew was "in" on the story.

Cotton cranked up the engine to be sure everything was all right and let it run for a few minutes in the garage, using methyl alcohol for fuel as the factory had recommended. Then we shut it off and I called Mike Boyle in Chicago.

"We're all ready to run," I told Mike, "and if you can get down here tomorrow I'll cut a couple of fast ones for you."

"I'll be there before noon," promised Mike.

He walked into the garage about eleven o'clock the next morning and spent several minutes examining the car very carefully. Then he said,

"Let me hear her run."

"Un momento, senor," replied Cotton, rather flippantly.

I turned the switch and he gave the crank a quarter-turn, expecting the engine to take hold immediately as it had the previous day. Nothing happened. He tried again and soon we were taking turns at the crank, working until our arms gave out. We stopped long enough to check everything and tried again with no better results. We were still trying to start it when the sun went down that evening. Mike was on his way back to Chicago in disgust.

His parting shot was, "If you ever get it running, give me a ring."

During the day we had done everything—absolutely everything—to get the car started except change spark plugs. We had no reason to suspect them of causing the trouble because they were brand new and had fired perfectly the previous afternoon. The next morning, however, Cotton decided to start from scratch and the first thing he did was put in new plugs. Then he gave the crank a quarter-turn and the engine roared into life immediately. It sounded perfectly wonderful. Each of us breathed a tremendous sigh of relief. During the next five minutes we started that engine and shut it off at least a half-dozen times. Then I phoned Mike again.

"If you're sure it will run this time," he said, "I'll be down as fast as I can get there."

"It'll run all right," I promised.

We started the engine again, as soon as I had hung up the receiver, just to make certain. I also wanted to get a little more familiar with the car before Mike arrived and I took it out on the track for several laps at moderate speed. It was all I could do to resist the temptation to "cut a fast one" before Mike arrived. Driving that car was really fun, but I finally coasted into the pits and cut the switch.

Five minutes later, Cotton said, "Let's be sure." He gave it a quarter-turn. It started immediately and we knocked off for a sandwich and coffee while waiting for Mike.

He reached the track early in the afternoon and, without any preliminaries, instructed us to get her going.

Cotton gave the crank a quarter-turn and nothing happened. He tried again with the same results.

"It looks like I made another trip down here for nothing!" exclaimed Mike.

"Just give us another minute or two," said Cotton, giving me a big wink. "I forgot to change plugs."

I still didn't know what it was all about—and I doubt if Cotton did, either, at that particular moment. But he slipped in another new set of plugs, twisted the crank and we were off. I warmed up the engine for a couple of laps and then did four in a row at better than 127 miles an hour before coming in.

"That's good enough for me," said Mike. "Put her in the barn." And he went back to Chicago. We rolled the car back to the garage and then put on our thinking caps in an effort to solve the mystery.

It had to be the plugs which were causing the trouble, but

both sets we had taken from the car appeared to be perfect at first glance. It was only after a very close inspection that we discovered an almost invisible film on the electrodes. Subsequent tests proved this film materialized about eighteen or twenty minutes after the engine was turned off, although nothing of that nature developed while the engine was running. As soon as the film formed, it served as a conductor of electricity and caused the plugs to act the same as if they had filled with oil.

We checked with the Maserati factory and learned that this happened only when methanol—another name for methyl alcohol—was used as fuel. With this knowledge, we rigged a little tank under the hood for a small supply of gasoline and connected it to the carburetor so that we could switch from methanol to gasoline for a few minutes to clean the plugs before turning off the engine. From then on, our starting problem was a thing of the past. To this day, however, I have never heard a satisfactory scientific explanation of the phenomenon.

As we continued preparations for the race, an oil leak developed in the rear main bearing. Cotton was reluctant to make a single unnecessary change in the car, however, and we finally agreed to install a six-gallon auxiliary oil tank rather than fool with the bearing. This was necessary because the rules of the race prevented any car from getting additional oil from the pit after the race was under way.

The front wheels of the Maserati also had a tendency to shimmy a bit when starting or stopping at speeds under sixty miles an hour, but it handled beautifully at racing speed and I didn't have the slightest doubt of my ability to win with it.

We qualified easily at 128.977 miles an hour. That put us on the outside of the front row, the ideal spot, in my opinion, because it's possible to go into the turn faster from that position. I said as much to some of my friends and the next thing I knew they were making wagers that I'd be out in front of the pack at the end of the first lap. Unlike most other sports, there never has been any real gambling in connection with a 500-mile race. But small, friendly wagers were not uncommon and now I was "on the spot" because I had opened my big mouth once too often. With the best car in the race, plus my favorite starting position, why shouldn't I take the lead immediately? At least that was their reasoning. As far as I was concerned, the only lap I was determined to lead was the last one—but I didn't want to let my friends down.

The Maserati differed from most of the American race cars in that it had four forward speeds. As we rounded into the main straightaway on the pace lap, the other boys shifted into high. I stayed in third and jumped down on the throttle with everything I had when we crossed the starting line. This gave me tremendous acceleration as I headed into the first turn, but the next few seconds were the busiest of my entire life.

Never before had I driven the Maserati with a full fuel tank. This time, with brand new tires as an added hazard, I had fifty-eight gallons of methanol aboard and that much fuel weighs approximately four hundred pounds. As I hit the turn, the back end of the car seemed to take complete charge and slid right out from under me. I don't know exactly what I did to avert disaster. But somehow—possibly by instinct and with a lot of help from "the Man Upstairs"—I managed to get the car straightened out before it could slide into the wall and cause the biggest pileup of cars in the history of championship racing. All of the way down the backstretch I thought of myself as being the world's biggest damn fool and I didn't even challenge Jimmy Snyder or Louie Meyer for the honor of winning the first lap. For one hundred miles the three of us ran almost nose-to-tail. Snyder had to stop for tires on the thirty-seventh lap and I managed to get around Meyer in time to take the lead as Jimmy coasted into his pit. I widened the gap to thirty seconds before making my own pit stop after sixty-nine laps. This put Meyer into the No. 1 position. But he had to stop, too, after four more laps. Rex Mays, who managed to go almost to the half-way mark before making a pit stop, took command temporarily. Then Snyder, coming up fast again, overtook him to regain the lead. When Mays stopped for tires and fuel, Meyer moved back into second place. I was right behind him at the 250-mile mark. Snyder's second pit stop gave Meyer the lead again, but he already was showing signs of tiring.

His car was an ill-handling brute compared to mine. He had to fight it around each turn while the Maserati was easing through them as if it was on rails. I was just ready to pass him —with the idea of picking up some additional lap prize money —when the yellow warning light flashed on as the result of a three-car crash which took the life of Floyd Roberts. I wasn't in a position to see exactly what happened, but I could tell the accident was a bad one as I cut inside the burning wreckage of Ralph Hepburn's car a few seconds later. Bob Swanson had replaced Ralph behind the wheel three laps earlier and had lost control of the car while coming out of the southeast turn, blocking the course directly in front of Roberts. When the cars collided, both burst into flames. Swanson was thrown out on the track and Roberts, still in his car, crashed through the outer guard rail to his death.

Chet Miller, close behind Roberts, swerved to the left in order to avoid hitting Swanson. Miller's car jumped the inside rail and turned over. Actually, I didn't know Roberts was involved at the time. I could see the Swanson and Miller cars, but Floyd's car had rolled down an enbankment and was out of my range of vision, although the smoke and flames from it were very much in evidence.

I received the bad news about Floyd when I made my second pit stop and it came as an awful blow to me. He was an honest, straightforward guy—the salt of the earth—with tremendous ability. We had been close friends for several years and I had gotten him his first chance to drive at Indianapolis for Earl Haskell in 1935.

I made my pit stop about a dozen laps ahead of schedule in order to take full advantage of racing rules, which require all cars to proceed at reduced speed under the yellow light. With only seventy-three more laps to go, I thought another full tank of fuel would carry me to the finish. When Meyer saw me in the pit, he did the same thing. His crew did the job a full minute faster than mine did, however, and he enjoyed a lead of sixty-eight seconds when both of us where running again. Now I really had my work cut out for me.

If his car had handled well, I probably never would have closed the gap, but he was experiencing more and more trouble on each trip around the course. I picked up as much as two seconds on some laps and finally caught him with seventeen laps to go—right on the main straightaway. He made a desperate bid to regain the lead on the very next turn, but got into a skid and tore the tread from his right front tire. The time required for him to limp the two miles to his pit and change the tire enabled me to gain a lead of more than two minutes. I needed every second of it, too, because eight laps later I suddenly realized I was running out of fuel.

I signaled frantically as I neared my pit. Cotton, moving as fast as I'd ever seen him move, dumped in a few gallons of the precious liquid and I was able to regain racing speed before Louie could overtake me. He was close enough, however, for one final effort to snatch the victory away from me. Like a true champion—bidding for an unprecedented fourth 500-mile title, instead of playing it safe for a sure second place—Louie refused to accept defeat. Three laps before the finish he barreled into the north turn at top speed, still trying to catch me, and spun. The car slid to a stop along the inside edge of the track, with Louie uninjured. It was his last race, but no competitor in any branch of sports ever reached the end of the championship trail with greater fighting spirit.

No one else was in a challenging position and I eased off the throttle during the last couple of laps with a lead of almost two minutes over Snyder. Cliff Bergere was another full lap behind and Ted Horn was fourth.

I didn't even feel tired as I made a couple of "safety" laps and headed for Victory Lane to face the sports writers, cameramen and radio commentators. In fact, the most important thing on my mind was the question of how Mauri Rose was doing in my pay car. As soon as I had signed to drive the Maserati, Rose had agreed to drive my car on a percentage basis

250

and I knew he had been doing a good job even though the car now was four years old.

There was a lot of noise and confusion as I coasted through the Victory Lane gates. The first close friend I saw was Joe Copps, who had succeeded Steve Hannagan as the Speedway's publicity chief.

"How's the pay car doing?" I shouted.

He cupped a hand to one ear and said "What?"

I repeated the question and got the same result, even though I was fairly certain he could hear me. It suddenly dawned on me that he didn't know what I meant when I called it the pay car. That was my own pet name for it and not many people knew it. So I got Joe's attention again and shouted: "How is Rose doing?"

"The last time I looked he was eighth," said Joe. That was good news, because I thought he would have trouble even finishing tenth against the many news cars in the race.

By the time I had managed to get that information, however, I'd brought the Maserati to a halt in the fenced-in enclosure and the press and radio boys were swarming around me. Boots was on hand to give me a kiss. Then we posed together for the newsreels and I took the car back to the garage. Unlike in 1937, this time I felt like a million dollars. I stayed up most of the night to celebrate and had a barrel of fun at our usual buffet supper for all of our friends.

CHAPTER 28

FOR many years the Firestone Tire & Rubber Company had been using the Indianapolis Motor Speedway as an outdoor laboratory. Its racing division specialized in building

251

tires which would stand up under the terrific heat and strain of a 500-mile race—a test which many experts regarded as being equal to 50,000 miles of ordinary highway driving. The experience gained in this manner enabled the company to keep ahead of the universal trend toward faster passenger cars.

Soon after the 1939 race, Firestone was ready to introduce a new type of tire-and-tube combination in the interest of greater safety in highway travel. Its engineers had designed a tire which minimized the hazards of a sudden blowout. Even when one of these did blow out, approximately half of the air was trapped for several minutes by a special cord-bound air chamber inside the inner tube, giving the driver ample time in which to reduce speed and maintain control of the vehicle.

To aid in the introduction of this product, I signed up to make a safety tour covering approximately half of the United States, demonstrating the tire and speaking at schools and luncheon clubs. The tour started in August at a rather moderate pace and was a lot of fun for a while. I described many of my racing experiences while giving my safety talk and I demonstrated the tires' extra safety qualities by blowing them out deliberately—at high speed—with the aid of dynamite caps placed in the casings.

Karl Kizer and I had formed the K and S Film Company earlier that year to make and sell movies of the race. I showed these films at most stops on the tour and the program was accepted so well that requests for my appearance began rolling into Firestone headquarters at a remarkable rate. According to the schedule arranged for me by Ralph Failor of Firestone, it was necessary to make three and four talks every day. It seemed as if everyone wanted to entertain us, too, and it was a tough job, "playing a new team" every night before moving on to the next stop on our crowded schedule. In order to get any rest at all, I finally turned our white Cadillac over to Failor and bought an airplane so that Boots and I could fly from one city to the next while the crew brought the equipment by road. If we kept one person from being seriously injured or killed, however, the effort was worth-while.

252

I've never ceased to be amazed by the high percentage of drivers who apparently fail to realize they can always keep out of trouble by doing two simple things. The individual who keeps his mind on his job when he is behind the wheel of his car—and who treats other drivers with the same common courtesy he would show them in his own home—isn't likely to be involved in any serious accident.

During the winter, I learned by the grapevine that Maserati was building a new car with four valves per cylinder and an increase of almost ten per cent in horsepower. That sounded to me like the hottest possible car for the "500" and I was interested in buying it. The only catch was that it might be eligible for only one Indianapolis race because Speedway officials had indicated they might change the specifications after the 1940 event. I didn't want to pay the price for a car which couldn't be used for at least two years. Eventually, the Speedway assured me the "specs" would remain the same for 1940 and 1941. By that time, the car had been purchased by a group of Argentine sporstmen for Raul Riganti and it was too late to order a duplicate one.

There was no choice for me to do anything but drive the same car which had carried me to victory the previous year. Remembering that I had "spread myself too thin" in 1938, I discontinued the safety tour in time to get myself in good condition. I even rigged up a steering wheel, mounted on a special frame with a hydraulic shock absorber, so that I could exercise at home in a manner which would strengthen my wrists and arms. I did a lot of actual driving at the track during the month of May, too, to make sure that I would be ready for the chance to become the first man in Speedway history to win two consecutive races.

Two weeks before the race, Riganti arrived with the new Maserati and it was everything I had expected. It made me sick to see it in the hands of someone else. Two other Maseratis, similar to mine, were entered by the Frenchmen, Rene Dreyfus and Rene Lebegue. Additional international flavor

253

was provided by two Alfa Romeos with Chet Miller and Al Miller in the cockpits.

The Frenchmen encountered all of their bad luck before the race. One was forced out of the starting lineup by faster cars, after it had qualified. The other, which had qualified fast enough to assure it of a starting position, broke a connecting rod and tore a hole in both sides of the crankcase. Because the cars were identical, however, it was possible to use the good engine as a replacement for the damaged one and the two drivers took turns in the car during the race to take tenth place. Riganti experienced more trouble in getting accustomed to the track and crashed on the southeast turn early in the race.

I expected Rex Mays to provide my most serious competition and I wasn't disappointed. His Bowes Seal Fast Special was the only car in the race, except Riganti's, which had an edge on mine in horsepower. It was the same car Meyer had driven the previous year, and its handling qualities had improved a great deal. Rex also had one other advantage. Because he was using gasoline for fuel, he could go the full five hundred miles on a single pit stop. I was using methanol. It didn't give me nearly as much mileage, although it reduced engine temperature, and I would have to make two stops.

My plan was to run approximately 121 miles an hour, so that I would finish with an average of 119, including pit stops. Rex started off at better than 122, however, and I stepped up my own speed in order to keep right on his tail. I'd learned my lesson in 1938 and certainly wasn't going to let anyone get as far ahead of me as Roberts had in that event. Rex apparently didn't enjoy the pressure from behind and didn't even challenge when I passed him on the thirty-fourth lap. Once in front, I eased off to my scheduled 121 average and Mays seemed to be content to protect his hold on second place, at least temporarily. By the time it became necessary for me to make my first pit stop on the seventy-fourth lap, I had lapped everyone except Mays and he was forty seconds back. I should be running again in second place before the other fellows could close the gap. Harry Bosey shoved a jack under the axle

254

and Henning changed a right rear tire while Bob Jackson took care of the fuel hose with the help of Charley Beinke. Pem Cornelius handed me some cold water. Bill Hunt and Ford Moyer shouted advice at me. As the crew finished servicing the car, however, my engine died for some unexplained reason. Cotton cranked it five or six times without success, screaming at me each time to "pump up the air pressure." I had done that instantly, but he came around to the side of the cockpit to see for himself while Bosey gave the crank another turn. This time, the engine roared into life again. My blood pressure had been mounting with each second of frustration. Mauri Rose, Ted Horn and Joe Thorne all had moved ahead of me—along with Mays—during the extra thirty seconds required to get my engine running. The car already was in gear and I let out the clutch just as Henning reached the side of the cockpit. My right rear wheel ran over his foot and knocked him down. But I was on my way again and overtaking the leaders steadily.

Mays came into the pits on lap 100. That put Rose in the No. 1 spot. But he, too, coasted into the pits four laps later and I was out in front of the pack again on lap 105—after Horn and Thorne also had paused to refuel. With everyone back on the course, I was a full lap ahead of Mays. He had a 49-second edge on Horn, who was thirty-six seconds ahead of the fourth-place Rose.

The weather began to look threatening and I was faced with the task of increasing my lead as quickly as possible so that I could make my second pit stop without losing first place in case it started to rain. A wet track would bring out the yellow flag, requiring all cars to reduce sped and maintain their respective positions. If the yellow flag caught me out of first place, I wouldn't have a chance to regain the lead unless the track dried off.

Actually, it turned out to be much easier than I anticipated. During the next forty laps I added a minute and fifteen seconds to my advantage and was 2:32 ahead of Mays, in second place, when I pulled into the pits on lap 144. Cotton dumped

255

in fifty gallons of fuel in quick order and I was running again with a lead of more than a full lap on the entire field.

Ten minutes later, a light rain began to fall. Seth Klein unfurled the yellow flag immediately and I eased off to about 105 miles an hour. That cut my average from 118.958 to 114.277 at the finish, ending all chance of a new record. The checkered flag came as somewhat of an anti-climax. But as it dipped in front of the nose of my car it made me the first driver in Speedway history to win two consecutive races and also placed me on a par with Louie Meyer as the only three-time winners. With engine specifications unchanged for the following year, there seemed to be no reason why I couldn't win for the fourth time in 1941.

CHAPTER 29

AFTER making a number of personal appearances before luncheon clubs and groups of automotive engineers during the first couple of months following the race, I felt in need of a little vacation. Boots suggested it would be fun to spend a week end with the Horace Millhones at Akron, Ohio, and we arrived on a Friday evening, early in August. The next morning I drove out to the Firestone plant to say hello to some of my friends. One of the first to greet me was Leonard Firestone.

He expressed considerable interest in my plans for the 1941 race and asked me to make sure to see Lee Jackson, the sales manager of the company, before leaving the plant. Jackson didn't waste any time getting to the point.

"How would you like to organize and direct our proposed aviation division of the Firestone Tire and Rubber Company?"

Mrs. Shaw watches as W. S. checks his blood pressure prior to the 1941 race.

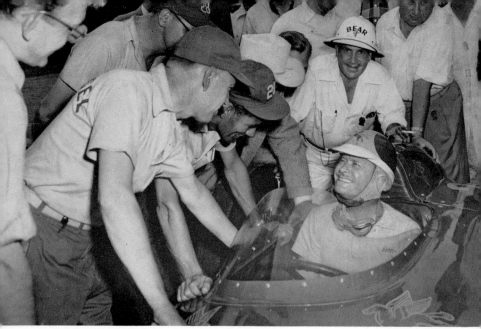

W. S. after a ride in the Cummins Diesel. 1952.

At the wheel of a Corvette, with Mauri Rose alongside. 1953.

Talking with Chief Mechanic Cotton Henning, a close associate during the operation of the famous Maserati Special, which W. S. drove to victory in 1939 and 1940.

Official Starter Seth Klein, Benson Ford, Clark Gable and W. S. at the Speedway when Benson Ford drove the pace car in 1950.

Henry Ford II, and W. S. in the Lincoln pace car, ready for the start of the 1946 race. The AAA official at the extreme right is Jack Mehan who served in the same capacity in the 1947 and 1948 races.

From left to right: General Jimmy Doolittle, W. S., Henry Ford II, and Tony Hulman at the Speedway in 1946, when Henry Ford II drove the pace car

W. S. at his desk in the Firestone plant, after accepting the job of organizing and directing its aviation division in 1940.

Examining some of the tires developed by the aviation division of the Firestone Tire & Rubber Company.

Flagging in the winner of Chevrolet's All-American Soap Box Derby at Akron, Ohio, in 1953.

Donald Strub, winner of the 1948 Soap Box Derby, receives the National Championship Trophy from T. H. Keating, Chevrolet general manager, with W. S., who acted as Referee, looking on.

W. S. and his son, Bill, with Miss Frances Welker admire a goat which was placed in their hotel suite as a joke when they were in Akron, Ohio, in 1950 for the Soap Box Derby finals.

W. S. talking to a crippled boy who viewed the 1949 Soap Box Derby with his nurse from a special vantage point.

Rex Mays helps his mechanic make a final check of his Bowes Seal Fast Special. 1948.

Life Magazine

After emergency repairs, Duke Nalon's car leaves the pit during the 1947 race.

Life Magazine

Emergency repairs being made on a race car by members of the pit crew.

Life Magazine

After a final check-up, the crew pushes Herb Ardinger's Novi Special to its starting position at the Speedway.

Life Magazine

A member of the pit crew holds up a blackboard advising his driver that he is starting his 58th lap.

Life Magazine

With Ted Allen, AAA representative, during a special wartime "500" mile tire test conducted for Firestone in cold weather. Although not a competitive event, W. S. often referred to it as the toughest "500" he ever drove.

W. S. with a special hydraulic steering wheel which he used to prepare himself for a race while he was at Firestone during World War II.

From left to right: W. S., Tony Hulman and Al Bloemker in 1953.

W. S. with two earlier "500" winners, Ray Harroun and Ralph De Palma, during the filming of a special wartime film for Firestone's "Crucible of Speed" movie.

O'Dell & Shields

Duke Nalon's Novi Special crashing in flames on the north turn of the Speedway. Mauri Rose is seen zooming by on the inside. 1949.

Bill Holland drives through the flaming fuel from the wreckage as it flows across the tracks.

O'Dell & Shields

The flaming car seconds after it came to a stop against the Speedway's outer retaining wall. Nalon has just escaped from the wreckage.

All that remained of Nalon's car after the flames had been extinguished.

O'Dell & Shields

O'Dell & Shields

Duke Nalon

O'Dell & Shields

Troy Ruttman

O'Dell & Shie

Lee Wallard

O'Dell & Shields

Bill Holland

O'Dell & Shields

Bill Vukovich

O'Dell & Shie

Jack McGrath

Johnnie Parsons

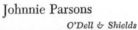

O'Dell & Shields

Life Magazine

On a fence separating the speeding cars from the spectators, a starling turns its back on the noise of the 1947 Memorial Day Race.

Left: W. S. and Raymond Firestone congratulate Bill Vukovich in "Victory Lane" after he won the 1954 race. *Right:* W. S. and his son Bill try out a motorcycle in the garage area of the Speedway. Watching are Frank Meunier and R. G. McMahan of the General Petroleum Corp. 1954.

W. S. with Carl Stockholm. 1954.

W. S., Ray Grimes and Ernie Roose at the Chrysler Corp. proving grounds just before their fatal airplane flight. 1954.

he asked. "We believe it can be developed into something big. You did a good job for us on the safety tour, everyone seems to know you because of your success in racing and you have had enough flying experience to know your way around in that field. How about it?"

"Do I have to give you an answer right now?" I asked.

"Not right this minute," he said, "but we would like to know as soon as possible, if you're interested. Why don't you think it over and let me know what you have decided on Monday?"

Early Monday morning I was back in Mr. Jackson's office.

"If you'll guarantee to give me a leave of absence next May, so I can race at Indianapolis again, I'll take the job," I told him.

"That's all right with us," he said.

"When do you want me to start?" I asked.

"Right now, if you're ready," he said.

As the result of that decision, our week-end visit to Akron was extended to more than five years. I was so busy I had no opportunity for recreation and regular exercise during the fall and winter months. In April, however, I made arrangements for my steering wheel exerciser with the hydraulic shock absorber to be brought to Akron. I spent about thirty minutes on it each morning and was in fairly good condition when I drove into Gasoline Alley at Indianapolis on May 2 to start preparations for the race. It was like starting a wonderful vacation, although a lot of work remained to be done.

Cotton had the Maserati ready to run, I was rarin' to go and I had an irresistible urge to "cut a couple of fast ones" as soon as the car had been warmed up properly. No one knew, better than I, what a silly idea this was. But it felt so good to be behind the wheel of a race car again, that I threw caution to the winds. I knocked off one trip around the course at about 130 miles an hour and headed into the first turn for another quick lap at an even faster pace. Almost before I knew what was happening, the car was broadside on the turn. The back end never did get all the way around, but the car slid sideways for more than six hundred feet before I was able to straighten it out as it lost momentum. The tires looked like four bunches of calico.

257

There was no rubber left on them at all. But the car itself appeared to be undamaged. Fortunately it hadn't touched a thing on its long slide.

I acted more sensibly during the remainder of the pre-race period and qualified easily for my favorite position on the outside of the front row. For several years I had made a practice of balancing my own wheels. Some one else probably could have done the job just as well for me. But I had once run into trouble because my wheels had not been balanced properly and I had handled that particular operation myself ever since that experience. This time, after our race-day tires had been mounted in the Firestone headquarters at the track, I took all the wheels to our private garage on Gent avenue to do the job. All except one rear wheel checked out perfectly. For some reason I couldn't get it to stay in balance, although it appeared to be all right in every other respect. It was the first time I had experienced a thing of that kind and I didn't know what to do about it. I'd get it in perfect dynamic and static balance, run it a little while and then discover that it had lost its proper balance. Finally I got it in balance again and marked it in chalk on the outside of the tire: "OK—Bal—Use Last." The others I marked simply: "OK—Bal."

A few days before the big event, some inconsiderate lug stole the shoes I had worn in every race for many years. They were old and oil-soaked, with dirt and aluminum ground into the leather. But, to me, putting on those shoes was like putting on impenetrable armor—not that I was superstitious, but those shoes and I had gone through a great many contests all over the country without serious damage. I've never missed anything quite as much and their loss upset me more than I cared to admit at the time.

On the day of the drivers' meeting, I walked into the garage to check on something with Cotton and there on the work bench sat a pair of identical shoes. For a minute I thought they were the ones which had been stolen. Close inspection revealed they weren't, but I learned that Ford Moyer had bought a pair as nearly like mine as possible. Then he had spent a good

258

part of two days rubbing oil and dirt and aluminum dust into the shoes so they'd look "natural." Ford had done a lot of things for me since we had started racing together almost twenty years earlier. He had taught me a lot about racing cars and engines. He had served as my mechanic, off and on, for years. But I don't believe he or anyone else ever did anything for me which affected me so deeply. Even if the new shoes couldn't be expected to have the "protective" qualities of the original pair, I certainly was touched by Ford's understanding.

Late in the afternoon, all drivers were given AAA permission to make final carburetion runs. The Maserati performed perfectly and we pushed it into the garage for the night. Sam Hanks wasn't as fortunate. On what was to be his final pre-race trip around the course, his crankshaft broke. The car looped at the start of the southwest turn and crashed through the inner guard rail.

In order to be near the track during the month of May, Boots and I had persuaded Mrs. Ferguson to let us occupy a room in her home in Speedway City. On the morning of the race I awakened about six o'clock and was taking a shower when I suddenly heard fire engines clamoring for the right-of-way. My first thought, as I reached for a towel, was the garage area. For years it had been like a bomb, with only a single spark needed to set off all of the fuel and oil stored around the place.

Before I could finish drying myself, there was a knock on the bathroom door and Mrs. Ferguson shouted, "The garages are on fire."

I pulled on some shoes, jumped into my trousers and buttoned my shirt as I ran out of the house without even kissing Boots goodbye. Black smoke was pouring out of the south bank of garages when I arrived. George Barringer's four-wheel drive Miller Special, as well as three cars which had not been qualified for the race, were burned beyond repair. The place was a shambles with other race cars, parts, spare wheels and additional equipment scattered throughout the area. Firemen already had succeeded in checking the spread of the flames, however, and by eight o'clock the blaze was extinguished.

Fortunately my own crew had been on hand when the excitement started. They had pushed the Maserati to a safe place and carried the jacks and spare wheels out of danger. They also had salvaged my helmet and shoes, although the shoe laces were burned to such an extent that replacements were necessary.

Even with the one-hour postponement granted by race officials, it took a lot of teamwork by everyone concerned to get ready for the start. While Colonel Art Herrington and his technical committee checked all of the cars involved, those of us who had escaped without serious loss made arrangements to share our equipment with others not so lucky. It was quite a scramble, getting everything assembled in the pit. I didn't notice at the time that the markings on my tires had been obliterated by the water from the fire hose and the hands of the men who had removed them from the danger zone.

Instructions for all cars to assume their starting positions came as a welcome relief from the strain under which we had been working. Our gang all had changed into clean race-day uniforms, which consisted of light blue shirts and matching trousers with a thin white pin stripe. We really looked smart. Apparently we were none the worse off because of the fire and I was as confident of winning as I ever had been in my entire life. In fact, I was even a little cocky and I made every effort to be as nonchalant as possible for any psychological advantage that it might give me.

For many years it had been customary to push all cars to their starting positions. Instead of letting my crew take care of this chore in the usual manner, however, I had Cotton crank the engine. Then I backed the car, under its own power, to my front-row starting spot. I blew a kiss to the cameramen at the starting line, punched the ignition cut-off button to kill my engine and casually lighted a cigarette. Bradshaw, my former boss at Perfect Circle, walked up for a final good-luck handshake. Finally the signal was given for every driver to start his engine. Cotton spun the crank and I turned on the ignition switch with all the confidence in the world—but nothing happened. We tried again as other cars began to pull around us for the start of the pace lap. Some other member of the crew relieved Cotton with the crank as he neared the point of exhaustion. Still nothing happened. In desperation, they abandoned the crank and started pushing me. If my engine failed to take hold before I reached the pit wall opening, between the track and the garage area, I would be flagged off the course and out of the race even before it was officially under way. The car hadn't rolled fifty feet, however, before the engine came to life. I was able to overtake the field in time to assume my regular starting spot. My worries, at least for the moment, were over.

Rex Mays took the lead on the first lap. I was right on his tail with Mauri Rose a close third. We ran that way for thirty-eight laps, only inches apart most of the time, and were at a distant point on the track when Joe Thorne, Emil Andres and Louis Tomei tangled in a spectacular accident on the north turn. When we closed in on the stragglers, as we started to lap the field, Mays eased off the throttle in order to pick a good spot to pass them. I did the same thing. But the instant I lifted my foot, I could almost feel Rose charging from behind. He sailed right ahead into the heavy traffic, passing Rex and me at the same time.

That made me mad.

I was perfectly content to let Rex lead the race during the early stages, postponing what I believed would be a final duel between us for victory. The time for that, in my opinion, would come after I had made my last scheduled pit stop. But I certainly had no intention of letting someone else set the pace for both of us, especially in a car which I thought was definitely inferior to my own. I zoomed around Rex, too. The hole Rose had found in the heavy traffic, however, already had closed. It took me several seconds to find an opening and Rose was about a quarter-mile ahead when I finally passed the last car between us. Five laps later I "sucked him under," going by him like a fast freight passing a tramp. He finally broke an oil line on the sixty-second lap.

261

Mays had made his first pit stop on lap 64 and Harry Mc-
Quinn was my nearest challenger—a little more than a lap behind—when I had to pause for fuel and tires. I thought sure
he'd take the lead from me before I was rolling again. But my
pit crew did such a smooth job that I was able to stay in first
place by a margin of ten seconds.

By the time it was necessary for me to make my second stop,
after 138 laps, I had piled up a lead of more than two minutes
on every rival. Cliff Bergere was second, Mays third and Rose
fourth as a relief driver for Floyd Davis in another car entered
by Lou Moore. Bergere had not made a pit stop and apparently didn't intend to make any. But again my crew did a beautiful job and I had a comfortable lead of more than one full lap
on everyone in the race, with fresh rubber, plenty of fuel and
only sixty-two laps to go.

As I swung into the main stretch on my 152nd lap, the car
seemed to sway a little bit, as if a sudden gust of wind had
given the tail a little extra push toward the outside of the track.
But it wasn't the wind. I found out that much on the next
turn. As I headed into it, some of the spokes of the right rear
wheel tore loose at the hub and caused the tail of the car to
slide toward the outer wall. For an instant the Maserati acted
as if it wanted to roll over with me. Although the wheel didn't
actually fold under the car, it had been weakened too much to
support the weight of the car properly through the turn. I
tugged on the steering wheel in an effort to keep the car off the
wall and relaxed my pressure on the throttle at the same time,
but I was traveling much too fast to avoid a spin under those
conditions. The car did a half-loop and hit the wall tail first,
rupturing the fuel tank. Then it bounced off the wall and spun
again before hitting the concrete barrier a second time. Fifty
gallons of methanol poured from the battered tank. Only God
knows why it didn't catch on fire. If it had, it doesn't take
much imagination for anyone to realize what my fate would
have been—because I was paralyzed from the waist down.

The wheel which had given me so much trouble when I had
tried to balance it, apparently had been faulty even at that

time. Because my chalk marks of warning had been erased during the fire, the wheel had been stacked in the pit with the others and finally had been placed on the car during my last pit stop.

One of the braces for the fuel tank apparently had come in contact with my spine like a sledge hammer when the tail of the car hit the wall. I felt certain my back was broken and I wouldn't even let the emergency crew touch me until medical aid arrived because I knew how much damage could be done by moving a person in that condition. It was only a matter of minutes, however, until an ambulance reached the scene and the doctors handled me as carefully as a new born baby. Taking plenty of time, and supporting almost every inch of my body with their hands, they managed to get me on a stretcher for the ride to the hospital.

My mind was in a turmoil. Although I was comparatively free of pain, I couldn't move my legs. What if my bowels and kidneys also were paralyzed? What if I could never race again? What if I was destined to be a wheel chair invalid for the remainder of my life? All of these thoughts flashed through my mind, over and over. At the same time, I couldn't keep from thinking about all of the cash which had been knocked out of my hands in the crash. My share of the prize money, for winning, would have been "peanuts" compared to what I would have been able to get for endorsements of certain products as the Speedway's only four-time winner with three in a row to my credit. At a conservative estimate, I would have been in a position to collect between $150,000 and $200,000 simply by signing my name to some contracts.

Instead, it was Rose—destined to score two other Indianapolis victories later in his career—who won the race that day after passing the tiring Bergere on the 163rd lap. Cliff did succeed in becoming the first driver of a gasoline-powered car to go the full five hundred miles without a stop. Dave Evans had done it exactly ten years earlier in a Cummins Diesel. But Cliff had become ill during the late laps and was forced to be content with fifth place. Mays, Horn and Hepburn all passed him to finish in that order behind Rose.

At the hospital, X-ray examination revealed a compression fracture which had wedged together my first, second and third lumbar vertebrae to cause the paralysis. That condition had to be corrected before they could even put a cast on me. Acute shock and my upset mental state complicated matters.

E. Vernon Hahn, a neurosurgeon who later became one of my closest friends, was the doctor in charge of the case. He called in Charles F. Thompson, an orthopedic consultant, and my medical "board of strategy" also included Rogers Smith. Rog was a friend of long standing as well as the doctor who served as chief of the Speedway's medical staff. No one ever was in better hands. Together they performed miracles and at the same time steered me safely through several periods of extreme depression when I became despondent because of my failure to improve as rapidly as my temperament demanded.

I may have hindered them more than I helped them. On that first night in the hospital, particularly, I know I was quite a problem. Despite all of the medication they prescribed to induce sleep, I developed a craving for a mint julep, something I rarely drink. Boots finally smuggled one into my room, after extracting a promise that I would be a model patient during the remainder of my hospital stay. Then for two or three hours I tried to wiggle my toes—and finally succeeded before dozing off. On the following morning, it was quite a relief to discover that my internal organs were functioning properly again. At the end of another twenty-four hours I was able to move my legs slightly, although they felt weak and numb. During the next four days, the wedged vertebrae gradually separated as the result of continued treatment and I was put into a cast from my hips to my shoulders. That was an awful experience and my mental condition wasn't helped any by Dr. Hahn's statement that I probably would have to wear it for at least six weeks and then take it easy for another month or so.

If they really thought it necessary for me to get a lot of rest, however, they made a mistake by telling me I could sit up for a couple of hours each day. By June 8, I had talked them into letting me leave the hospital to continue my convalescence at Mother's home on Fortieth Street in Indianapolis. In a couple of days, I felt almost as good as ever, despite the handicap of the cast. Early the following week Boots and I drove to our home in Akron and the following Monday I resumed my normal working schedule for Firestone.

I had to attend several War Products meetings at Wright Field and, especially on hot days, I began to notice people moving away from me. Although Boots was able to bathe me fairly well under the cast, she couldn't quite reach every part of my body. Johnson's baby powder helped a lot, but it didn't prevent unpleasantness entirely. I made it a habit to warn every one present at committee meetings I attended and I also tried to choose an isolated seat whenever possible.

The cast was driving me crazy, however. It made my body itch constantly and I would have gone completely nuts if I hadn't figured out a way to scratch the spots that itched. Working for hours at a time, with a penknife, I dug little holes in the cast at half-inch intervals. Horace Millhone helped me on several occasions. It wasn't long before it looked like a sieve and we celebrated Fourth of July that summer by removing the cast altogether without medical help—or even medical permission.

CHAPTER 30

MY job as head of Firestone's aircraft division was my first experience as an important cog in a large organization. During my first few weeks on that assignment the previous fall some of the other executives made no secret of the fact they thought I was acting like a young bull in a china shop. This was understandable to some extent. I was expected to form an organization of people already working for Firestone. That meant it was necessary for me to raid other departments and "Shanghai" help in any manner I could. Naturally, I wanted the best men and women available.

In the beginning we had nothing to offer the aviation industry, in addition to tires for transport planes, except wheels, tires and brakes for small private aircraft. I had sailed into the markets we had for those products immediately. With war fires burning all over the globe, however, military aircraft seemed to offer the best possibility for future business. Even before the 1941 race, I had started renewing contacts at Bell, Curtiss-Wright, Republic and other companies most likely to be given major government defense contracts. Scattered through these various organizations were friends I had known for a number of years. My racing background and reputation also made it easy for me to strike up new friendships with other individuals who might be the source of future business. I had asked a lot of questions in an effort to find things they needed which we could build. Now, in the late summer of 1941, only two or three months before Pearl Harbor, these preliminary activities were starting to pay dividends.

All of us in the racing business were called upon frequently to do something that never had been done before. Usually we were able to improvise some device or method which would solve each problem as it arose. Even though our solutions were not always regarded as "good engineering practice," they usually worked. That experience now proved to be invaluable. My complete lack of knowledge concerning the way things had been done before, enabled me to come up with some simple solution to problems which had been regarded as difficult. I soon gained somewhat of a reputation among engineering groups in the various plants as an idea man and this opened additional doors. One example involves the difficulties encountered with the Bell P-39 on the sod fields of England. After a heavy rain, with our accepted type-2 or streamlined tire for military aircraft, these planes would sink into the sod to such an extent that it was extremely difficult to move them into take-off position on the runways.

Sal Salisbury had mentioned this problem to me, and I was sitting in the Bell Aircraft office in Buffalo thumbing through the rotogravure section of a Sunday paper while waiting for him to keep an appointment with me, when a photo of a bomb-loading trailer happened to catch my eye. The tires on it were small but very squat and they spread the weight of the load over quite a lot of ground.

"Why wouldn't a tire like this do the job on the nose wheel of a P-39?" I asked Sal, when he joined me.

"It probably would," he said, "if you had a wheel to fit it which would absorb most of the landing shock to prevent injuring the tire and tube."

I made a quick sketch of a wheel I thought would be strong enough and then talked with Sal about the regular landing gear tires.

"Several years ago," I said, "we used to race on the Ascot track in California with a special tire which was designed to provide maximum traction on left turns. Because we were turning to the left all of the time, the tire had been built with a special shoulder on one side. It gave us much better traction than anything else we ever used, and a tire with such a shoulder on each side should be perfect for these planes."

I made a rough sketch of such a tire, with "flying buttresses" supporting the shoulders. Sal improved my work with a few deft passes of his pencil and I took both sketches back to Firestone engineers.

Byron Shin, who headed our wheel and brake department, took one look at my sketch of the low-profile wheel and said, "I think you've got something here you can patent."

"Forget about the patent," I replied. "Let's just get busy and make enough of these wheels to get the planes off the ground over in England."

Jim Hale, chief engineer of the tire division, said the tire I had seen in the photo of the bomb-loading trailer was one being built in our English plant and it would not be difficult to get it into large-scale production quickly in this country. I took the other sketch of the landing gear tire to the art department and they moulded a quarter-section of the tire out of clay. Quite obviously it was the answer to the problem. We called it the channel tread tire because its imprint in the mud was like a square-shouldered straight-sided channel. Within a few days the tires and wheels were adopted as standard equipment and replacement for every P-39 that had been manufactured. In the meantime Shin had applied for a patent in my name, but I assigned it to Firestone immediately.

Another problem which I had a hand in solving involved self-sealing fuel tanks. The Germans had been using them for some time before our air force did anything about it. The self-sealing fuel cell which finally was approved, however, was impractical because it reduced the plane's fuel capacity too much. The specifications called for a cell which was something on the order of a sponge rubber and neoprene sandwich, seven-eighths of an inch thick, with an outer covering of horse hide. Because of special treatment given the hide for this purpose it absorbed moisture from the air and often became extremely heavy. The first company to come up with a better product was sure to get almost all of the business it could handle and I had everyone in the plant working frantically until we perfected a satisfactory five-sixteenth inch fuel cell with an outer cover of specially prepared nylon. These cells were capable of sealing holes created by as many as three "tumbling" 50-calibre machine gun bullets, which means that they were hitting the cell walls flat instead of point first. They unquestionably saved the lives of a lot of our pilots and I'm proud of my small part in their development.

The Aviation Division of the Firestone Company grew so rapidly from its very meager beginning in 1940 that, as the end of hostilities neared, it was building 90 per cent of the wings for the Curtiss-Wright C-46; self-sealing fuel cells for almost every type of military aircraft; tires as large as ninety-six inches in diameter for the big bombers, barrage balloons and dozens of other rubber and metal parts.

But it wasn't all work at Akron. We had a lot of fun, too, on week ends when it wasn't necessary for me to keep my nose to the grindstone. We were guests of the Millhones for almost three months while looking for a place to live. Then we rented the furnished home of a family which was going to Florida for the winter, and in the spring we finally were able to get settled in one of Akron's new apartments. Akron is in the snow belt. On almost every winter morning the ground was covered by a fresh blanket of clean snow. It was a beautiful scene and the maid had instructions to stay in bed until at least eight o'clock every day so that Boots could prepare breakfast herself and enjoy it with me in an atmosphere of cozy privacy which was difficult to attain at any other time.

Most of Firestone's top brass made no secret of the fact that they believed I lacked the necessary "dignity" for someone in my position with the company. But that didn't alter our mode of living at all. I had purchased a motorcycle and Boots enjoyed riding behind me in tandem fashion. Horace Millhone also had one, with a side car for Mary, and we often shattered the quiet air of the countryside with impromptu races. Boots often rode on my shoulders for an extra thrill and anyone who saw us probably thought we were part of a stunt show.

The Millhones lived in an old rustic house on the edge of a park in Cuyahoga Falls. A spring, which provided approximately 250 gallons of water every minute all year long, at a constant temperature of fifty-two degrees, fed the trout pool and swimming pool. Horace and Mary loved to entertain. It wasn't unusual for them to invite as many as forty or fifty guests for a week-end party of swimming, fishing, target practice and square dancing. Everyone seemed to be interested in firearms during those war years and on one afternoon while shooting at targets I noticed Boots coming down the steps from the house with six or eight full liqueur glasses on a tray, balancing it on one hand at about shoulder height, in true professional style.

"Hold it, Honey," I shouted. Then, using a target pistol, I shot each glass off the tray from a distance of about 40 feet.

Such a stunt wasn't too unusual at one of the Millhones' parties and I didn't realize I had impressed any one particularly by doing it. Our house guest that week end, however, was Bill Curlett, an old friend from California. A week or two later he sent the Millhones a dozen new liqueur glasses with a note saying: "If Wilbur Shaw is going to continue attending your parties I'm sure these will come in handy."

Tom Milton, one of my early heroes and also the first two-time winner of the "500," was among the Millhones' guests on another occasion. Like many other athletes, I had made it a practice to skip rope as part of my usual conditioning routine. Mary Millhone was quite proficient at this also and the two of us were putting on a show. Although Milton unquestionably is a little more modest about it, his competitive attitude is much like mine: "anything you can do, I can do better." Most good race drivers—and champions in all sports—apparently feel that way. My performance was a challenge and Milton, who had not skipped rope for many years, spent most of the evening trying to duplicate our rope tricks.

Boots and I had accepted an invitation to spend New Year's eve of 1943 in Buffalo with Herb and Emily Fisher. He was a former Indianapolis resident, working as chief test pilot for Curtiss-Wright, and we were friends of long standing. We went to the theater and then brought the New Year in properly. After dinner the following night—New Year's Day—Herb said he was sorry he hadn't invited Don and Helen Berlin as week-end guests, too. Don was a prominent aviation engineer with General Motors in Detroit.

"Let's get 'em on the phone, anyway," I said, "and wish them a Happy New Year." It was only ten or eleven o'clock, but apparently they'd had a rough night on New Year's Eve and had turned in early. When they finally answered the phone, all of us talked to them. Herb was the last to add "his nickel's worth," and as he hung up the phone he said, "Wouldn't it be

270

fun to hop on a train for Detroit and get them out of bed personally?"

Boots wasn't sure it was a good idea. She had never met the Berlins. But the three of us out-voted her quickly.

"There's a train out of here about midnight," Herb said, "and it only takes about five hours."

It was a scramble, but we made it and managed to get a few hours of sleep on the way. In Detroit, we grabbed a cab and went straight to the Berlins' home. It must have been a little after six o'clock in the morning.

"Are you sure you know what you're doing?" Boots asked as I reached for the doorbell.

"They'll get a big bang out of seeing us," Herb assured her.

"Mr. and Mrs. Berlin are still sleeping and I don't believe they want to be disturbed this early," the maid told us, when she answered the door.

Herb finally convinced her that they wouldn't mind our early-morning visit and I helped him enlist her aid in making it a real surprise party. First we went to the kitchen and each of us got a pan and a soup spoon. Then we took off our shoes and went upstairs to the Berlins' bedroom. I pounded on the door, pushed it open and all of us paraded in, making as much noise as we could. Up and over the bed we marched, in our stocking feet. It must have been quite a shock to Don and Helen, but they joined in the celebration immediately and we had a lot of fun together all day long.

During the tension of the war years, nothing seemed to do as much good for me as a chance to blow off a little steam occasionally in that manner. Most of the time I was working fourteen and fifteen hours a day, flying thousands of miles every week in order to keep Firestone's delivery of military aircraft supplies on schedule.

On one occasion, flying across Texas to join Boots in Palm Springs for a long week end of sunshine while en route to Los Angeles on business, I decided to brush up on my blind-flying technique. I removed the cushion from the seat, so I would be sitting too low in the cockpit to see what few landmarks existed in that part of Texas, and got on the El Paso radio beam. My only mistake was that I didn't realize what a whale of a tail-wind was helping me along. When I finally came "out from under the hood," in order to make my approach to the landing field, there was no sign of El Paso ahead of me—where I felt sure it should be. I already was west of El Paso and didn't know it. I called the tower for instructions, but the instructions I received didn't make sense at all.

I thought I knew the El Paso territory by heart, having flown over it many times, but the rugged mountains looming ahead of me were quite unfamiliar. After getting a glimpse of them, I was thoroughly confused. To complicate matters, it was beginning to get dark and my fuel supply was almost exhausted. Something had to be done, and quickly.

After making a 180° turn, I saw some lights south of me and headed for them. They came from a small village in a narrow valley, with a railroad track running through it. On the edge of the village was a cow pasture—complete with cows—but it was the only fairly clear area I could see which might be large enough for me to land safely. As my wheels were about to touch the ground, I punched the radio button again to tell the El Paso tower what I was doing. At the same time, my right wing tip nicked the branch of a small tree and tore my antenna loose. Later, I learned the message had not been received.

Even in the loneliest spots there always seems to be a certain number of curious youngsters who appear out of nowhere when anything out of the ordinary happens and this was no exception. As soon as I heard them chattering in Spanish, I knew the final instructions from the tower had caused me to veer too far south and carried me across the border without the formality of obtaining clearance from the proper authorities. By the time I had inspected my damaged wing and checked my meager supply of fuel, most of the villagers had reached the scene. Temporary repairs would be difficult and I had no idea of where to look for aviation gasoline in this isolated area. A great deal of gesticulation, plus a few quick sketches with pencil and paper, enabled me to get across the idea I wanted to

272

get to a telephone as soon as possible. They led me to the only one in the village. It was a direct line to one of the mines in the mountains, but the man at the other end at least could speak English. He also had some usable gasoline, although it would be almost morning before one of the villagers with a burro could complete the round trip.

Small towns are the same all over the world, I believe—friendly, curious and anxious to help anyone in trouble. It was impossible for me to get word of my plight to any of my friends in the States. But I had no difficulty finding someone who would take me in for the night. Nothing better than adhesive tape was available to repair the damaged wing tip, but enough of it was rounded up in the morning to do the job. I also repaired the antenna and radioed El Paso to report what had happened. By that time, Ross Hadley and some of my other friends in Los Angeles were preparing to form an aerial search party. Fortunately, Boots had been spared any anxiety because she had retired the previous night before the late news broadcasts had revealed I was missing. Her friends had thought it kinder to let her sleep, because nothing could be done in my behalf until daylight. Even before getting my message in the morning, via El Paso, however, Boots said she knew I was all right because something inside her always let her know when I wasn't.

The engine seemed to run well on the gasoline obtained from the mine. Villagers herded the cattle to one side of the small pasture. Then I took off with a crippled wing and a prayer, hoping the adhesive tape would hold and that those great big mountains would stay where they were while I circled to gain sufficient altitude. It was a happy, lucky man who landed in Palm Springs later the same morning and the ribbing I've taken through the years as the result of this incident has kept it fresh in my memory. Believe me, my friends in aviation have never let me forget it.

Gradually, the tide of the war began to turn. Victory seemed to be only a few months away and Firestone officials began to prepare for the resumption of normal business. During the win-

273

ter of 1944–45 they asked me to make a special 500-mile test of a new type of synthetic tire for use on passenger cars and arrangements were completed for the use of the Indianapolis Motor Speedway. It was the longest, coldest 500-mile high-speed run I ever made in my life. The temperature was about five degrees above zero and the absence of competition made it seem like 5,000 miles instead of 500.

Firestone wanted to be sure, however, that its new tire had all of the safety and durability characteristics which laboratory experiments promised. They also wanted to film the test for use as part of a promotional movie to be called "The Crucible of Speed." Others assigned leading roles were Ray Harroun, winner of the first 500-mile race; Ralph DePalma, one of racing's most popular early-day drivers; Cliff Bergere, who had driven more miles on the Indianapolis Speedway than any other competitor; Johnny Moore, head of Firestone's efficient Racing Division; and Richard Beach, the only professional actor in the entire cast, who played the part of an inquiring reporter.

What impressed me most about the test on the Speedway, however, was the physical condition of the famous plant. There were big crevices in the track surface on the turns, which had to be patched before we could start the test, and grass was growing between the bricks on the main straightaway. The old wooden grandstands looked as if they were about to fall apart. Apparently no maintenance work of any kind had been done for almost four years. It reminded me of a dilapidated back house on an abandoned farm. A lot of money would be necessary to make another International 500-mile Speed Classic a reality. The depressing scene actually haunted me in my dreams for several nights.

During the preceding year, I had talked to Captain Eddie Rickenbacker on several occasions about the Speedway's future —and also to Joe Copps, the Speedway's publicity chief. Rick, who owned the plant, had done a superb job of guiding the "500" safely through the difficult depression years, when other tracks throughout the world were being converted into real

274

estate developments. Since the outbreak of World War II, however, it had been necessary for him to devote all of his time and energy to the management of Eastern Air Lines. He wanted to sell the big 433-acre plant rather than tackle the expensive task of restoring it to usable condition. After having had a chance to inspect it, I didn't blame him a bit.

But, to me, the track was the world's last great speed shrine, which must be preserved at any cost. I felt that all I was, or ever hoped to be, I owed to the Indianapolis 500-mile race. I accepted the situation as a personal challenge and started a one-man crusade to get the job done. The final shots necessary for the completion of the Firestone film were to be made in a New York studio and I took advantage of the opportunity to see Rick again. It was time to get down to brass tacks.

"How much money will it take to buy the Speedway?" I asked.

"I'll sell it for exactly what I've put into it," he replied, quoting a specific figure. He refused my request for a definite option, however.

"I don't want to give anyone an option," he said, "but I believe you are the most likely person in the world to round up sufficient financial backing to swing the deal and I'll give you every possible consideration because I'm sure you have the necessary ability to run it. I'll also let you examine the books at your convenience, so you'll be able to present an accurate picture of the Speedway's financial possibilities to any prospects."

With the facts and figures obtained through Rick's cooperation, I went back to Indianapolis and talked with officers of the Indiana National Bank to learn how much money could be borrowed on the property. Then I prepared a detailed prospectus, showing the Speedway's receipts and expenses since 1928, as well as my own estimate of the cost of putting the plant in useable condition again. These I sent to more than thirty firms and individuals who might be willing to invest $25,000 or more in the project. The response was very gratifying. It looked as if the necessary capital was available.

Within a few weeks, however, it became evident the plan was not practical if the 500-mile race itself was to be given first consideration. Too many of the firms displayed a definite determination to control Speedway policy in an effort to advertise and promote the use of their own particular products. I tried desperately to correct this situation, but by mid-summer it appeared to be almost hopeless.

I had refused to consider suggestions from friends, who had proposed the name of this or that individual capable of swinging the entire financial deal alone, for that very same reason. But VE day, on May 8, already was history. It was only a matter of days until the world also would celebrate VJ day on August 15. Seth Klein, who also had been trying to find a buyer for the Speedway, had talked to Rick about the possibility of becoming general manager and getting the necessary repair work started for another "500" under the Rickenbacker regime in 1946, if a change in ownership did not materialize. Rick continued to postpone any announcement of his intentions along this line, however. With all of the work to be done at the Speedway in order to make a 1946 race a reality, time was running out on all of us. Something had to be done quickly.

Together, on a hot summer night in August, Boots and I reviewed the names of every prospect suggested to us and I recalled Homer Cochrane's earlier urgings that I talk with a prominent Terre Haute business man by the name of Anton Hulman, Jr. I had never met Mr. Hulman, but Cochrane, an Indianapolis investment broker, was confident the two of us would make a good team.

"Tony is about your age," said Cochrane. "He's a good business man and a former football and track star at Yale. He enjoys hunting and fishing as much as you do. He's a Hoosier who is interested in civic affairs. And I think he has the financial ability to swing the deal if you can interest him."

Unlike most of the individuals on my original list of prospects, Mr. Hulman apparently had no important business interests in anything connected with the automotive industry. He would be free to do whatever was necessary for the good

276

of the Speedway and racing in general, without any selfish interests to influence his decisions. The more I thought about him, the more I became convinced that he was the one to do the job and the following day I asked Homer to arrange an appointment.

It was more than a month before Tony and I sat down to talk things over, however. I had too many other things to do—and worry about—during the intervening thirty days.

Before I got the burning desire to save the Speedway, Boots and I had decided, now that we were "settled" for the first time in our sixteen years of married life, that it was high time we had a family. Dr. Klingler already had told us a Caesarean section would be necessary. He also had assured us there was no reason to expect any complications and had set a date in early September for the birth of our son—I didn't even consider the possibility of having a daughter instead. But the tragic end of my first marriage always was in the back of my mind.

Firestone officials also wanted me to make some additional tire tests at high speed on the Utah Salt Flats. I was anxious to get this chore out of the way immediately. One thing after another delayed our departure for Utah, however, and it was about the third week of August before I finally headed westward. Ten or twelve days would be necessary to complete the tests and Mary Millhone decided to accompany me—with her two youngsters—so that they could spend the time visiting her parents in Salt Lake City. Four-year-old Madelon entertained her younger brother, Malcolm, every mile of the way by singing "Bell Bottom Trousers" over and over.

I checked with Boots by phone as soon as we arrived and learned that everything was all right at home. But the Salt Flats were too wet to attempt any high speed run immediately and we did nothing but "sit on our hands" the following day, Friday. Boots called about five o'clock in the evening and responded to my "hello" with a question which almost knocked the telephone receiver out of my hand.

"Are you ready to become a father on Tuesday?" she asked.

277

"Why? What's the matter? Aren't you all right?" I exclaimed.

"Don't get excited," she said. "There's nothing to be alarmed about. But when I went in for my weekly examination this afternoon, Dr. Klingler said that he didn't think it would be safe to wait until the date he had given us earlier. He wants me in the hospital on Tuesday, and I told him I'd let him know if that was all right as soon as I talked with you."

I told her I'd start back to Akron immediately in order to be sure of getting there in time and then I called Mary. She wanted to be on hand for the big occasion, too, so I picked up all three of the Millhones later in the evening and hurried home. It was a good thing I didn't waste any time. Bill, being a true Shaw, had a mind of his own. No doctor was going to tell him when to be born. He kicked up such a ruckus the morning after I arrived that we had to get to the hospital in a hurry.

All of my worries proved to be unfounded. Everything at the hospital went as smooth as silk. At ten o'clock in the morning I became the father of Warren Wilbur Shaw, Jr. There were no complications of any kind and I was as proud as if I had just created the entire universe.

A few days later I drove back to the Salt Flats to finish the Firestone assignment. They still were too wet for our use, so we moved our headquarters to Nevada and made the tests on the Tonapah Highway near Las Vegas, during the second and third weeks of September. In contrast to the winter run at the Speedway, temperatures ranged from 87 to 108 degrees. Then I returned to Akron again and concentrated on the Speedway problem during every moment I could spare from my regular Firestone duties.

278

CHAPTER 31

ARRANGEMENTS for my first meeting with Tony Hulman were made quickly. A few days later I picked up Cochrane in Indianapolis and we drove over to Terre Haute together. Tony was waiting for us in the office of Hulman & Company. With him were Joe Cloutier, Leonard Marshall, Joe Quinn and Tom Doherty. When I shook hands with Tony, he told me he had been a regular spectator at the Speedway ever since Rene Thomas's 1914 victory in a Delage and we seemed to hit it off right from the start. He impressed me particularly with his interest and sincerity. For more than thirty minutes, I presented every fact and figure at my disposal to give him a complete picture of the Speedway's financial record in former years—and its potentialities.

Then Tony and the other members of the group questioned me for almost two hours about everything connected with the operation of the track and the race itself. I answered to the best of my ability and it was evident they were becoming increasingly interested. Finally the discussion turned again to the financial prospects of future 500-mile races.

"With proper management," I said, "I don't see how you can fail to make money on your investment."

"I don't care whether or not I make any money out of it," Tony replied. "The Speedway always has been a part of Indiana, as the Derby is part of Kentucky. The 500-mile race should be continued. But I don't want to get into something which will require additional capital each year to keep it going. I'd like to be sure of sufficient income so we could make a few improvements each year and build the Speedway into something everyone could really be proud of. We'll drive over to Indianapolis soon to take a good look at it, and then let you know what we think of the idea."

That's the way matters stood when I headed back to Akron that night. I couldn't take the time to accompany Tony on his personal inspection of the plant, but Cochrane made the necessary arrangements with Al Rickenbacker, Eddie's brother, who was in charge of the property. A few weeks later, through Cochrane, Joe Cloutier made arrangements to meet with me again at the Antlers Hotel in Indianapolis. Together, we listed every possible expense item in connection with a 1946 race and Joe seem to be satisfied that he had the complete financial picture. He sounded extremely encouraging to me and I called Rick later that night to tell him it probably would be only a few more days before everything was all set.

"If you let Paul Davis know how things are going," he said, "he'll keep me informed of your progress." Davis, an Indianapolis attorney, also was secretary of the Speedway corporation.

Cochrane phoned me the following night. "It looks like it's a deal," he said. "I just talked with Joe Cloutier and he told me the only thing Tony still wanted to do was make sure Indianapolis bankers would approve a loan for part of the purchase price. We'll talk with them tomorrow."

No hitches developed and all of the interested parties finally got together to wind up the transaction on November 14 at the Indianapolis Athletic Club. Boots and I left Akron two days earlier, with the baby, and drove to our farm near Crawfordsville, Indiana. My mother and step-father had been living on the farm ever since I had purchased it following the 1941 race. Boots and Bill planned to stay with them while the final phases of the deal were being worked out in Indianapolis.

The climax to all of the many weeks of negotiations came about four o'clock in the afternoon. With everyone in agreement concerning the financial details, Joe Copps was called into the room to aid in the preparation of a statement for the press. Joe had flown to Indianapolis at Rickenbacker's specific request to handle this assignment and Tony asked him if he had any suggestions to offer concerning the new setup. I thought Tony was referring to ideas about publicity and promotion. But Joe apparently believed Tony was asking for his opinion concerning the selection of officers for the new corporation. This hadn't even been discussed by any of us, although it was understood I was to be the general manager. I had intended to suggest that Pop Myers be named president because of his familiarity with Speedway affairs since its very beginning. Tony, of course, would be chairman of the board and I probably would have the title of executive vice president as well as general manager. The other positions would be filled by Tony's associates.

"In my opinion," said Joe, "Wilbur is the only logical choice as president and general manager. The important thing is to have someone at the head of the organization who can carry part of the publicity burden and get along well with the press. Although Mr. Hulman probably is well known in Indiana," he continued, "Wilbur is a national figure—as a matter of fact, an international figure—and he is better fitted to do the public relations job which must be done in order to make your 1946 race a success."

After a little more discussion, the Terre Haute group withdrew from the room. When they returned, the statement for the press was completed with the new officers listed in this manner: Tony Hulman, chairman of the board; Wilbur Shaw, president and general manager; Pop Myers, vice president; Leonard Marshall, secretary; Joe Cloutier, treasurer. Eloise (Dolly) Dallenbach, Pop's private secretary during most of his long career with the Speedway, would be asked to return as office manager.

The first important step in my long campaign to preserve the 500-mile race had been successful. But I don't remember experiencing any particular feeling of elation. My mind was too busy groping for the answers to the hundreds of problems which had to be solved before we could even open the Speedway gates to the public. I called Boots to give her the good news and promised to join her at the farm later that night after taking Joe Copps to the airport. On the way, I told him of my earlier plan to suggest that Pop be named president, before matters had come to a head so quickly during the meeting.

"If I had known that," Joe said, "I would have been reluctant to say what I did. But, as it turned out, I'm sure the Speedway is much better off. Pop's connections and his counsel will be very valuable. But it's going to take a lot of hard work and someone with a lot of drive to get the job done in time for a 1946 race."

The list of things requiring immediate attention seemed endless. I also had to devote part of my time to Firestone's affairs during the remainder of 1945 and the "Duesenberg days" of 1931 seemed short in comparison with my working schedule during the next few weeks.

First, we reopened the Speedway's downtown office at the old location, 444 North Capitol Avenue. Jack Fortner, who had held the same position prior to the war, agreed to return as Superintendent of Grounds and tackle the job of getting the plant in good physical condition. Don Burge, the best ticket man in Indianapolis, took charge of that department with Frances Derr as his assistant.

Requests began to roll in by the dozen for special magazine articles concerning plans for the resumption of the annual race. Some of the major publications sent staff men to Indianapolis to interview me. But most of the requests were for articles to be written by our own publicity staff. The only trouble was, we didn't have one. Joe Copps and the Hannagan organization were not in a position to handle the job on such short notice. Pressure from other agencies all over the country was terrific. But the new regime, so far, was 100 per cent Hoosier and I had a feeling that it would be well to keep it that way.

One of the early applicants was Al Bloemker, who had opened his own public relations office in the Circle Tower a couple of months earlier, after twenty years of experience on the editorial staff of the Indianapolis Star. While trying to make up my mind which of the major agencies should be signed to take over such duties, I asked Al to fill some of the story requests already on hand. It was evident from the start that he had a good knowledge of what had to be done—plus the ability to do it—and the other applicants were forgotten quickly.

The really tough problem was to find a contractor who would guarantee to finish the necessary rebuilding program in time for the race. The Paddock and grandstand G had to be replaced for safety reasons. The other six old wooden stands and the Pagoda required major repairs. One contractor after another told me there wasn't enough of the right kind of steel available in the entire country, because of priority regulations, to build the two new stands we needed. Finally Harry Tousley walked into the office after an inspection tour of the plant with Fortner.

"I suppose you know you can't possibly get the steel you need to build the type of stands you want at the Speedway," he said.

"That's all I've heard for the last two weeks," I replied.

"Anyone who told you that, told you the truth," he said, "but there is steel available, even if it doesn't fit the specifications. It seems to me that the only solution to the problem is to design the stands around the kind of steel that is available. If you are willing to do that, I think we can get the job done for you by race day."

"How soon can you let us see some plans?" I asked.

"As soon as we find out exactly what's available in the way of steel," he said.

By early January, Harry had everything down on paper and all of the necessary material lined up for delivery as needed. I gave him the go sign after checking with Tony and Joe. The necessary excavation work was started the same day and the race with time was under way.

Carload after carload of new lumber, as well as everything which could be salvaged from the two stands torn down, was used to strengthen the old stands with Fortner hiring every available carpenter for the project. Another crew cleared the grounds of the tangled brush and weeds and dead trees. Ticket sales boomed. By March it was evident we wouldn't have

283

enough seats to accommodate much more than half of the crowd which wanted to attend. Even the seats in the two new stands still under construction had all been sold. That's when the present parquet section came into being, along the inside rail of the main straightaway, in the area used formerly for reserved parking spaces from which race fans could watch the action without leaving their cars. A parquet section, with fourteen rows of individual chairs on raised platforms, would enable us to put seventy people in the same area formerly occupied by a single automobile.

Fortner's army of carpenters took over that project, too. For a while we sold seats even faster than we were able to build them and we might have been caught short on race day except for a strike at the nearby Allison plant of General Motors. Every striker who knew the difference between a saw and a hammer was invited to work at the Speedway and many of them did.

Grandstand G was only a stone's throw from Pop's residence on the Speedway grounds. Even on the days I was too busy with other matters to get to the track, he'd give me a blow-by-blow report of the progress being made. Starting in late April, he would conclude each report by shaking his head, sadly, and saying, "They're never going to make it by race day, Wilbur." For a while, I didn't do anything about such pessimism except to tell him to quit worrying. Finally it began to get on my nerves and I lost patience with the Grand Old Guy.

"Quit saying that," I barked at him. "Even if that is your honest opinion, keep it to yourself. Such a statement can't possibly do us any good and it might cause us a lot of harm. That grandstand is going to be ready for people to use on race day if I have to hire a whole army of husky laborers to hold the supports in place."

It was, too, although Pop came very close to being right. Tousley's workmen didn't even have time to remove the wooden forms from around the last of the concrete they poured before the gates were thrown open on the morning of the race. In the meanwhile, everyone connected with the racing fraternity had converged on the track for the start of practice on May 1. Every time a driver turned a lap at anything near racing speed, every workman laid down his tools and watched. It was a mighty expensive way to get things done, but there was no alternative.

The mechanics in charge of the race cars were having their troubles, also. With the exception of Lew Welch's Novi Special and Lou Fageol's twin-engines car, almost every entry was of pre-war vintage and replacement parts were hard to get. Veteran drivers were scarce. More than twenty ambitious youngsters, whose desire to drive race cars had been shelved by necessity during the war, applied for permission to take the driver's test and nine succeeded in earning positions in the starting lineup. Any last minute stimulant to public interest which might have been needed was provided when Ralph Hepburn qualified the Novi Special at an average of almost 134 miles an hour for a new track record on the Sunday prior to the race.

On May 30, 1946, for the first time, the Speedway actually had as many people on hand as Hannagan and Copps usually had claimed were there. Traffic was tied up for miles in every direction as cars full of impatient fans crawled toward the various entrances. Frankly, the Speedway staff was overwhelmed by the tremendous turnout. But everything went off on split-second schedule.

For the pace lap, we had turned to the No. 1 family of the automotive industry and invited Henry Ford II to lead the field in a Lincoln. Because of wartime restrictions, no automobile manufacturer had been able to place anything new on the market. But it was no secret that young Ford was ready to show his rivals something new in the way of aggressive leadership as soon as the production race could be resumed. In January, he had been honored by the United States Junior Chamber of Commerce as the nation's "outstanding young man of the year."

The pre-race pageantry reached its climax with James Melton singing the traditional "Back Home Again in Indiana." As the last words drifted away, I stepped to the microphone to give the command for which everyone was waiting.

It's difficult to describe the mingled emotions I experienced at that instant. I had a tremendous feeling of satisfaction for my part in making the big show possible again. The record-breaking turnout was particularly gratifying. On the other hand, I was definitely worried about how many of the race cars, most of them from five to eight years old, would be able to go the distance and really make a contest of it. And almost over-shadowing these thoughts was a feeling of envy as I looked over the starting field. I could see every driver in the cockpit of his car, tense and impatient to get under way. Many were old rivals of mine. I'd have traded places, gladly, with any of them, and paid a bonus to boot, for the privilege of replacing Ted Horn behind the wheel of the car in the No. 7 starting position. It was the Maserati in which I had crashed while leading the 1941 race, after I had driven it to two of my three Speedway victories. I felt like a helpless little boy, about to burst into tears, because his playmates had grabbed all of his toys and were running away with them. Then I glanced at the pace car and realized that, for one lap at least, I'd be out in front of the pack again. Turning back to the mike, and taking a deep breath, I gave the traditional command:

"Gentlemen, start your engines."

As they roared into life, I climbed into the pace car and we rolled slowly toward the first turn with the field strung out behind us. We were nearing the third turn before all of the stragglers were able to find their proper positions. With all thirty-three cars finally in perfect formation, we swung through the fourth turn at steadily increasing speed and crossed the starting line at ninety miles an hour.

The race was on!

Mauri Rose set the pace for the first eight laps with Rex Mays right on his tail. Horn was having ignition trouble and his Maserati was the first car to make a pit stop. I ran down from the starting line to see what was wrong and my hands itched to help Cotton Henning change the faulty magneto, but

286

I wasn't eligible even to hand him a wrench. Despite exceptionally fast work, Horn was five laps behind when the job was completed and Hepburn had worked his way to the front in the powerful Novi. Paul Russo crashed on the north turn during his eighteenth lap and was taken to the emergency hospital with a broken leg. Twenty minutes later, Rose hit the wall at almost the same spot without being injured. As Hepburn's brakes began to wear out, George Robson forged to the front. Cliff Bergere also set the pace for a few laps before a broken connecting rod forced him to the sidelines.

As the half-way mark was reached, with mechanical trouble beginning to take a terrific toll of cars, the race developed into a duel between Robson and Jimmy Jackson. After making his only scheduled pit stop, Jackson tried desperately to close the gap, but was handicapped by carburetor trouble. He wasn't as unfortunate as most of his rivals, however. One after another, they dropped out of the running until only nine cars remained in competition with 100 miles still to go. At that rate—six withdrawals every 100 miles because of mechanical ailments—only three would be running at the finish. But the epidemic of engine trouble suddenly came to an end. All nine cars were able to complete the gruelling test with Robson getting the checkered flag a half-lap ahead of Jackson, Horn finished third, despite the time lost as the result of his magneto trouble. Emil Andres was fourth and Joe Chitwood fifth.

The Indianapolis Motor Speedway had successfully cleared its first big hurdle under new ownership and I was out on my feet, more exhausted mentally and physically than I had ever been in my life. In fact, my mind had been in such a turmoil for several days that I had sent an S.O.S. to Carl Stockholm in Chicago. I wanted him with me so that he could stop me any time I made a wrong move or gave a wrong command. I knew I could rely on his judgment and I was afraid I might collapse at any moment. I wasn't the only one in that condition, either. On the morning of the race, after the gates had been thrown open, I had walked into Jack Fortner's office and found him with his head on his desk, crying like a baby.

287

CHAPTER 32

AS the result of our experiences during the hectic six-and-a-half months leading up to the 1946 race, it was evident the Speedway management faced three major problems. Many things still had to be done for the comfort and convenience of the spectators—another traffic jam, particularly, would be disastrous from the standpoint of public patronage. More new stands and other expensive improvements were needed. Assurance of additional prize money was necessary to stimulate the building of new racing equipment and to encourage the continued participation of outstanding drivers.

Top men from all of the law enforcement agencies and several independent traffic engineers helped Safety Director Joe Quinn work out a complete new traffic pattern inside the Speedway grounds so that twenty-one lanes of traffic could pass through the Speedway gates simultaneously. Tony, Joe Cloutier and I mapped a long-range maintenance and rebuilding program. Then we tackled the problem of prize money.

Despite a bonus payment by the Speedway for the 1946 race, which had boosted the total prize money to an all-time high of $115,450 at the time, there were rumors of a possible drivers' strike in 1947. Hepburn, with whom I had dueled on many occasions during my own racing days, apparently was the leader in the formation of an organization called ASPAR (American Society of Professional Automobile Racing). With Hep as president, the group had asked and received assurance of prize money amounting to forty per cent of the gate receipts from promoters in charge of 100-mile championship races at

288

dirt tracks throughout the country. The object was to force the Speedway to accept the same terms.

Part of my duties for the Speedway was as a goodwill ambassador, making speeches throughout the country in order to create more interest in the "500." My schedule called for a trip to Los Angeles during the winter and I made arrangements to meet with the ASPAR group on that occasion to explain the Speedway's unique position.

"I know exactly how you fellows feel," I told them, "because I've been on your side of the fence most of my life. If we could run the 500-mile race under the same conditions as other promoters operate on the dirt tracks, we'd be glad to go along with your request. They pay a small percentage of their receipts, or a very nominal fixed fee, for the use of tracks which, in most cases, are state-owned property. These tracks were built for other purposes, with the taxpayers' money. They are being maintained with the taxpayers' money.

"Operation of the Speedway is an entirely different matter. Even without considering our original investment, our annual expenditures amount to several hundreds of thousands of dollars for taxes, maintenance, improvements and personnel to make one big race a year possible. An agreement such as you are demanding could kill the 500-mile race in a single year—and if you kill it, you'll be sounding the death knell of all auto racing.

"Most of you haven't had a chance yet to become well acquainted with Tony Hulman," I added. "We've given a lot of thought to the question of prize money and we are willing to guarantee a $75,000 purse, not counting $20,000 in lap prize awards and all of the usual cash prizes offered by accessory companies. I can give you Tony's solemn promise, too, that the Speedway will pay as much additional prize money each year as sound economic procedure permits. If you'll agree to go along with us on that basis, I feel sure you'll be satisfied with the way things turn out next May."

Entry blanks were placed in the mail as usual, about January 1. Some car owners and drivers returned them promptly

289

with their entry fees. A few more arrived during February and March. It was evident, however, that ASPAR leaders intended to carry out their strike threat. The deadline for entries was at midnight on April 15. At the usual closing time, five o'clock, we had a total of thirty-five, including enough good cars to assure a much better race than that of the previous year. ASPAR leaders claimed they had approximately thirty others, although they actually had only about half that number. In order to give them every opportunity to change their minds, Al Bloemker and I kept the office open until midnight, but nothing happened.

Everyone connected with the situation, on both sides, was under a terrific strain during the remainder of April and the early part of May. ASPAR tried its best to fight its battle for recognition through the pages of the daily newspapers. It was extremely difficult to resist the temptation to answer some of the ridiculous statements made. But the Speedway maintained an attitude of calm silence along with an open-door policy which welcomed sincere discussions with ASPAR leaders interested in finding a solution to the problem. Their campaign, intended to convince the public that a 1947 race was impossible without their participation, collapsed when the time trials got under way. Ted Horn qualified my old Maserati for the pole position. Cliff Bergere and Herb Ardinger qualified the Novi Specials. Mauri Rose and Bill Holland earned starting positions with Lou Moore's new front-drive Blue Crown Spark Plug Specials. Those five cars alone were enough to assure fans of a whale of an automobile race and the starting lineup was increased steadily with $1,500 in special prize money posted by the Speedway on each qualifying day.

Ralph Hepburn and other ASPAR representatives talked frequently with Speedway officials—collectively and individually —in an unsuccessful effort to obtain concessions. When they finally realized that none would be made, they indicated their willingness to compete under the original provisions of the entry form. By that time, however, there was no possible way for them to get into the race without the written permission of every original entrant.

Discreet investigation indicated this was almost impossible, although there did appear to be an outside chance of obtaining the necessary waivers if ASPAR would agree to two specific stipulations. One was that no ASPAR car, regardless of its qualifying speed, could crowd any of the original entries out of the starting lineup if they had met the minimum requirement of 115-miles-an-hour in the time trials. The other was that no ASPAR car could share in the special qualifying awards originally posted by the Speedway.

When ASPAR representatives accepted the first stipulation, but balked at the second, Tony Hulman dug into his own pocket to post duplicate awards for that group. Then, with the groundwork laid for a possible solution to the problem, the Speedway and ASPAR officials arranged an open meeting to consider the best method of procedure with press and radio in attendance. The session had not been in progress very long until Hepburn asked me to undertake the job of getting the necessary signatures.

"No one connected with the Speedway has any right to ask a bona fide entrant to sign a waiver," I explained. "Our entry form is the same as a contract between the Speedway and the entrant. It says the Speedway will not accept any entries after midnight of April 15 and we have no right to ask for permission to accept additional entries now. That's up to ASPAR or some disinterested party."

"Because of the ill feeling which has developed between ASPAR and the other drivers," said Ralph, "I believe some neutral person would have a better chance of success. Will you suggest someone?"

"How about Bill Fox of the Indianapolis News?" I asked.

Other members of Hepburn's group nodded their approval and he said, "That suits us if he'll do it."

Bill was taken completely by surprise and it was several seconds before he responded to the suggestion.

"The 500-mile race is much more important than any of us,

individually," he said, finally. "If everyone here will help me, I'll take the assignment with one stipulation. It is going to be a difficult job and I want it clearly understood that I am not accepting in order to be on the inside track for any news which may develop as the result of this situation. I'll keep the Speedway management posted concerning my progress, with the understanding that all statements for press and radio be given to all of us simultaneously by Al Bloemker."

Because of personal threats attributed to a few hot-headed ASPAR members, Bill's job was not an easy one. In each case of this kind, however, he managed to bring the interested parties face to face with satisfactory results. After forty-eight hours of hard work, involving dozens of telegrams and long-distance phone calls, the necessary waivers were obtained for all of the seventeen ASPAR members who claimed they had cars ready to run. Twenty-one of the original entries had earned starting positions, leaving twelve spots open with the race only two days away. ASPAR's comparatively weak position during all of our discussions was revealed when only nine of the post-entries were able to run fast enough to equal or surpass the 115-mile-an-hour minimum speed requirement. It's interesting to note, too, that none of the ASPAR cars finished among the first five in that 1947 renewal of the "500" which was given a special touch of glamour by the Borg-Warner Corporation.

The famous Borg-Warner victory trophy had been placed in competition many years earlier. Each winner of the race had his "mask" or profile placed on the side of the huge silver cup and also received a smaller replica of the award as a permanent record of his victory. Beginning in 1947, however, Borg-Warner officials decided to make a bid for additional publicity concerning their part in the Speedway program by inviting some of Hollywood's most beautiful actresses to make the trophy presentation in Victory Lane. Carole Landis was their first choice. And in subsequent years this same touch of glamour has been provided by Barbara Britton, Linda Darnell, Barbara Stanwyck, Loretta Young, Arlene Dahl, Jane Greer and Marie

Wilson. Miss Stanwyck also played the leading role opposite Clark Gable in a race movie made at the Speedway by Metro-Goldwyn-Mayer under the able direction of Clarence Brown.

It was in 1947, too, that an invitation to provide the pace car began to take on the importance with which it has been regarded ever since. Nash made such excellent use of the honor, in its publicity and advertising, that other manufacturers were quick to follow a similar pattern when they were invited to pace the race—Chevrolet, Oldsmobile, Mercury, Studebaker, Chrysler, Ford and Dodge. Each year, the Speedway made an honest effort to select the most deserving car on the basis of its contribution to automotive progress and this policy added considerable prestige to our invitation.

For the first twenty-three laps of that 1947 race, Cliff Bergere set a fast pace in his Novi Special before experiencing supercharger trouble. Ted Horn had tough luck right at the start, for the second straight year, because the tricky control valve on his auxiliary oil tank had been turned the wrong way. This little mistake caused too much oil to be forced into the crankcase and his emergency pit stop left him almost four minutes behind the leaders. The sturdy old Maserati, which still occupied a warm spot in my heart, again was destined to be defeated. Any concern I had in regard to Horn's bad luck, however, was knocked completely out of my mind by Shorty Cantlon's fatal crash on the No. 1 turn during his fortieth lap. While trying to avoid two cars, which had gotten into momentary trouble immediately in front of him, he had hit the concrete retaining wall almost head-on. Shorty and I had been such close friends, over such a long period of time, that the accident almost knocked the props out from under me. Because of the many race details requiring attention, I had to force myself to put Shorty's death out of my mind temporarily—and even then I found myself thinking about him repeatedly in spite of the increasing tension created by the controversial "E-Z" duel which was shaping up between Bill Holland and Mauri Rose.

They were team mates, driving "twin" cars owned by Lou

Moore. Rose was a veteran of ten Indianapolis races. Holland was a rookie, making his first "500" appearance. With Rose right on his tail, Holland had moved into the No. 1 spot when Bergere's car faltered. Holland had received exceptionally fast service—seventy-two seconds—when he came into the pits almost thirty laps before Rose found it necessary to stop for new tires. Although Rose then led until his own pit stop, the work on his car required almost two full minutes and Holland enjoyed a lead of sixty seconds with only forty laps (100 miles) to go. Barring accident or mechanical trouble, they seemed certain to finish in that order because the third-place Horn was three minutes farther back.

Moore gave both of his drivers the "OK" sign so that they would know their only job was to maintain their present positions. They could run two or three miles an hour slower, thus reducing the possibility of engine failure or accident, without being overtaken. When neither man gave any indication of easing up on the throttle, Moore erased the "OK" from his blackboard and replaced it with "E-Z." I happened to be looking toward the pits and saw Moore hold up the sign as Holland passed. I think he held up the same sign as Rose came down the straightaway, but I can't swear to it because I was looking elsewhere at the time. It has been a matter of argument among the racing fraternity ever since.

I feel sure, however, that Moore didn't care which of his cars finished first. Approximately $60,000—almost every cent he owned—was wrapped up in those two automobiles and his major concern was to keep them running in one-two position for the remainder of the race. The one thing in the world he didn't want to happen was to have Rose and Holland engage in a last-minute duel, which easily could end in disaster.

Holland has no one to blame, but himself, for what happened. In all fairness to Bill, however, I must admit he very probably would have won without difficulty if he and Rose had been driving for different car owners with separate pit crews interested only in their particular entry. When Moore flashed the "E-Z" signal, he certainly had no reason to believe that his two drivers were not fully aware of their relative positions. It was posted in full view on the special drivers' scoreboard hanging on the corner of the judges' stand at the starting line. The board showed car No. 16 (Holland) in first place, with a big "0" under the 16 to indicate that he led by less than one full lap. It showed car No. 27 (Rose) in second place with a figure "2" under the 27 to show that he held a lead of more than two laps over the third-place car. The manner in which the scoreboard was operated for the particular benefit of the actual contestants had been explained in considerable detail at the annual drivers' meeting the previous day, although Holland said later he had not heard any explanation of that kind.

Anyone interested in defending the actions of either Holland or Rose, however, should remember one important unwritten rule of racing. Once a race is under way, the driver of a car is complete "master of his ship" so long as he does not violate the rules of competition. He is subject to immediate disqualification if he fails to comply with the flag signals given to him on the orders of the chief steward; but no driver is required to comply with any instructions given by his pit crew unless he wishes to do so.

Holland responded to Moore's "E-Z" signal by reducing his speed almost three miles an hour. Rose continued to run at the same speed he had been traveling for the last hour and began to cut approximately one and a half seconds off Bill's lead every lap. With twenty laps to go, thirty-two seconds separated the cars and Rose had absolutely no way of knowing how fast—or how slowly—Holland was running. But after another five or six laps, as he came out of the northwest turn and onto the main straightaway, Mauri was in a position to see Bill going into the southwest turn. Mrs. Holland already was on her way to "Victory Lane" in order to pose with her husband in the usual manner for newspaper and newsreel photographers. The sight of Holland's car, however, was all Rose needed to close the gap relentlessly. He said, later, his only thought was that Bill was having engine trouble—and that here was his opportunity to score his first clean-cut "500" victory after sharing honors with Floyd Davis in 1941.

On the 190th lap, with only ten to go, Rose was only thirteen seconds out of first place and moving up fast. Half-way through the 193rd lap, on the backstretch, Mauri passed Holland without a challenge because Bill apparently thought he still was one full lap ahead. The finish, with Rose winning by a comfortable margin, was a terrific let down for the spectators who had worked themselves into a frenzy in anticipation of a thrilling neck-and-neck battle right down to the wire. But it was a race they talked about all winter long.

CHAPTER 33

WITH the Speedway fulfilling Tony Hulman's promise to pay "as much prize money as sound economic procedure permits," the drivers divided $137,425 at the Victory Dinner and all of our plans moved along in orderly fashion. No major problems, comparable in magnitude with those of the two previous years, developed for the 1948 race and another record-breaking crowd seemed to be assured for the resumption of the Rose-Holland rivalry.

Ralph Hepburn, back in the cockpit of the Novi Special, was another favorite. Despite the satisfactory solution to the ASPAR situation, he had elected to remain on the sidelines the previous year because both Novi cars already had been qualified by other drivers. Now, after a two-year layoff from actual competition, he was looking forward to the chance of breaking his own track record. On the first Sunday afternoon designated for time trials, he warmed up the car for a few laps and apparently decided to cut a couple of fast ones before making his official run. It was about one o'clock and the fans still were streaming through the gates.

Several railbirds clocked Hep at 133 miles an hour on one practice lap and he seemed to give the big front-drive Novi even more throttle as he headed down the backstretch. You could hear him ease off as he neared the northeast turn and get on it again a few seconds later—in the usual manner of anyone at the wheel of a front-drive car, which requires a steady pull through the turns to avoid disaster. Suddenly there was a squeal of tires losing their grip on the track surface, followed by an even mightier roar of power from the engine as Hep tried to pull out of trouble, and then complete silence—a chilling, cruel, haunting silence which seemed to cast a spell over everyone on the grounds.

Within a matter of seconds, emergency equipment was on its way. But Hep was beyond help. The car had dived below the white line, marking the inside of the turn, and then shot toward the outer retaining wall at a 45-degree angle. The impact was so great that it had knocked Hep's helmet and goggles from his head. He was slumped in the cockpit when the ambulance arrived. Death had been instantaneous. I walked to where my car was parked in the garage area and climbed into the front seat. Sitting there, alone, I recalled our many experiences together—as well as our strained relations during the ASPAR episode—and I cried for at least five minutes. No accident on any track ever had a more depressing effect on the racing fraternity. All of us felt as if we had lost a brother. I don't believe a single wheel turned at the Speedway during the remainder of the day and Hep remained in our thoughts long after the 1948 race became history.

Rose won, for the second straight year, setting a new track record of 119.814 miles an hour to finish more than a full lap ahead of Holland without difficulty. Bill had to work hard all of the way, because his car developed a tendency to jump out of gear. Duke Nalon placed third in the Novi "twin" to Hepburn's car and Horn was fourth.

Holland finally joined the exclusive list of Speedway winners in 1949, after Nalon had crashed in what probably was the most spectacular one-car accident of the track's entire history. With Nalon, Rex Mays and Jack McGrath in the front row of the starting field, none of the officials expected anything but a perfect start at the usual 90-miles-an-hour speed. More than a hundred feet before reaching the starting line, however, Nalon charged past the pace car at approximately 120 miles an hour with several of his rivals in close pursuit. For twenty-three laps he set new records every time he circled the course. Then, as Nalon swung through the north turn, near the spot where Hepburn had wrecked the previous year, the rear axle broke.

The left rear wheel came off and bounced high into the air. The car traded ends immediately and hit the wall, tail first, on a sharp angle. At the instant of impact, the left front wheel also was torn loose and the car burst into flames as sixty gallons of methanol poured from the ruptured fuel tank. Like a blazing meteor, the car scraped along the wall for almost a hundred feet. Nalon, badly burned but not critically injured, scrambled out, taking refuge behind the wall. A mass of flame, three feet wide and eight feet high, blocked the track as the fuel flowed across the course toward the infield grass. Some drivers had no choice but to drive right through the fire. Others, with time to reduce their speed, swerved inside the white line to avoid the flames.

Within a few minutes, however, the blaze was under control and another Rose-Holland duel began to develop for the third straight year. With 100 miles to go, Rose was fifty-one seconds behind and starting to make his final bid. Holland was going like the wind, increasing his average on each lap. During the next fifty miles of desperate driving, Mauri was able to shave only three seconds off Bill's advantage. With forty miles to go, the Rose car began to show definite signs of trouble. Eight laps from the finish, it rolled to a stop on the backstretch, with its magneto torn loose from its mounting. Holland finally was able to ease up for the first time and win by more than three minutes over Johnnie Parsons.

Veteran drivers whose careers dated from that exciting period prior to World War II had won their last Indianapolis race. Other outstanding newcomers of the post-war era—including Parsons, McGrath, Lee Wallard, Troy Ruttman, Bill Vukovich and Walt Faulkner—were ready to dominate the spotlight in the years to come.

Similar changes were taking place among the Speedway's own staff. "Miss Dolly" had retired after the 1947 race in favor of Frances Welker. Jack Fortner's death in 1948 resulted in the appointment of Clarence Cagle as superintendent of grounds. Cotton Henning left a big gap in the list of top-flight mechanics when he passed away a few months after returning with me from a tour of European race courses and automobile plants.

Boots had been urging me to slow down. And there was nothing I wanted more than an opportunity to enjoy family life with her and our son Bill. In the spring of 1948, we finally built a ranch house type home of our own, north of Indianapolis. And because of all the headaches connected with its construction, we certainly deserved a get a lot of pleasure out of it.

For sixteen years we had felt we shouldn't have a family until we were settled in a comfortable home with sufficient room for the baby. When we planned Bill, we thought we probably would be with Firestone for the rest of our lives. But Bill was only a little more than three months old when my new Speedway responsibilities made it necessary for us to move back to Indianapolis. For two months, our "home" was the Antlers Hotel, complete with nursing bottles, formula hot plate, bassinet and all of the other equipment necessary for a youngster of Bill's tender age. Boots had quite a time keeping the bottle washing department separated from the diaper washing department in our one-bathroom suite without kitchen. It was a far cry from the way we had planned Bill's routine so carefully. Baby sitters were scarce, too. But Cotton Henning lived at the Antlers at that time and Harry Hartz usually stayed there whenever he was in Indianapolis. We drafted them as often as possible so we could slip down to the dining room for an occasional meal together. Cotton, especially, was as patient as an attentive grandmother. He'd sit with a book or a paper in one hand, reading, while he pushed Bill's bassinet back and forth.

In February, Pem and Florence Cornelius invited us to use their home while they enjoyed a six-weeks vacation in Florida. A few days before they were due to arrive back in Indianapolis, Bill Hunt walked into the Speedway office and tossed a set of keys on my desk.

"I've been transferred to Arizona and we're leaving immediately," he said. "I don't know how long we'll be gone, but I'll appreciate it if you'll take over our house until we return."

It was in the country, near White River. It was filled with antiques and pieces of this and that, which Bill had made in his own workshop over a period of many years. Being country people at heart, it was a real treat for us to move out in the open with spring "bustin' out" all around us. We loved it, there.

All of this time, we owned a house in Indianapolis at 4519 Guilford Avenue. I had bought it in 1938 as a home for Mother and as a stopping place for us whenever we were in town. After she had moved to the farm near Crawfordsville, however, we had rented it to the Overstreets. We couldn't expect them to move until they had a definite place to go and rental property was hard to find at that time. It was early fall before we were able to move into our own home while getting ready to build exactly what we wanted.

Jack Dyer finally found the perfect spot for us—eleven acres of rolling land, with beautiful sycamores. Williams Creek ran through the front pasture. Boots spent many hours putting her ideas for our home on paper. She finished the plans while I was on a three-day business trip to Detroit and showed them to me when I returned. She'd thought of everything and I turned her drawings over to Charles Ward, our architect, without making a single change.

300

Getting a house built so soon after the war was a project almost as difficult as the Speedway stands, despite Harry Tousley's constant cooperation. Because we had sold the Guilford Avenue property and agreed to vacate it by May 1 during that spring of 1948, it was touch and go right up to the last minute. A detailed description of our experiences during the last few months would "out-Blanding" Blanding's story. When moving day arrived, the new owners carried their possessions in the back door on Guilford Avenue while we moved ours out the front door. It took weeks to unscramble our personal belongings and the job was complicated by the fact that our new home was far from ready.

The kitchen and one bedroom and the trophy room could be used. The remainder of the interior of the house still was under construction. Each evening Boots would shovel debris from the living room, where the carpenters had been working, in order to clear a path to the bedroom. I was too busy at the track to be of much help. Neither of us got as much sleep as we needed, either. We had to be up and dressed at seven o'clock each morning before the carpenters returned, because we didn't even have a door on the bedroom at that stage of the project. The trophy room was full of our furniture. By race time, a second bedroom was finished sufficiently for use as a temporary living room and that's where we entertained our guests. Rough wooden forms, which had been used by masonry workers to allow for the insertion of round windows in our bath rooms, served as cocktail tables.

A few weeks after the race we invited the Speedway "family" to a furniture-moving party. It was great fun, at least for us, hauling furniture out of the trophy room and deciding where to put each piece. Our only trouble was that we didn't have nearly enough furniture for all ten rooms. But we decided to be in no hurry to get the place fully furnished. Instead, we followed a policy of adding each new, or old, piece only when we happened to see something we felt we just "couldn't live without." Our collection, consequently, is purely Shaw—any old period—but we've loved every piece of it. Like Bill, our

301

home was worth waiting and planning for. Our roots were finally down, back where we had started on good old Hoosier soil. Boots and I both were looking forward to a chance to enjoy more of each other's company than ever before, with Bill's presence adding to the pleasures of family life.

The year 1951, however, brought a lot of heartaches and finally my own collapse. After an illness of many weeks, Mother died in March. That blow was softened to some extent because I had become reconciled to it while watching her grow steadily weaker despite excellent medical care. The unexpected death of Dad, only six weeks later, was a real shock. He had appeared to be in excellent health at Mother's funeral and, although we had not spent much time together since Mother's second marriage—except on brief hunting trips as often as I could accompany him—we always had felt extremely close to each other.

On that last week end in April, with a terrific month of work ahead of us, Al and Katie Bloemker had arranged for the use of a cottage on quiet Lake Ridinger in Northern Indiana. Boots and Bill and I, along with Mary and Ed Sullivan of Indianapolis, completed the party and we made the trip on a Friday evening. We were sleeping late on Sunday when an Indiana State Trooper knocked on the door.

"Mr. Shaw," he said, "I hate to be the bearer of bad tidings —and maybe I should try to break the news more gently—but friends of your father found his body this morning in a hunting lodge near his home in Vernon. Apparently he'd had a stroke or a heart attack."

I thanked him and walked back to the bedroom, in a daze, to tell Boots. Al drove me into the little lakeside village of North Webster so that I could make what arrangements were necessary by telephone. Then we returned to the cottage for another twenty-four hours because I didn't want to see anyone or talk to anyone until I had my emotions under better control. The following morning we drove straight through to the funeral home in Vernon and on Tuesday afternoon we laid Dad to rest alongside Mother in the little cemetery on the bank of Mus-

302

catatuck River, which is a beautiful part of the great outdoors he loved so well.

When the track opened for practice three days later, I welcomed the thousand-and-one problems which would require so much of my attention. Once again, everything went smoothly. Walt Faulkner, who had broken Hepburn's qualifying record the previous year, watched Nalon set a new mark and then raised the standard even higher with one-lap and four-lap averages of 138.122 and 136.872 miles an hour, respectively.

Parsons, striving to repeat his 1950 victory, stayed right on the heels of the leaders on race day for sixty laps before magneto trouble forced him to the sidelines. Wallard, with one of the most courageous performances in Speedway history, boosted the race record to an amazing average of 126.244 although two shock absorbers were out of commission and his brakes were virtually useless at the finish.

After the physical and emotional strain of the last three months, it was a relief to relax during June and July. Each year I had whittled away at my long list of speaking engagements and there was nothing of major importance on my calendar except Chevrolet's annual Soap Box Derby Finals at Akron, Ohio. I wouldn't have missed that for anything in the world.

A couple of weeks before the Derby Finals, however, the Speedway lost another veteran member of its staff with the death of Don Burge. With ample training under his direction, Frances Derr was ready to carry on in his place. But the relentless inroads made by death among my relatives and friends and associates gave me cause to wonder where it would strike next. I didn't even consider myself as a possible victim and the knockout punch it swung in my direction at Akron came as a complete surprise. The fact that I didn't stay down for the full count of ten is still regarded as a miracle by some members of the medical profession.

CHAPTER 34

HARRY HARTZ was responsible for my first appearance at the Soap Box Derby Finals. He had been invited to serve as official starter for the 1937 event, a few weeks after I had scored my first "500" victory, and he asked me to accompany him. I was fairly certain I could have a lot more fun doing something else that week end, but Harry was insistent.

"You'll really enjoy it, Wilbur," he said. "The kids are wonderful to work with, and the race means as much to them as the '500' does to us."

I finally agreed to go and got one of the biggest thrills of my life out of that first trip to the Derby Finals. I've been a regular ever since, officiating at all but two of the events, when it was impossible for me to attend. In my opinion, it's the finest competition in the world for boys. Chevrolet certainly deserves all of the publicity it receives for sponsoring the nation-wide program. I'll be the proudest dad in all of the United States if Bill can win it when he becomes old enough to take part. In addition to stimulating the development of skill and good sportsmanship, it emphasizes the value of ingenuity and perseverance.

It was a real privilege to associate with the ambitious youngsters from every section of the country, and a lot of fun, too, to work with the inner sanctum of the Soap Box Derby management. This "terrible trio" consisted of Myron E. Scott, Derby general manager; Bruce Overbey, Derby track manager; and Violet Brewer, Derby secretary. They must have spent hours, or possibly weeks, dreaming up some of the gags they pulled on me. No one ever appreciated a good practical joke more than I did, however, even when I was the victim. Scottie and I, particularly, enjoyed ribbing each other. His official title is assistant advertising manager of Chevrolet. In 1948, when Chevrolet was the pace car at Indianapolis, Scottie was driving me around the track on a quick inspection trip. I was in a hurry, but apparently he wasn't. Twice I urged him to get going. Each time he increased his speed only five or six miles an hour.

"Listen, Featherfoot," I finally exclaimed, "if you can't put more pressure than that on the accelerator, move over so I can drive."

Scottie complied without any argument. When I went to Akron for the Derby Finals later in the year, however, he turned the tables on me beautifully. Before a crowd of three hundred—press, radio, magazine and special guests such as Jimmy Stewart and Jack Dempsey—he presented "Featherfoot Shaw" with the most unflattering award I have ever received. It was a knobby, plaster cast in the form of a bare right foot, painted pink, with a feather sticking out of the heel. It was mounted on a small pedestal and the whole thing was encased in glass. I still have it on display at home, with my regular Speedway trophies.

My reception at the Mayflower Hotel, when I went to Akron for the 1949 Derby Finals, is another occasion I'll always remember because of a Scott-Overbey-Brewer gag. By that time I had learned it was well to be prepared for anything which might happen. But I was caught completely off guard when I entered the hotel room reserved for me.

Merely by opening the door, I tripped a switch which exploded a bomb and started a hidden record-player with blaring sound effects of a screaming woman, police sirens, horns, bells, train whistles and every conceivable type of noise at full blast.

The room was a shambles, with burlap window draperies and a potato-sack rug. A long-dead poinsettia reposed on the battered orange crate which served as a coffee table. Dozens of live "fruit flies" played tag around a dish of rotten bananas. A woman's intimate apparel hung from the various pieces of

305

broken furniture. Torn and scorched sheets were on the bed and the pillow case was smeared with lip-stick. The windows were boarded up with two-by-fours. Pictures were askew on the wall. The mirror was cracked. A sign on the toilet read "out of order." Many hours of work and planning had been necessary to make the hilarious idea such a tremendous success from the standpoint of the "unholy three" and the Mayflower management, who had enjoyed the proceedings from various observation points. I'm sure they felt amply repaid by my complete consternation and voluble reaction.

"Scottie, you old goat," I said, after everything had been restored to normal, "that's the damndest stunt I've ever had pulled on me anywhere. You and your gang certainly went to a lot of trouble, didn't you?"

"Nothing's too good for Shaw," he replied—and I'd already given him a flying start on another gag he used the following year. On that occasion, as I opened the door and walked into my hotel room—a little cautiously, I'll admit—a live billy goat in the far corner lowered his head and prepared to charge. On the wall, stretching from one corner of the room to the other, was a big sign: "From one old goat to another—Welcome to Akron."

Chevrolet's All-America Soap Box Derby Finals in 1951 were scheduled for Sunday, August 12. On Saturday afternoon, I had attended a "Hawaiian Luau" press party and gorged myself with fruit until my stomach started to rebel. I didn't want any dinner that night, but I did eat an order of milk toast before retiring early. In the morning I felt much better. Boots, Bill, Fran Welker and Clarence Cagle had made the trip to Akron with me. The program wasn't scheduled to start until one o'clock, but I wanted to be on hand early. Bill and Clarence decided to accompany me. Boots and Fran planned to follow a little later with Jo and Lee Copple. A last-minute addition to the party was an old friend who had arrived that morning from the Philippines and I promised to meet him at the gate with a ticket.

Bill and Clarence had seats on the edge of the track in front

306

of a section of the grandstand reserved primarily for the use of actual Derby contestants as they were eliminated from competition. Fran and Boots had been invited to sit with Mrs. Scott on the opposite side of the track. As the official referee, garbed in black-and-white checkered shirt and sun helmet, my place was at the finish line after participating in the opening parade down the hill. As starting time approached, however, I still was at the foot of the course, chatting with friends. The job of obtaining an extra ticket and meeting Tom at the main gate had consumed more time than I realized. Someone finally tapped me on the shoulder and said, "The parade is about to start. They want you at the top of the hill right away."

A glance at my watch made it clear I had no time to waste. Like a "ruptured duck," I took off on a dead-run up that long 1,265-foot incline. There was only a two per cent grade on the first part of the run. But the center section of the course was six per cent and the last 365 feet had been built on a sixteen per cent rise. My heart and lungs were working overtime when I reached the top. An open convertible, with my name on it, was waiting for me. The driver already was behind the wheel and the engine was running. I climbed up on the back of the rear seat as a feeling of nausea began to sweep over me. Sharp chest pains added to my discomfort. But I forced myself to smile and I waved to the spectators on both sides as we moved down the course. Boots told me later that my face was "pea green" and she knew I was ill when I passed the spot where she was sitting. At the foot of the hill I saw Clarence and Bill sitting near the side of the track. Climbing out of the convertible, I walked over to join them and slumped into a chair next to Clarence.

"I guess the heat's got me," I said.

"You're not too hot," said Clarence. "You're sick."

"I'll be all right as soon as I get a little rest," I replied, "but, I've got to get out of here right now because I think I'm going to vomit."

I walked behind the bunting-draped guard rail, which protected the electric-eye of the photo-finish apparatus, and stretched out on the ground. The parade, still in progress, seemed endless and I didn't want to cross the track to the rest room until it was over. When the last car finally passed, Clarence steered me across the course and into the little track office under the stands. Boots arrived at about the same time. Overbey already was on his way to the official announcer's stand to request that any doctor in the crowd come to the finish line immediately. It was fortunate that Dr. Louis E. Brown, Jr., of Akron, responded promptly. By the time he arrived, however, I was bathed in perspiration and the pain in my chest was becoming almost unbearable.

Scottie came in at about the same time to see if he could be of any help, but I got rid of him in a hurry.

"Listen, Buster, you've got a show to put on," I told him. "Get out there on the track and keep it running on schedule. There's a doctor here to take care of me."

One look was enough for Dr. Brown to diagnose my trouble as an acute coronary occlusion.

"Get an ambulance, quick," he commanded. "This man needs oxgyen and immediate hospital attention." I blacked out before the ambulance arrived, but I did recover consciousness for a few seconds during the ride to the hospital.

Dr. Brown was slapping my face and he and Boots both were shouting at me, "Keep on fighting! Wake up! Keep on fighting!" Then everything went blank again and I don't remember anything until after I had been placed on a hospital cart and taken to an elevator.

This time I awakened with Dr. Brown kicking and hammering on the elevator door, imploring the operator to hurry. Several people were on the elevator when it arrived.

"Get the hell out of the way," ordered Dr. Brown. "I've got a dying man here." Then, directing his attention to the operator, he said: "Get me a room—any room—immediately."

Dr. Brown asked me to sit on the edge of the bed while he gave me some additional medication. While he still was working on me, Ray and Laurie Firestone walked into the room.

"Ray, you're looking at the silliest S.O.B. in the whole

308

world," I blurted out, before he could even say a word. Then I blacked out again and it was three long days before I knew very much about what was going on. During that time, everything possible had been done to aid my recovery. The adjoining room had been made available to Boots. She had kept in close touch with my medical friends in Indianapolis and had been guided by their advice. Ray and Mr. Thomas, Chairman of the Board at Firestone, made it possible for us to have everything we wanted from the hospital. Mr. Keating, Mr. Fish and other Chevrolet officials also hovered over me like mother hens. Dr. Brown remained in attendance almost constantly and several top-flight specialists were summoned from other cities.

After we knew that time and rest would be the most important factors in my recovery, we enjoyed our "vacation." Living quarters were arranged for Boots in a lovely suite of rooms in the nurses' home across the street. She was permitted to be with me from early morning until late at night. Even her meals were served with mine and I can't remember any other time in my life when we had spent so many days together. Boots read five books aloud to me. Laurie joined us every afternoon at four o'clock for our "cocktail hour," always with a fresh bit of fruit or a wonderfully funny story. It may be hard to believe, but we really enjoyed ourselves after the first bad days.

By the end of a month, I was ready to be discharged with the knowledge that a long period of convalescence was ahead of me. The hospital staff headed by Worth L. Howard, executive director, gave me a going-away luncheon with steaks and a big cake. For another week, although still bedridden except for a few minutes each day, I was the guest of the Firestones in their home. When Boots finally was convinced I was strong enough, they took me to the airport in an ambulance and carried me aboard the Firestone plane for the trip to Indianapolis. Boots had made arrangements for another ambulance there. As it turned into our winding lane, Boots told the driver to cut across the lawn and pull right up to the back door. Lottie, our housekeeper, held the door open while they carried me into the kitchen on the little cart. Tears were streaming down her cheeks.

"What's the matter, Lottie?" I chided her. "Aren't you glad to see me?"

"I surely am, Mr. Shaw," she sobbed. "I just seem to be overcome."

Clarence also was on hand for my return home. He and Boots helped me to my feet and Boots said she thought it would be all right if I sat out on the front porch for a few minutes.

"Then you're going straight to bed for a couple of days more," she added.

I've seen a lot of magnificent scenery on my repeated travels from coast to coast and my two trips to Europe, but none of it was quite as beautiful as the view from my own front porch that afternoon. Harry Tousley had knocked himself out to enlarge the porch during our absence, as we had planned earlier. Fran Welker and Katie Bloemker had decorated the flower boxes. The changes made our home even more attractive than before and I was mighty happy to be back.

It was mid-October before I was able to leave the house for brief intervals and another month before I drove a car again. Boots accompanied me on my first trip to the office, soon after Thanksgiving Day. By the first of the year I was anxious to get back into harness. But I heeded the advice of Dr. Rollin Moser and my many close friends in the medical profession, who were regular weekly visitors. As soon as I felt myself becoming the least bit tired, I took time out to rest. At first, two or three hours of work was all I could stand each day. Gradually, this period lengthened. By April I felt almost as strong as ever, but the big test still was ahead.

"You've got to be extremely careful until after the race," the doctors warned me. "Keep your mind free of worry and don't exert yourself, regardless of what happens. If you can avoid a setback during all of the tension and activity connected with preparations for the race," they added, "there's no reason why you shouldn't do everything you formerly did, before many

310

more months go by. It looks as if you're going to be as good as new."

I did my best to follow their advice to the letter. About the middle of May, when the pressure really was building up to its usual peak at the Speedway, I called on Carl Stockholm again to ride herd on me. Mary Hulman had loaned me a "golf cane," which could be opened up to form a seat, and I made good use of it.

The car everyone was talking about that year was the Cummins Diesel Special. The Cummins Engine Company of Columbus, Indiana, had decided to use the Speedway as an outdoor laboratory and proving ground for its product, as many of the pioneer automobile manufacturers had done during the early years of the track's existence. Don Cummins, the company's vice president in charge of engineering, was directing the project. He had chosen Freddie Agabashian as the driver of the heavy car, which weighed several hundred pounds more than the conventional entries. A speed in excess of 134 miles an hour probably would be necessary to qualify for a starting position and there was considerable speculation concerning whether or not the Cummins car would be fast enough.

On the first day of time trials, Agabashian climbed into the cockpit for the supreme test. He took two quick warm-up laps and signaled for the green flag. Clockers could hardly believe their eyes as their watches revealed an average of more than 139 miles an hour on the first official trip around the course. Three more fast laps followed and Agabashian had set the car on the pole for the race with a 10-mile average of 138.010 for a new track record. Bill Vukovich and Chet Miller raised the mark still higher on subsequent days. But the car I was itching to drive was the Cummins Diesel and a few days later I did. Even though I didn't put as much pressure on the throttle as Freddie had applied, it was a perfectly wonderful feeling to be back on the track and running at high speed.

Race day dawned with hardly a cloud in the sky. The pre-race ceremonies moved along on split-second schedule. Such former race drivers as Tom Milton, Harry McQuinn and Earl

311

Cooper headed the capable staff of AAA officials. The Purdue University Band swung through its sixty-minute program. With all cars in position, Morton Downey climbed on top of the concrete wall in front of the judges stand and sang "Back Home Again in Indiana." Then it was my turn.

As I had done in 1946, and every year since, I stepped to the microphone and took a deep breath to make sure I was in full control of my emotions. A little more than nine months earlier I wouldn't have given a plugged nickel for my chances of being on the starting line when the 1952 race got under way. But I'd won my fight and no longer was there any doubt in my mind concerning the future. I was in the groove again, with the green flag flying and a clear course ahead.

Out of the corner of my eye, I could see P. O. Peterson at the wheel of the Studebaker convertible, which had been chosen as the pace car because of that company's many important contributions to land transportation over a period of a hundred years. Alongside the car, with a smile on his face to reassure me that everything was all right, stood Carl Stockholm.

Thirty-three impatient drivers and 175,000 spectators were waiting for me to say the magic words. But I took another second or two to look down the track toward the spot where Boots and Bill were sitting in a box near the first turn. Even though I couldn't actually see them among the restless mass of humanity on hand for the big event, I waved in their general direction. Something inside me recorded their instant reply.

Facing the starting field again I suddenly realized that the feeling of envy, which I'd always experienced in former years at this particular moment on every May 30th, was gone. I was completely happy. I had my family—and my health—and my home—and my exciting job of building the annual 500-mile race into an even greater attraction each succeeding year.

With a feeling of sincere gratitude to God, I lifted the mike to my lips and gave the traditional command:

"Gentlemen, start your engines!"

EDITOR'S NOTE: On October 30, 1954, Wilbur Shaw made arrangements for a flight in a single-engine private plane to the Chrysler Corporation's new proving grounds near Chelsea, Michigan. Ernest Roose of Indianapolis, a close friend who had painted the L. Strauss & Company portrait-trophy of every 500-mile-race winner for the last seven years, accompanied him. Ray Grimes of Greenfield, Indiana, was the pilot. At the proving grounds Mr. Shaw drove one of the new Chrysler sedans on a special test run. Then he and his two companions headed homeward in the late afternoon. The sky was overcast, with a ceiling of seven or eight hundred feet, when the plane passed over Fort Wayne at an altitude of 6,000 feet on its flight southward. The temperature on the ground was two or three degrees below the freezing point. Snow was falling and two other planes in that vicinity reported "icing" conditions. No one knows exactly what happened during the next few minutes. From a point about fifteen miles south and slightly east of Fort Wayne, however, Grimes contacted Baer Field by radio to ask if there were any "holes" in the overcast which would enable him to make a visual landing. The answer was "no." Then Grimes requested permission to make an instrument landing and this was granted immediately. Whether or not the wings of the plane were becoming coated with ice is a matter of conjecture. But the plane carried no equipment to correct the situation if it did develop. And at nineteen minutes after four o'clock it crashed to earth in a cornfield near Decatur, Indiana, carrying all three occupants to instant death.

INDEX

315

317

319